The
Colton
Letters

The Colton Letters

Civil War Period
1861-1865

Compiled and Edited by Betsey Gates

MP McLane Publications
Scottsdale, Arizona

Address editorial and general inquiries to:
McLane Publications, P.O. Box 9-C, Scottsdale, AZ 85252

To purchase books, contact:
McLane BookSales, P.O. Box 25556, Tempe, AZ 85285
1-800-949-1555

Publisher's Cataloging in Publication
(Prepared by Quality Books, Inc.)

The Colton letters : the Civil War period / Betsey Gates
p. cm.
Includes index, glossary.
Preassigned LCCN: 92-62703.
ISBN 1-881502-01-5

1. Colton Family--Correspondence.
2. Ohio--History--Civil War, 1861-1865--Personal narratives.
3. United States--History--Civil War, 1861-1865--Personal narratives.
I. Gates, Betsey, 1927-
II. Title.

E601.C65 1993   973.7'81   QBI92-20353

Casebound International Standard Book Number: 1-881502-01-5

Library of Congress Catalog Card Number: 92-62703

Illustrations and Map of Sherman's Raid by Quick Carlson
Cover Painting and Sheldon's Military Portrait by Tom O'Mary

First Edition 1 2 3 4 5 6 7 8 9 10

In fondest memory
of Mom

Gertrude Caroline Gates

who
together with her female ancestors
displayed the wisdom
to preserve and protect
these letters

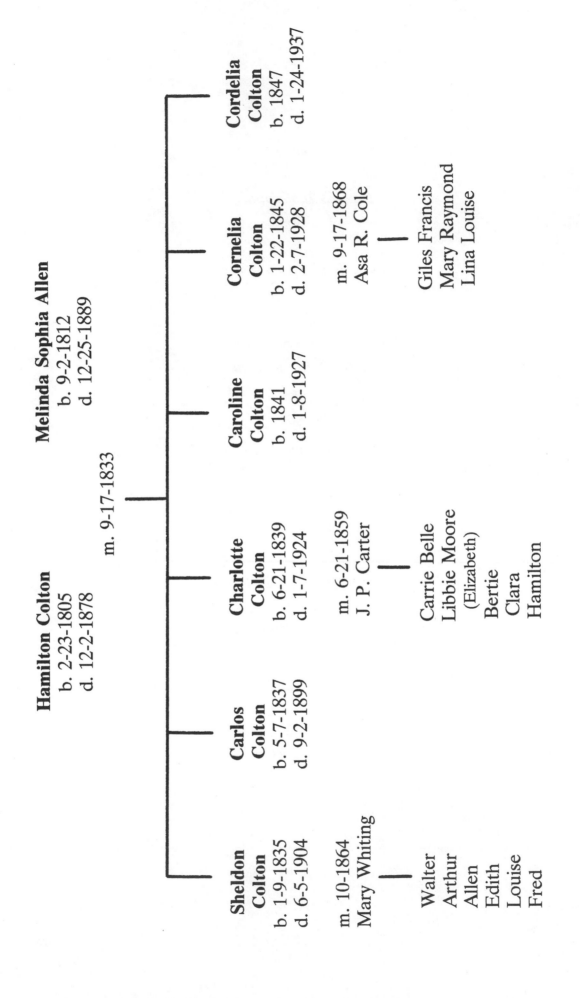

Hamilton Colton
b. 2-23-1805
d. 12-2-1878

Melinda Sophia Allen
b. 9-2-1812
d. 12-25-1889

m. 9-17-1833

Sheldon Colton
b. 1-9-1835
d. 6-5-1904

m. 10-1864
Mary Whiting

Walter
Arthur
Allen
Edith
Louise
Fred

Carlos Colton
b. 5-7-1837
d. 9-2-1899

Charlotte Colton
b. 6-21-1839
d. 1-7-1924

m. 6-21-1859
J. P. Carter

Carrie Belle
Libbie Moore
(Elizabeth)
Bertie
Clara
Hamilton

Caroline Colton
b. 1841
d. 1-8-1927

Cornelia Colton
b. 1-22-1845
d. 2-7-1928

m. 9-17-1868
Asa R. Cole

Giles Francis
Mary Raymond
Lina Louise

Cordelia Colton
b. 1847
d. 1-24-1937

INTRODUCTION

This book consists of a small portion of the more than 1,000 letters (written between the 1830's and 1920's), by members of the Colton family of Milan, Ohio, their relatives and friends. The focus of this volume is the Civil War period of 1861-1865. These documents are of historical content, adding one more authentic chapter to the voluminous recording of a tragic yet compelling time for our country and our people. *THE COLTON LETTERS* is not about the Civil War per se, although many descriptions from the field of battle, as well as encampments and military events are included. This is rather the selected chronicle of an average family, struggling to retain a sense of normalcy during this devastating period of America's history. Ordinary activities of life are discussed between sisters, brothers, parents, relatives and friends. Moral values and strength of family are constantly apparent.

The Colton letters travelled through a long and thoughtful route. Family members corresponded with one another almost on a daily basis, detailing their experiences, thoughts and feelings. By request, these letters were then returned to the mother, Melinda Sophia, and kept in safe keeping in the family home in Milan. After Melinda's death, the daughters of the family continued this practice of collecting and preserving the letters, which were eventually stored in huge cartons in the attic of the Colton home. Cornelia presented over a thousand letters to her daughter, Lina Louise, who was later blinded and could not read them. She in turn gave them to my mother-in-law, who was not able to read them due to poor eyesight. Many cartons of letters were thus preserved and protected, but not read by anyone outside of the immediate Colton family.

A twist of fate brought the letters into my possession, when a bicycling accident put me in traction for a period of six months. My mother-in-law, recognizing the avid interest I had in these family treasures, presented the disorganized collection she had stored in her basement. Many years and thousands of hours were spent reading and collating these documents. I came to know the Coltons intimately through their words, their poetry, their individual styles and personalities. Many of the letters had to be read with the assistance of a magnifying glass. Some were written in normal fashion, then written again crosswise over the previous words, thus making them almost works of art. Paper was precious and not to be wasted.

This collection dates from the 1830's, and continues until 1927. The final letter refers to the birth of my husband, Sheldon Gates. He was named for his great-great uncle, Sheldon Colton, who fought on the side of the Union in the Civil War, was wounded at the battle of Kernstown, captured by the Confederates, and managed to escape to freedom. As Sheldon writes to his mother on April 19, 1862

> . . . During the action the Lt. Col. came along and ordered our company to be moved a little to the left. In the meantime Capt. Lewis had got hold of a rifle and was fighting on his own hook so I took command and executed the movement. Just after this I concluded to see if my revolver would reach the enemy and had drawn it and was stooping forward slightly to get a look through a rail fence behind which we were standing when a ball struck the pair of scissors I have carried so long in my vest pocket breaking one point and bending the other. The force of the ball was partially broken by my pocket diary. It then glanced down penetrating my body about two inches forward of the joint of the hip bone, passing around the bone in a semicircular direction, grazing it as it went along and lodging about two inches around the joint of the bone.

Sheldon's recovery from these wounds was slow and painful. Despite his handicap, he served for many years in the Adjutant General's Office in Columbus, Ohio.

In preparing this volume, I chose to present the letters <u>as</u> <u>written</u>, without deletions or corrections in grammar or punctuation. The charm of the actual handwritten letters cannot truly be captured in printed format, therefore photographic copies of letters by the major authors have been reproduced, so that you, the reader, may respond to the style and personality of each individual: Sheldon — upright, methodical, dedicated and quietly poetic; Carlos — more flamboyant, but a most thoughtful son; Lottie — a shy, loving mother, somewhat insecure; Lina — bright, feminine, observant, with a charming sense of humor; Nelia — sweet, musically talented, sensitive to her father's criticisms, a descriptive writer; Delia — the youngest (Dee Pet Daughter), but a no-nonsense, hard-working protector of the parents.

And now, the family history. On September 17th, 1833, Melinda Sophia Allen was united in marriage with Hamilton Colton according to the form of Solemnization of Matrimony prescribed by the Protestant Episcopal Church of the United States of America. John O'Brien, Minister of Trinity Church of Monroe, Michigan presided. Melinda and Hamilton raised six children, Sheldon, Carlos, Charlotte (Lottie), Caroline (Lina), Cornelia (Nelia) and Cordelia (Delia). Known sisters and brothers of Melinda were — Sophia Melinda, Wealthy Clarinda, Lucy Lorinda, Cornelia Lucinda, George, Hiram, Almira and Frances Louise. The sister and brother of Hamilton were Clarinda (C.Bill) and Carlos (C. Colton).

Family stories, passed down from Nelia to her granddaughter, relate that Hamilton and his brother Carlos were both in love with the same girl. Carlos wrote many letters to Melinda, but it was Hamilton who finally won her heart and hand. Carlos later married Sophia Melinda; they named their son Hamilton (Hammie) in honor of the brother. The two young cousins, Carlos and Hammie, served in the same regiment at Camp Lawrence in Maryland, until Hammie died of typhoid fever.

For clarification, the headers used in this book identify the eight members of the primary family, using their <u>exact</u> signatures. Other letters receive the designation Relative or Friend. The reader will please be cautioned not to confuse the Hamilton and Carlos of the older generation with Carlos and Hammie, their sons. Hopefully, this book may find its way to existing, unknown members of the Colton family. Perhaps, also, some readers may discover their own ancestors among these pages.

The Coltons were a religious, literary, patriotic and hard-working family, ever loyal to and supportive of one another. Many letters refer to bouquets or sweet-scented shrubs that were sent from those at home in Milan to members in other cities. This was a family custom, a means of reminding those who were distant of the love and caring that would always come to them from the homestead. Even a single Fall leaf placed in a letter would carry with it memories of childhood, the warm hearth, music shared, frolicsome games and tender moments.

Through the challenging years of the war, the Coltons survived on the produce from their small farm, but primarily on financial contributions from their sons. Letters rarely arrived without a $3.00 or $5.00 contribution. The daughters, after completing their educations in the Normal School, became teachers or copyists in the Adjutant General's Office in Columbus, Ohio, barely subsisting on minimal salaries or occasionally being supported by relatives of larger means. In a letter (not included in this volume), Hamilton writes to his son Carlos

> . . . your Uncle & Aunt are entitled to some courtesy from us, we are under many obligations to him especially, he never had anything but what I was welcome to the largest half of, & there have been numerous instances where that disposition has been of much service to me & mine, when sickness & adversity have borne heavily upon me, & neither of you that we now lean on could even help yourselves — to him we are indebted for uniform kindness & good will for more than a quarter of a century & it would grieve me much if any child of mine should fail to show them proper respect . . .

Sheldon, Lottie and Nelia married and raised families of their own. Carlos remained a bachelor; Lina and Delia were maiden ladies, living out their years together until Lina's death in 1927. Delia stayed on alone in the family home until her death ten years later. Unfortunately, a relative who inherited the homestead burned the remaining letters in a huge bonfire, together with other effects not considered of value. We are indeed indebted to Cornelia, for her foresight in passing on to younger generations those letters which have made this book possible.

The Colton home in Milan is of wood frame, with a four-columned front portico. It is situated on a large lot with huge trees, next to a ravine. One of Delia's fond memories concerned the peony bushes her father had planted on the four corners of the property. Many years later, these were inadvertently cut down. Mysteriously, forty years after Hamilton's death, the peony bushes reappeared in their original locations. Cordelia's photograph albums and the family Settle (a long, wooden rocking bench with high back, arm rests and cradle) were donated to the Milan Historical Museum. Milan, Ohio is most noted for being the birthplace of Thomas Alva Edison, born in the same year (1847) as Cordelia Colton.

For one hundred years, the letters in this volume had not been removed from their cardboard cartons, unfolded, organized or read by anyone. My journey into the Colton family archives has been a special privilege, as well as responsibility. In my possession are beautifully preserved, historically important documents — letters written on the field of battle, reference to helping to inaugurate "Ancient Abraham", descriptions of the capitol in Columbus, with its Lunatic Asylum, Blind Asylum and Camp Chase, accounts of military celebrations and a parade featuring a model of the famous iron ship, the "Monitor". For those scholars interested primarily in specific battles, personnel or troop movements, the Index will provide a helpful guide to individual letters of such details. A Glossary defines words or phrases, perhaps unfamiliar today, but commonly used in the 1860's.

This book would never have been completed had it not been for the encouragement of my husband. Thank you Shel, for being my guide and computer guru throughout this project. Thanks, also, to daughter Lori for inspiring an interest in genealogy, to the many loving friends and family members who shared their wisdom and enthusiasm, and to the Milan Historical Museum and Milan Public Library researchers.

Now, dear reader, travel with me through this previously undiscovered and unexplored saga of a loving and dedicated family. In the modern world in which we live, the art of letter writing has been replaced by the telephone, computer and FAX machine. Words have become utilitarian and time-saving. This book will return you to the tormented era when our country was split apart — but it will also place you in a time when communication was flowing, poetic and personally revealing. Let the Coltons, in their own words lovingly preserved, lead us into this gentle account of a time past, but long remembered.

The Coltons

H. Colton

M. S. Colton

Nelia.

Sheldon Cotton.

Carlos

[photographs of Lina and Lottie not found]

Delia.

1861

The Confederate States of America declare a provisional government, inaugurating Jefferson Davis as President on February 18.

On March 4, Abraham Lincoln is inaugurated, in Washington, as President of the United States.

The Civil War begins when Southern guns fire upon Fort Sumter, April 12. Major Robert Anderson surrenders the Fort on April 14.

Harper's Ferry arsenal and the Norfolk Navy Yard are seized for the Confederacy in mid-April.

Confederate and Federal armies meet at Bull Run on July 21. After a battle of several hours, Union troops retreat to the Potomac.

George B. McClellan is appointed to command the Army of the Potomac.

Kentucky maintains a neutral position until autumn, when both Confederate and Union armies build their forces throughout the state. General Felix Zollicoffer, with a strong force of Confederate troops, occupies the town of Somerset, forcing the Federal division to retire.

Hamilton, Melinda and three of their daughters reside in the family home in Milan, Ohio.

Delia attends school and helps her parents on the farm.

Lina and Nelia study at the Western Reserve Normal School, training as bookkeepers and teachers.

Lottie and her husband J.P. Carter, reside in Milan with their young daughter, Carrie Belle, and new baby, Libbie Moore.

Sheldon works as bookkeeper for the firm of Raymond & Jones. On December 8, he is appointed 1st Lieutenant of the 67th Regiment, Ohio Volunteer Infantry, Co. K.

Carlos works on the Toledo Blade newspaper, and later is employed by the insurance firm of Brown & Colton.

Milan Jan 18th 1861

Dear Carlos

I received your letter
yesterday noon. I have only been
skating once since you were here
It is pretty good sleighing here now
although it has not got smoothed
over
quite enough yet. I am afraid if
you should come here once to wash
my face you would not want to do
again for I would not let you off so
easy as to agree not to wash your
face or throw you down because
"it would get your clothes wet. no
indeed not I. I believe in paying
folks back in their own coin. I am
taking writing lessons of Mr P. R.
Spencer now and hope that by the
time I write next time I write to

(Delia)

Milan Jan 18th 1861

Dear Carlos

      I received your letter yesterday noon. I have only been skating once since you were here It is pretty good sleighing here now although it has not got smoothed over quite enough yet. I am afraid if you should come here once to wash my face you would not want to do again, for I would not let you off so easy as to agree not to wash your face or throw you down because "it would get your clothes wet" no indeed not I. I believe in paying folks back in thier own coin. I am taking writing lessons of Mr P.R. Spencer now and hope that by the ~~time I write~~ next time I write to you I can write better than I do now, at least I can try, as there is nought like trying you know. Mr Spencer is one of the queerest men I ever saw, he talks so much that we can hardly write, he will give us a copy and by the time we get one line about half written he will say "now if you will please cast your eye on the blackboard, I will try & explaine this copy" and then he will go on "and talk and talk" untill we get so tired, then he will go through with a long explanation and put in all the big words he can think of If I did not know him I should think he was crazy, he is a monomaniac on writing, I should judge from his actions. Tell Sheldon Pa says if we had Mr Brainard there to teach grammar, and Mr Spencer to teach writing he should think we might go it. I do not know as I can think of any thing further to write about tonight only to add that I am well, "and hope you are enjoying the same blessing". I have not got anymore to say so good bye love to all

                    from Delia

Lina

Milan Feb. 24th 1861

Dear Brother.

      I really did <u>not</u> intend to so long delay replying to your last letter, and ought long before this to have acknowledged receiving your "<u>little &</u>", and returned my <u>heartfelt</u> thanks for the same, believing that " 'tis better late than never" I now offer my thanks for your liberal present, and think as you do "that it was far better than <u>cutting</u> <u>me</u> off with a <u>shilling</u>. Had that been the case I fear I should present a poor looking spectacle as a bride. You spoke in your last letter about telling the family there of matters. My objection was the reason you have of Mr Chase's family hearing about it, for it would of course come back here immediately. I gave Nelia liberty to speak of it but do not know whether she has or not. I had just as soon Uncles' family would know of it. I felt, at first, that there had <u>not</u> better be anything said about it at present, but now do not care.

The Dr. thinks the closing of your letter to me was done in <u>good</u> <u>style</u>. I think so too, and sincerely hope, your wishes for us may be realized.

Neely writes that she is enjoying her visit very much. I intended to have written her today and may possibly, yet, but there is not enough to write about to make even one letter interesting. I suppose she is a little disappointed not to have some more skating. Deely would not give it up last week, until three or four boys got into the canal. She then concluded that it was <u>not</u> very good skating. Pa wants a three oclock dinner to day, so shall be obliged to put by my writing, and give orders to <u>Bridget</u>.

After dinner.

Don't you think we have an enterprising set of vestry men in our church? We have been obliged to do without services two or three times, because <u>there was no wood</u> to make fires with. We could not be there at all to day. I went to the Presbyterian church this morning and heard a good sermon by Mr Walter.

Nelia's presence has not been much required as Organist, tell her that last Sunday afternoon, we had singing downstairs by the <u>choir</u> minus herself, Delight and Mr Carter.

I have been to Nette's a number of times lately, spent most of Monday evening there. She has a cousin here — Carrie Prentice — a very pretty girl, and I guess quite as full of mischief as Nette herself, she is to remain here for sometime yet.

Mr Carter's family are well. Carrie Belle is now quite an important member of the household, being full of fun and frolic. I will write to Neely the forepart of the week as Ma has been writing her today, am indebted to Sheldon will write as soon as I can.

Give much love to all the family.

Lina

Sheldon Colton (signature)

Toledo, O. Feb. 24 1861.

Dear Mother:

I have concluded to write you a small letter before church time this morning. I have not time to write a great deal, as I intend to go to church and to a Masonic funeral this afternoon. One of the oldest masons in the place died day before yesterday, and is to be buried today by the Knights Templar, of which order he was a member. I presume it will be a large funeral. I do not know whether you knew him or not. His name was E.B.Dodd — he was usually called Capt. Dodd. He lived here a good many years, and was a highly respected citizen.

It is a beautiful day here, and I hope will continue so, as we shall have to walk three or four miles.

I do not know what Father's ideas are exactly, in writing as he sometimes does. In his last letter he intimates that my life insurance policy will some day be assigned to "whom it may concern" — and in Nelia's letter he says that she may invite Carlos' and my particular friends to make you a visit as you would like to get acquainted with them or something to that effect. If he has an idea that I am going to ask any one of my young lady friends to share my poverty at present, he is entirely mistaken. If I thought enough of a young lady to wish to marry her, I should think too much of her to ask her to share my lot under the existing circumstances.   But more than this.

"The hallowed form is ne'er forgot
That first love traced."

and the memory of the only one that I ever really expected and intended to call my own is much stronger than any feelings I have had toward any young lady since she took her departure for that better land where I hope some day to meet her.

I have some lady friends here whose society I prize very much and respect them highly but that is all.

I do not know what ideas Carlos may have on the subject. I have said but very little to him about it.

It is church time and I must close, as I wish to get around in time. I am getting along very well at my new boarding place — one of the young ladies is a member of the Episcopal Church here, and the gentleman and lady boarder — Mr & Mrs Dr Briggs are also.

Nelia says she wishes the vacation was a week longer than it is.

Mr Raymond's crazy brother was buried yesterday, his death is a great relief to all concerned.

Love to all.   Yours truly,
$3. enclosed.   Sheldon Colton.
I enclosed a Harper to put in the mail for Lina today.

13

Sheldon Colton. (signature)

Toledo, O. March 3 1861

Dear Delia:

I am going to write a few lines to you today so that I can send some money to "The Old Folks at Home."

Nelia is getting along here very well. Makes a good many acquaintances, and seems to be enjoying herself generally — I think she is not in much of a hurry to go home, as she says she is going to stay here till Saturday.

I presume Hammie will go back again with her and make you a visit. I hope you will see that he enjoys himself well, and does not get into trouble if he does.

I went to Church this morning at the Presbyterian, formerly the Bethel, to hear the funeral sermon of Capt Dodd.

I presume I shall go over to the Episcopal Chapel this afternoon, as they want me to sing in the choir there.

Tomorrow morning I expect you will get up early and hurrah for Lincoln and keep it up all day as he will be President then I presume, unless something very bad should happen to him in the meantime.

Mr. Raymond has gone down to Washington to see to things generally and help inaugurate "Ancient Abraham" if necessary.

I am the head man in the firm now that he is gone. Mr Jones does not come down to the yard, and I have it all to see to so that I have my hands full, but I guess I can keep it moving.

We have had very pleasant weather for about a week until today, when it commenced raining and has kept it up pretty steadily all day.

The ice is all out of the river here now, and I presume the skating is done with here and at Milan. I got my skates fixed over, and strapped a while ago and have had them on only once since, and then for only about ten minutes.

I must close and take this to the P.O. and get ready for church.

Give $3. of this bill to Father and $2. to Lina.

Love to all.

Yours truly,
Sheldon Colton.

A. W. COLTON,
SHIP BROKER & INSURANCE AGENT
Water Street, between Jefferson & Madison
TOLEDO, OHIO

1861

Dear Brother

      When at Utica I noticed that our Uncle had on his table the best Potatoes I ever saw, they are a variety imported from Chile not long since and sell for seed at $4 per Bu I received a letter from him yesterday in which he says that in consequence of my admiration of them he has sent me by Rail Road a Bul of them, and if you have a vacant corner on your Farm I will send you a sample, when received, for cultivation.

      I cut the enclosure from a New York paper thinking that perhaps Sheldon might want to avail himself of the offer. Abram has been quite sick but is now better. We are expecting Annie home next week, as for myself I am almost worn out with hard work being this spring rather more than my usual share Abram has had <u>his</u> House painted and renovated as good as new

                Yrs. Carlos Colton

Relative

Toledo March 5 1861

My dear Brother

In looking round at the evil signs of the times I am forced to the conclusion that there is one community that will have more real & tangible causes for seceding than have yet been given by any of the subjects of Coltendom & Ebony — as soon as Mr Lincoln gets the hang of the New School House and begins to look about him he will, I take it <u>at once</u> devote his attention to the kingdom of Milan and the long suffering inhabitants thereof, and I fancy I can see the astonishment with which he will discover in that locality above, in his dominion, an emaciated Porcine Female with only a very diminutive lacteal appendage surrounded by a legion of diminutive grunters struggling for the chance thereat. Assuming the Population at one with the Cyphers I assume it as a fixed fact that old Abe can by no possibility split the Log in such a way that each one can have a rail or even a splinter if then it results that one gets the prize there will be 999 disaffected disappointed and maddened individuals rife for anything and in how pregnant examples what a Rabble can do in this year of grace 1861 when led on by defeated Demagogues, and taking warning by Mr. Buchanan fully I have determined before matters reach a crisis to throw reinforcements and supplies into Castle Dangerous at one of the extremes of the town. I have therefore issued General Orders, 1st that an ample supply of Provisions consisting one Bl of Extra Wayne Street Flour and one half Bl late caught white fish shall be despatched tomorrow and that the Commander of the Toledo High School Cadets with such Non combatants as may need an Escort proceed to the said Castle Dangerous, and hold the same against all comers until the said Provisions are consumed or they are regularly ordered to some other Fortress#

The detachment according to Southern precedent, consisting of
        Field officers ——————1
        Rank and file   0000000
        Non combatants   Quant suff
will take up their line of March on Saturday at 5 PM

I am in receipt frequently of Papers from the Reverend S W Brace (3 to day) I presume he intends coming here in the Spring and we will give him the best reception we can.

I see that in his list of relations he omits one who made some noise in the World by his exit in California at a Sheriffs Ball one fine morning, and I laughed to hear Sophia remark that he touched very lightly on <u>the poor relations</u>, and that she truly believed the Man was looking out for a helpmate, this view which Sophia & Melinda seem to have taken is confirmed by a family here from Utica who say that in this regard he has been making a Study of himself ever since his wifes death

I grieved to see the worldly tone of his Epistles in one of his Age and Profession

I know not whether you are aware that Hamie is a Candidate for Office under Old Abe, some of the leading Republicans (who are now in Washington) entirely without solicitation on our part took occasion to say just before leaving that his name should be placed on the roll of Candidates for a Cadetship I tell him that if he is perfectly satisfied he can go through with it mentally and physically, to go ahead. I can ensure him I think the Appointment during the coming year or whenever there is a vacancy in this District

Annie is in Detroit. Abram at Terre Haute
we are taking measures to get rid of one of our Boarders and may have to dispense with them <u>on both sides</u> and try how living by ourselves will answer for awhile.

This is a much larger Epistle than I am in the habit of writing and you will probably think like our Reverend Uncles using a large amount of verbiage for the substance

C

I cannot avoid repeating a remark once made to me by old Mr. Burt that for so likely a Man I had some relatives of whom it might be remarked en passant that they were rather an ordinary set and I am sorry to say that the acquired ones some of them at least have not improved the reputation, the way that one unfortunate has been saddled on to me would make me swear could I think I had the least chance of doing justice to the subject. I have from sheer pity done what I could but in justice to my own children have got to get rid of him in some way, and shall do so as soon as I can find any one needy enough to accept the small pittance allowed for Board by his employers, there are a half hundred Boys in the town whose friends would jump at the chance he has and furnish their own Board, the Boy would have gone to destruction at once had it not been for the oversight we had of him, all this will serve to explain an allusion I have made to dispensing with <u>all Boarders</u>

Carlos

Toledo March 9th 1861

Dear Father

      Considering a female equally as safe as <u>the</u> <u>mail</u> — sometimes — I send the enclosed valuables by Nelia — the 5 is for the usual purpose, the 3 is my offering to Mother, thinking she can get what she wants with it better than I can, not knowing any particular want. The bearer of these dispatches seems to have had a good time here in fact I believe she would most any where. She is just that kind of a girl. I send the letter from Insurance Company that you enclosed to me a short time ago. Mortimer asked his Co by letter a few days since about the recpt of your letters, has not yet got any reply. T. H. Hoag has recently got a new bookkeeper, he told me this morning he had intended to ask Sheldon to go with him but had a talk with Mr Jones and <u>concluded he would not take him away</u> <u>from there</u>. Sheldon attends to their business with as good a knowledge of it I think as either of his employers, and I believe to their entire satisfaction, he ought to have $1000 a year at least. I will send the amount of my insurance prm sometime this month. Love to all

                    Carlos

Carlos

Toledo March 19th/61

Dear Father

Hammie quite unexpectedly "came to hand" yesterday. I suppose it must have been pretty dull times for him particularly as he was not able to run about the City much. Sheldon recvd a letter from Lina today, he also got the last one — written over a week ago — from you & Nelia——If the girls go to the Concert expecting to see Mrs Mortimer and Mr Fuller from here they will be disappointed, as neither of them are going —— Dr Laird has written two or three times for Mr & Mrs M to go down. I have seen a programme with Mrs. M and Mr Fuller's names opposite some of the peices, and I suppose they will draw. Hammie says Lina and the Dr had a dispute about the propriety of his being a Minister of the Gospel, and she being the wife of such, and she says she won't. I sincerely trust she will make him renounce such an absurd idea or discard him, it seems to me the heighth of folly for a poor man to marry a poor girl, with the intention of living on the reluctantly-given alms of the parish, that supports them — Annie and Alpha are still absent — think they will return next week —— The weather is still wintry but I suppose and hope there will be a change for the better by tomorrow, the sky is clear and prospects fair for fair weather — please tell Nelia I will settle her Hack bill — Much love to Mother and all the family.

Carlos

I enclose a $5— bill ————

19

Milan April 2ᵈ 1867

Dear Carlo,

The country is safe... let Sumpter & Pickens... of the subomfunish chosen now, since the Sovereigns of Milan... the People — the Sovereigns of all power in this free happy country now in their might yesterday safe & serene. Content of... Milan elect St. Behruth perphrastic by the decides... of convote our How Williams... there will there think, on the... all the Candidate now dropped his Williams Behruth & Diols, the two forms being ahead, were taken for the three June true, which resulted as stated above, — the People thus showing their capacity

...my much from whether him an mean of getting on him the mind... want and unable to say... sometimes... figure to genering but the mother... done full while to claim him, or leaf... full very much... drawn him to the 27, to clothe... me unwilling... the truth, or before me done know what we have... without... any wholly... there I sometimes conclude that I do... time is pipping & the time opportunity when... for me should we... now... to wide... with now when is the poor master of Milan —

Yours affectionately
H. Colton

H Colton

Milan April 2nd 1861

Dear Carlos,

      The country is safe, let Sumpter & Pickens go to the rebels if the submissionists choose now, since the Sovereign of Milan — the people — the source of all power in this free & happy country arose in their might yesterday & after a severe contest of twelve hours elected S. P. Berkwith postmaster by the decided majority of <u>one</u> <u>vote</u> over Ham Williams — there were three trials, on the ~~first~~ second, all the candidates were dropped but Williams, Berkwith & Roiles, the two former being ahead were taken for the third & final trial, which resulted as stated above, — the people thus showing their capacity for self government by electing the only one of the numerous candidates who is totally unfit for the office, with this result I am highly pleased although I voted for Williams on the two last ballots — As stated some time ago I have had but little hopes for Carter, as the Choate faction, the most influential part of the Republican party opposed him on account of his connexion with Penfield, while Rag Tag & bobtail had their own candidates & he of course dropped between the two extremes ——— am very glad that I did not subject myself to the mortification of such an inglorious defeat— I couldnt help hoping against hope that Carter might get the office as it was so well known that he was the man for the place for it might have helped me a little as well as him & I can see nothing now that I can do but attend to your business as heretofore — & a kind of general operation in the kitchen. I have enough to do all the time & as the Spring advances shall have more than I can attend to but it doesnt seem to be exactly the kind of labor that I was intended for if indeed there was any special intention in my creation which I am at times inclined to doubt ——

      The chance of ever doing anything more here than I have been doing for the last three years seems to be getting "small by degrees" — & the question is whether there can be any object in breaking up & trying to do something somewhere else — my fears are that soon, if not now you & Sheldon would be burdened more than you would be if we should remain here so entirely dependent upon you. I am sensible that my business capacity has failed very much, but whether from an increase of years or from the rust of idleness am unable to say. I think sometimes that I ought to go away & test the matter but dont feel able to leave home, at least feel very much disinclined to do so, & to take it with me would insure the risk, as before stated, of increasing our expenses materially without insuring my ability to meet them — hence I sometimes conclude that I dont know what conclusion to come to — in the meantime time is passing & the time approaching when time for me shall be no more - & when it will matter little with me who is the Post Master of Milan —

                yours affectionately
                H. Colton

Sheldon Eaton

Toledo O. April 5th 1861.

Dear Mother:

Yours of March 24th was recd in due time, and I was much pleased to hear from you again.

I did not look for any other kind of shirting here, as I thought that would do well enough which you sent down, though I do not like it quite as well as I do the ones I now have.

I find that the bodies of some of my white shirts are coming to pieces but the bosoms seem to be as good as ever, and I do not know but it might pay to send them down and have them renewed in body — though they probably could not be in spirit very well under the existing circumstances. I suppose they could be retailed down there, but they could only be <u>hole</u> saled here.

The rest of my wardrobe, extensive as it is, is in a pretty good condition.

We have had some amusement here this week on account of Annie Garden's being here.

Tuesday night we all met at Mr Osborn's where I went for the first time, and had a good time, then Wednesday we were all invited down to Mr David Smith's where I had never been before, and Thursday night a few of us Milan folks met at Mr Chase's, and when we left there I went with Kent Hamilton to his boarding house — Mrs Scotts — where they had a Baptist sociable, and tonight I have an invitation down to Mr Eaton's — another strange place. So you see I am becoming acquainted and getting somewhat dissipated also, as I have been up till about twelve oclock for several nights now, and as I usually get up before six it makes my sleeping time somewhat short, and for the last few days I have had about all the work that I wanted to do in the office. The business season is about commencing —

and I presume we shall all be lively again soon, though we do not look for quite so much to do as we had last Spring when I came here to take charge of the books. When I left home, Father advised me to get rid of some of my modesty, and I think I have succeded admirably in doing so, for I begin to think I can do almost anything that is necessary.

I have been very successsful since I came here in getting along with business. I have had no trouble of any account in keeping my accounts, and have got along well with my employers so far.

One thing that suits me very well is that I am always a welcome visitor at Mr Raymonds or at least things have that appearance, for Mrs R. tells me to remember that I have a standing invitation to call there whenever I feel like it. And I find that I feel like it pretty often.

I have been very well ever since I came here, as I have not lost an hour's time in the office from sickness — So you see I am very comfortable, physically — and as my conscience is comparatively clear, I get along very well. Taking it altogether I am pretty well satisfied here, and am not at all anxious to leave. If it was so that you could all be here as well as not I would not feel like going back at all, but I am decidedly opposed to your leaving Milan as long as you can keep possession of the house there, for it costs a large amount of money to live here, especially if Carlos and I should happen to get out of work.

Enclosed find $3. to supply family want.

Love to all —

Yours truly
Sheldon Colton

Linas letter was rec'd

Carlos

Toledo April 10th 1861

Dear Parents

It seems you were troubled on the receipt of my last letter home with the idea that I was unwell, from the tone bad writing etc. I remember I was not feeling very well at the time though the bad penmanship might be partially accounted for in the fact that I was writing with a strange pen in Sheldons office. We had such dismally disagreeable weather through March my health & spirits were somewhat affected and suppose it is the case with most everyone. But I judge we are to have a change in the weather programme now as we had a beautiful day today———

Aunt Lucinda came down with her little girl yesterday, to make a short stay. A new boarding place has been found for Ben which he takes tonight I believe — A letter was recvd from Fanny Hyde yesterday written at request of Mrs Bill telling of an awful affliction that has come on poor Clarinda. It seems that for several years there has been a tumor in her right breast, which has been worse this winter than usual. Although she has been just as lively as ever — even when Annie was there. She showed no symptoms of disease. On consultation with Dr Clark of Detroit recently — it was decided that to save her life the breast would have to be <u>cut</u> <u>out</u>, which was done a week ago last Monday — at Hatties house, by Dr's Clark & Brown.

Carlos

The doctors and Phin being the only ones present. Mrs Bill and Hattie staying in other rooms — Mrs B. Said she was under the influence of Chloroform so that she was not sensible to pain, but that her groans were the most agonizing she ever heard. Fanny knew nothing of it till all was over, and never was so much astonished — Poor Phin! I feel sorry for him. Such a fine manly fellow as he is — and he has always had so much affection for Clarinda it must be a hard blow. I cannot but think that <u>we</u> have a great deal to be thankful for if we <u>are</u> <u>not</u> <u>rich</u> — with the exception of the common ailings of life, and comparative poverty, how marvellously we have escaped what <u>might have been</u>! And I trust God in his great mercy will continue to shield us all from the terrible calamities which are the lot of the more unfortunate — Clarinda was still quite low and nervous when Fanny wrote —— Sheldon got a letter from Nelia in which she spoke of the resignation of the talented! Mr Lewis — good! It is approaching the time for closing the mails & <u>I</u> must close — I hear that Joe Blinn is going into the dry goods business at Perrysburg with some one — Love to all

from your affectionate son
Carlos

I enclose <u>$5</u> —

Toledo April 19th 1861

Dear Father

The basket per Express arrived duly. And has been forwarded with the Trenton and Detroit packages to Mrs Slocum as requested. Postage paid. The flowers are beautifully sweet. and the Maple Sugar ditto. You might well feel proud to be the Maker of Sugar from trees of Your own planting. This is a glorious morning too beautiful for War. I write in a hurry as the Mail goes this Morning. Love to all I enclose $5.

Carlos

I Sent my premium recpt. to Mother two or three days ago.

26

Carlos

Toledo April 19th 1861

Dear Father

The basket per express arrived duly, and has been forwarded with the Trenton and Detroit packages to Mrs Slocum as requested, <u>postage</u> <u>paid</u>. The flowers are beautifully sweet — and the Maple Sugar ditto — you might well feel proud to be the maker of sugar from trees of your own planting — This is a glorious morning, too beautiful for War — I write in a hurry as the mail goes this morning. love to all

I enclose $5—   Carlos

I sent my premium <u>recpt</u>. to Mother two or three days ago —

H. Colton

Dear Carlos,

Your letter of yesterday with the usual & appropriate "consolation" was received in due course of mail ——

Likely you have heard about the war down South as I send the Milan Free Press to Sheldon — we are looking anxiously for the next number, I am more especially now as in trying to improve my facilities for news, have lost what little I had, they stopped the Fri weekly Blade — Sent one number of the Daily & quit — getting one & skipping two or three is not quite equal to the first arrangement ——

Milan bids fair to be well represented at the seat of war, a number have joined a Norwalk Company, & Sprague of Huron is now making up a Company he is said to be meeting with some success in this Town & the region round about not only as to numbers but especially as to the character of the recruits

You may have heard that Mrs. Dan. Hamilton tried to stop Will, who had enlisted at Springfield — She was too late — he had marched before she got there — She is said to consider it a greater affliction than any previous one, which have been many & severe ——

The most sedate & least suspicious one of our boarders wrote home last evening for leave to join — though if not suspicious himself his name is an auspicious one, Lafayette — there would be none from here of a more soldierly appearance ——

A young man from the County called last evening to bid Lina perchance a long farewell, it is to be decided to day whether his mother will spare him or his Father who is a Democratic Post Master ——

Therein consists the sublimity of the enthusiasm which pervades the Country, it has no regard to age, station or political associations. It will enable the Government if it chooses to do so, to make short work of this job, & prevent the need of such another one for a long time to come.

We have the power & prestige of the Government backed by the unanimous voice of millions of free men determined to remain free — with the sympathy of the civilized world — whether the struggle be long or short Truth & Justice will prevail ——

Yours
H. Colton

Nashville April 21st/61

My Dear Lina

It was with feelings of deep regret that I received your letter of the 11th inst. — To know that while you are yet so young your heart should receive such a blight. I cannot censure you dear Lina, for the step you have taken though I do not agree with you that you would be unfit to be a ministers wife — for dignity of character has from childhood been ascribed to you, by all your friends — but — if you feel unfit and unwilling to take upon yourself these vows — which would bind you to a Minister of Christ, I think you are justified in not uniting yourself to the Dr. expecially as he deferred his confidence until matters had gone so far — in that I think he wronged you — for I should consider Dr. C— and Rev Mr C— two very different characters — and between those who are candadates for the Holy estate of Matrimony there should be perfect confidence — Whatever course you may decide to pursue in the future — or whatever your fortunes — you have my heart-warmest sympathy and love — write to me freely darling just as you would talk to me if I was with you — and remember a Sister could not love you better than I have from your earliest infancy. You must all have pretty busy times if you have boarders and no kitchen help — How is your Mothers health now — and how does she your truest friend feel in regard to your affairs — I have never heard a word of your matters except in your own letters — Have not heard from Toledo in a long time. Hear from Fannie quite often now — which is a great gratification particularly now that Ma is with her — Have also heard from Lucy lately — John was not decided what he should do — But have not received one letter since the War excitement —

Relative

Oh Lina I do think this the most unjust War I ever heard of — the idea of what <u>has</u> <u>been</u> the United States — going to War among themselves. I for one am heartily sorry Lincoln ever entered the Presidential without the calling and decision of Congress. As I sit here — I can see several Flags of the Confederate States waving in the Breeze — which saddens my heart. Here as elsewhere there is a great deal of excitement. I hope Sheldon or Carlos Abram or Arthur will not <u>think</u> of volunteering — How long we shall remain here is a matter of great uncertainty — there was a rumor last week that supplies were being stopt from Cincinnati here — which is now dispatched — if that should prove true Henry will be thrown out of business. Father S. has written to Henry advising him to send Fannie and I there — if it is not perfectly peaceable — and pleasant here. I cannot bear the thought of going without him — and shall remain until something more decided remains — but I fear there will be difficulty in travelling from here North — after awhile if the excitement continues increasing. If I did not think it important for Henry to continue in business to provide our "daily bread" — I should urge him to go North — as it is I have nothing to say but quietly bide my time. I have so much war news from all parts to read I cannot do very much else — there are Extras published to the different daily Papers, so we abound in news — one half of which probably is not true — We are quite well and hope to hear from you all soon. I cannot imagine why I dont hear from Toledo —

Give much love to all from

Myra

Carlos

Toledo May 2nd 1861

Dear Sister Delia

      I am feeling pretty tired this evening as I have had a good deal to do for several days past and will only write a short letter this time. You will observe by my "Colons" on the envelope that I am still a "Lincoln" man for all Lincoln men and a great many others <u>too</u> <u>numerous</u> <u>to</u> <u>mention</u> are for "Our Country & death to Traitors." We had a very exciting time here for a few days before the 1100 troops left for Cleveland. I felt just as though I wanted to go with them & put in <u>another</u> <u>note</u> for Old Abe. Not in the ballot box but in the heart of one of vile traitors who are trying to plunge our people into Civil War, and ruin our great Country. Well, maybe I will be wanted yet but it dont look quite as much as if we were going to have a long war as it did a few days ago. I have been <u>fighting</u> <u>mad</u> for a week or more but am cooling off a little now. We are all anxious to have Myra come back — Aunt Sophia got a letter from her yesterday She was feeling badly —

I enclose a note to Pa.

Good night & Love to all

                from your brother
                Carlos

I went down to see Mrs Stevens Sunday — but she was lying down & I didnt see her Sarah wanted me to give you her love and says she wants you to visit her some time

           C

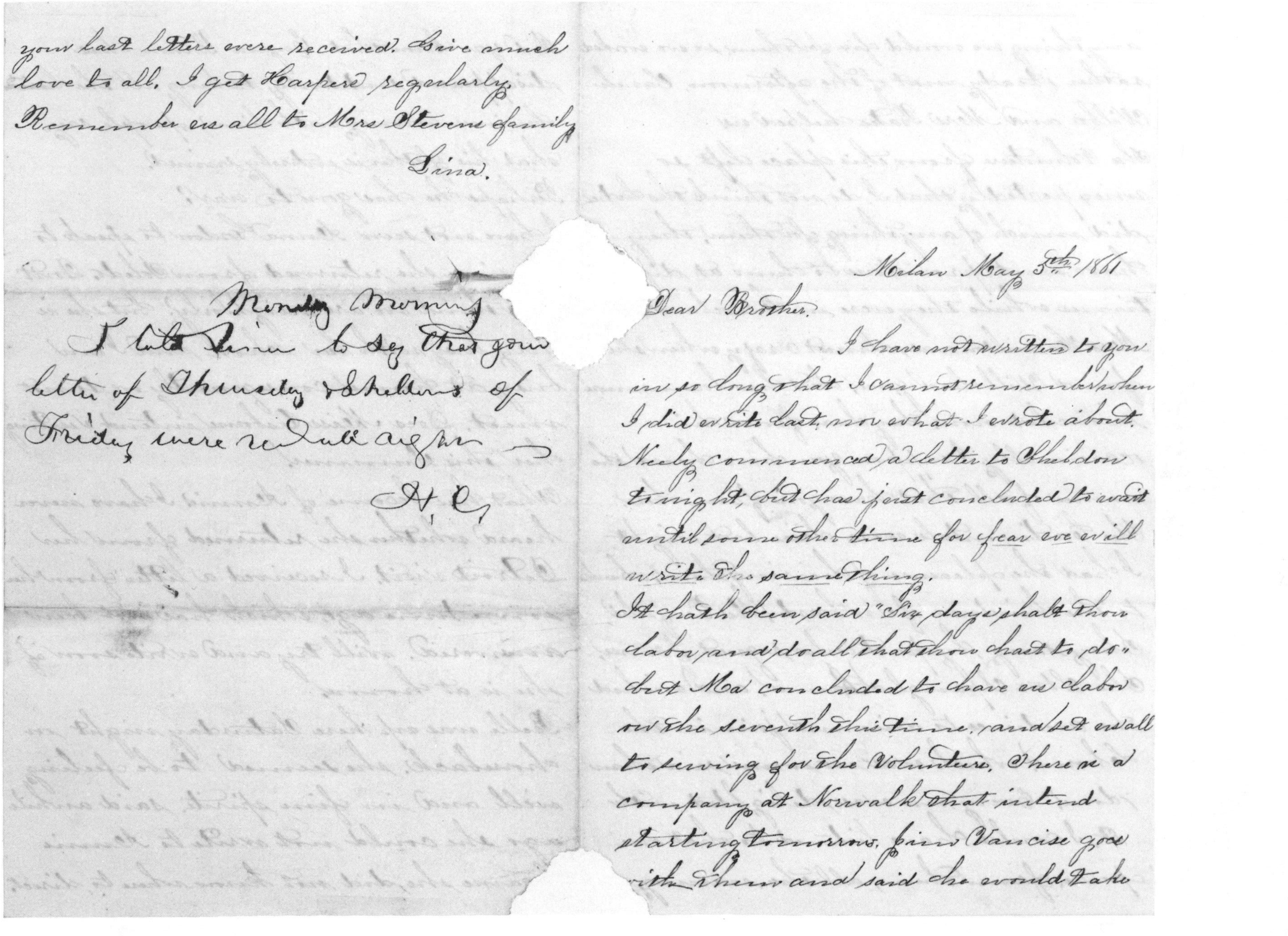

Lina

Milan May 5th 1861

Dear Brother,

I have not written to you in so long that I cannot remember when I did write last, nor what I wrote about. Neely commenced a letter to Sheldon tonight, but has just concluded to wait until some other time for <u>fear</u> <u>we</u> <u>will</u> <u>write</u> the <u>same</u> <u>thing</u>. It hath been said "Six days shalt thou labor and do all that thou hast to do" but Ma concluded to have us labor on the seventh this time, and set us all to serving for the Volunteers. There is a company at Norwalk that intend starting tomorrow. Jim Vancise goes with them and said he would take anything we could fix for them, so we worked rather steady most of the afternoon. Sarah Wilson and Mrs. Bates helped us. The Volunteers from this place left so unexpectedly that I do not think the ladies did much of anything for them. They have sent provisions to them at different times while they were in Cleveland. Mrs. Hamilton was almost crazy when she found Will had gone, but has become more reconciled now. They hear from him occasionally. I suppose you have heard the names of all that have gone from here. The Continentals were here last night. I had the pleasure of hearing them, thanks to the kindness of our boarder, Mr. Penfield. They sang, by particular request of course, the Star Spangled Banner, and wished the audience to arise and join in the Chorus, which was "no sooner said than done". Everyone was delighted with it. I could have listened to that one piece, from them, all the evening. Did you know that Eugene Brown has disappeared suddenly taking all the business money with him. People say that his father is entirely ruined. Perhaps he has gone to <u>war</u>? I have not seen Anna Gordon to speak to since she returned from Toledo. Don't you think we are neighborly? But she is very busy with her school and I am busy at home, consequently we do not meet. Does Miss Osborne intend visiting her this summer. What has become of Annie. I have never heard whether she returned from her Detroit visit. I received a letter from her some time ago which has not been answered. Will try and write soon if she is at home. Belle was up here Saturday night on horseback. She seemed to be feeling well and in fine spirits. Said awhile ago she could not write to Annie because she did not know where to direct, your last letters were received. Give much love to all. I get Harpers regularly. Remember us all to Mrs Stevens family

Lina.

Monday morning
I told Lina to say that your letter of Thursday & Sheldons of Friday were recd all right —

H.C.

Delia

Milan May 6th 1861

Dear Carl

I received your letter a week ago Saturday but did not answer then for I thought I would wait and answer it to day for there would be more to write about but I find there is not so I sit here on the front Stoop I have a beautiful scenery for the Apple, Peach, and Cherry trees are in blossom as far as I can see and the Oriole, Robbin, Wren and Catbird are flying past here and Singing. The Apple tree out by the Summer house looks Splendid It is full of blossoms Some are white and Some are pink Then look at the one nearly at the right of the one just mentioned which only bears once in two years it is crowded full of blossoms. There is a promise of all kinds of fruit both large and small and the Strawberries are in full bloom and look nice. I can not think of any more to write now So good bye from your

Sister
Delia

H Colton

Milan May 9 1861

Dear Carlos

A letter was received from you yesterday containing the usual amt. of "consolation" it found us comfortable as could be expected.

You say Aunt wants to know what your Mother thinks about war? — She has faith in God, Lincoln, Scott Anderson & Slemmer — & feels assured that they will bring matters around right as fast as circumstances will permit — She thinks that patriotism, a love of country & its defence on all proper occasions & by all available means is a constituent part of true religion, for example Jim Vancise has been for some time with a Company at Norwalk awaiting orders. We noticed that he was at home Sunday morning & your Mother called on her way to Sunday school to enquire what was the matter & whether anything was needed she found that he lacked something for the purchase of a revolver. She raised the necessary amount among the teachers & spent the remainder of the day with what help she could get readily, in fitting him out comfortably in the way of divers small matters that may be useful to him in this world or on his way to the next in case he should be hurried in that direction — She thinks farther that even if Parson Brownlows prayers may not avail much either in Tennessee as anywhere else, that it is better to have him on our side than against us — finally She thinks that Truth & Justice are attributes of Omnipotence & must prevail

My Sentiments}　　　　　　　　Yours affectionately
　　M.S.C. —　　　　　　　　　　　H. Colton

The folks intend to send the article they suppose Aunt means for trimming by Mrs. Hamilton as it is rather bulky for mail without a franking privilege ——

"Spauldings Cephalic Glue" is advertised here —

Toledo, O. May 13th 1861.

Dear Father and Mother:

I have had assurances that I can get a commission in the regular army of the United States if I will apply for one, and I would like to have you say what you think about my doing so.

You are perhaps aware that the President has ordered an addition to be made to the army, which will require about five hundred lieutenants, who will have to be mostly taken from among the people, as the officers now in the army will be taken to fill the higher offices.

I have written to you that I enlisted in a military company, but I am not at all sure that the company will go and if they do I would have to go as Commissioned Officer or Musician. This company is composed of too able men - some of them old military men - for me to even attempt to get an office, and I do not much fancy going as Musician, and the army Surgeons would not pass me into the ranks.

I do not intend to withdraw from the company in any event, if they are ordered out, unless I get a Commission.

Sheldon Paton

Toledo, O. May 13 1861.

Dear Father and Mother:

I have had assurances that I can get a commission in the regular army of the United States if I will apply for one, and I would like to have you say what you think about my doing so.

You are perhaps aware that the President has ordered an addition to be made to the army which will require about five hundred lieutenants, who will have to be mostly taken from among the people, as the officers now in the army will be taken to fill the higher offices.

I have written to you that I enlisted in a military company, but I am not at all sure that the company will go and if they do I would have to go as Commissioned Officer or Musician. This company is composed of too able men — some of them old military men — for me to even attempt to get an office, and I do not much fancy going as Musician, and the army Surgeons would not pass me into the ranks.

I do not intend to withdraw from the company in any event, if they are ordered out, unless I get a commission. The addition to the army is for three years or till the expiration of the war I believe, for which time the men would have to enlist, but an officer can throw up his commission at any time, I believe.

The advantages of going as an officer are "too numerous to mention," in all cases. It is perhaps a little more dangerous on the field, but not much, and the chances of being on the field at all are no more than even, as I might, if an officer — be stationed at some fort during the entire campaign.

My health has been so good during the past two or three years that I would anticipate no trouble on that ground, but rather an increase of strength from out door exercise.

The pay of a lieutenant is such that he can make from fifty to Seventy five dollars per month, and so I could do more for the folks at home than I do now, instead of doing less as the case would be if I should go in the ranks, and that is a great inducement to apply for the commission.

I would like to do what I can for my country in the present crisis, and have but little of the "sinews of war" at my command. I have an ordinary amount of sinews of body however, a cool head, and plenty of warm blood to spare if necessary. I hope I have courage enough to stand fire, but cannot tell till I am tried, as I have never been in any very dangerous positions.

I am not afraid to die, and not half as much afraid of pain as I used to be, and besides all that, the chances of getting hurt are small at any rate. If this war should last more than three or four months, the business of the country would be so prostrated that we might be compelled to give up our situations, and then our prospects would be rather slim, while the army under the present circumstances are pretty sure of good pay, especially while the private funds placed at the hands of the government hold out.

All that kept me from immediately applying was the thought of my Mother and Sisters, and how they might feel about it. I am very sure however that they would rather have me go as an offficer than in any other way.

I have said nothing about the glory, because I do not know that there would be much, and I am not particularly anxious for Military fame. I would like to have a reputation for courage for the sake of influence, because then whatever I might say in favor of peace and love to all men could not be attributed to cowardice.

One reason why I would like to go is that when not on duty I would have plenty of time to read and study.

I will not urge the case any farther but rest it till I find out your opinions if you answer in any reasonable time.

I suppose of course you saw "What a Mother thinks" in Saturday's Blade — if not you had better look it over carefully — let me hear what a Mother and sisters think in this case.

All well here.

Yours truly,

Sheldon Colton.

Your letters to Carlos and Myself read

M. S. Colton

My Dear Husband,

Sheldon had told very nearly what he had written in the letter you returned, & it seems to me now, when I hear him talk about it, & know what his feelings are, it would not be right to make the least objection to his going, if he gets a Commission, his Uncle & others seem to think, there is but little doubt about it, as they know of no one else in this part of the State that has any idea of applying, for the same — Sheldon feels that it is just such a life as will suit him, & that he would be happier, in such a situation, than he could be in any other, & if he should go, & continue to feel as he does now about it, I should try to be contented, his Uncle, Mr. Raymond, & Mr. Stevens will use all their influence in his behalf —

If there should be another call for Volunteers, Carlos says he "Shall most certainly go" but <u>he</u> <u>thinks</u> <u>Sheldon</u> <u>ought</u> <u>to</u> <u>stay</u> <u>at</u> <u>home</u>, — this is Carlos most busy time, & have scarcely any chance to visit with him yet. He will probably have more leisure time next week — I should feel a great deal more anxiety about Carlos, if he should go, for I do not think he could endure near as much fatigue & exposure, as Sheldon could, the evenings that he drills, here now, he comes in so tired, he can hardly speak — but he thinks he should grow stronger immediately, should he leave his office, & have more out door exposure but <u>I</u> <u>feel</u>, that he could not <u>endure</u> the <u>hardening</u> ——

Delia is enjoying herself finely, a part of the time with Kitty Chase at school & some times with Sarah Stevens at home — Mrs. Stevens was not as well again, for a day or two the first of this week, but was much better again yesterday, when I spent a part of the afternoon with her. I do not think best to stay with her but a little while at a time, for she <u>will</u> <u>talk</u> <u>too</u> <u>much</u> —

Lucy is in Perrysburg. Aunt, Delia & I will probably go up there sometime next week, — Aunt has a good deal of <u>visiting</u> marked out for us, & if you all keep well at home, think I shall enjoy myself pretty well, another week — Sheldon has Summer Coat, which I think will fit you, & he does not need it now, since he got his new suit. I will put it in a basket, with some other things of theirs, that they do not care about keeping here, & will send them the first of the week. I have taken Lina's shawl to the Dyers, but cannot have it until the last of next week —

For two or three days past I have been disappointed in not hearing anything from home — but have tried to think that you are all well, but too busy to write — Sheldon says you must not try to work when you are not able, for he can send you enough more at any time, to pay for hiring whatever you may want — Aunt is waiting for me to get through with my writing, so that she can write a few lines to Fannie — I must close now, with much love to all, Lottie & family included — Yours Affectionately

M.S.Colton

Perrysburg June 15th 1861

Dear Husband,

Sheldon & Arthur came up with
us Saturday evening, & returned on the Boat this
morning, yesterday afternoon, I walked with Sheldon
Arthur & Delia, up to Fort Meigs, then went down
the hill to Aurora Spaffords old place, but could
find nothing there but the old well, & the found
ation, of the chimney of Spaffords house, not a
vestige remaining of any other building on the
flats, except a part of the foundation of
Hollisters store, —— Lucy is very pleasantly
situated here, lives about a quarter of a mile
below Hollister, on the same street — John has
a very good situation as they now think, in
partnership with a young Man that he likes
very much, they are doing a good Cash busines
keep nothing on hand but dry goods ——
If you all keep well at home, think I shall
enjoy a weeks visiting here, shall probably
return to Toledo Saturday, or Monday if Carlos
can come up Saturday to return with Me —
The "Basket" arrived just in time to be opened
so that I could take out the flowers, & distribute

40

M. S. Colton

Perrysburg June 17th 1861

Dear Husband,

Sheldon & Arthur came up with us Saturday evening, & returned on the Boat this morning, yesterday afternoon, I walked with Sheldon Arthur & Delia, up to Fort Miegs, then went down the hill to Aurora Spaffords old place, but could find nothing there but the old well, & the foundation, of the chimney of Spaffords house, not a vestige remaining of any other building on the flats, except a part of the foundation of Hollisters Store.— Lucy is very pleasantly situated here, lives about a quarter of a mile below Hollisters, on the same street— John has a very good situation as they now think, in partnership with a young man that he likes very much, they are doing a good <u>Cash</u> business keep nothing on hand but <u>dry goods</u> — If you all keep <u>well</u> at home, think I shall enjoy a week's visiting here, shall probably return to Toledo Saturday, or Monday if Carlos can come up Saturday to return with me —

The "Basket" arrived just in time to be opened so that I could take out the flowers, & distribute   I left my boquet with Aunt, & the two that Nelia sent for <u>her</u> friends, was left in Abram's care to be given as directed, then took a part of the Currants & about a pint of the Strawberries, in a little pail, & Sheldon's boquet in my hand and started for the Boat. Sheldon could not leave his office in time to go up to the house, for me, but Charlie Chase took Delia & I with our luggage, in their buggy, to his father's Warehouse, where we remained an hour or more before the Boat left — Have been very busily engaged a good deal of the time in repairing the Boys Clothes, am now making some shirts for Carlos. If I should stay two or three weeks longer, should probably find enough to do for them, to keep me pretty busy, but I do not intend to stay longer than, sometime next week, & not as long as that, unless y<u>our</u> health improves. I have hoped all the time, that as the weather became warmer you would feel better, not have so much of the headache, write soon & often & let me know just how your are, or I shall not be contented to stay much longer — Delia has got over her homesickness, & is now enjoying herself well — If the girls can find a sample of the last Calico Shirts we made for Sheldon (I think they will find some in the flat round work basket in our bedroom) I would like to have a half yard more of it, (it was bought at James Lockwoods) sent to Toledo, that I can make him some collars, when I return there, I thought perhaps you could send it in the "Free Press".

Poe is expected here this week to attend Court, he is expecting now to be admitted to the Bar — If Addie does not come too I may <u>possibly</u> return with him & stay a day or two —

Lucy unites with us in sending love to <u>all</u>, & Delia sends her <u>special regards</u> to Miss Carree Bell —

As ever y<u>ours</u> truly & affectionate
M. S. Colton

41

Trenton, July 9th 1861

Dear Brother

I received a Toledo paper from you lately in which was a piece of poetry written, by Sheldon. It is a beautiful piece, and I am gratified to see that you are mindful of me, in my solitude. About the time I went to Detroit I received an Oswego paper from you, which I was very glad to get, and the Independent I receive regularly so the greater part of my reading matter comes from you.

I have heard lately that Sheldon is going to Washington, as private Secretary to Gen. Hill, I suppose the situation is a desirable one, particularly as he will not be called on to fight. I suppose Delia will not consider me very patriotic.

Clarindas health is very good but her right side is still weak, she is not able to do much work with her right hand. Phin still has the Office of Inspector, comes home saturday evenings and returns monday mornings. Is Melinda at home? if so give her my love and tell her that I am well aware that I have not answered her letter but shall endeavor to do so in the course of human events. I hope my friends will not infer from my silence that their letters are not acceptable, be assured that nothing short of a personal interview can be more gratifying to me. My time is principally occupied in domestic affairs not that my work is very hard, but after it is done for the day, I am unfit for writing, in short I am growing old. Do you hear anything of the Rev S.W.B it is now past the time that he spoke of coming West.

I shall be obliged to close as I have an opportunity of sending this to Trenton love to all, your Sister
C. Bill.

Autumn Leaves

They sent me a fading leaflet,
 From the scene of my boyhood hours,
Where the tall oak trees are waving
 Their boughs o'er the woodland flowers;
Where the robin and bluebird are singing
 The morning song of old,
And the honey-bee gathers treasures
 From cups of liquid gold.

And it spoke to me in whispers
 That only the heart could hear,
Of the scenes that memory clusters
 Around the homestead dear;
But not to memory only
 The gentle whisper came,
For Fancy painted a picture
 Worthy of golden frame.

She saw bright Nature's artists
 Busily working all,
Preparing colors and brushes
 To use in the coming fall.
Jack Frost, the master painter,
 Was soon to visit the land,
And they must all be ready
 At the wave of his magic wand.

And one little elf by moonlight
 Was busy the whole night long
Stealing from sleeping roses
 Some tints to rival the dawn;
Then back to the woods he hurried
 For a brush of thistle down,
And a smooth green leaf for a palette
 To mix his colors on.

From the first faint, reddening glimmer
    That tinged the eastern skies,
To the golden light of morning
    He mimicked the magic dyes:
Then threw down his little palette
    And hastily flew away;
For he must not be seen by mortals
    In the full broad light of day.

A little blue-eyed maiden
    Arose with the morning sun
And walking out in the garden
    She saw what the elf had done,
And she picked up the little leaflet
    With various tints o'er spread,
And as she musingly held it,
    'Twas thus to herself she said:
"In a distant, crowded city,
    'Mid the noise and bustle and heat,
My brother is daily toiling
    Far away from this cool retreat;
I will send him this little token,
    'Tis a trifling one 'tis true,
But 'twill speak to his heart of the homestead,
    The birds and the flowers too."

'Twas sent, and the weary brother
    Received with glad surprise
The gift of the little maiden
    For it brought sweet memories;
He has painted fancy's picture,
    And the words she spoke has told —
But memories are too sacred
    For the pen to e'er unfold.

              Sheldon Colton

Carlos

Toledo Aug 9th/61

Dear Father

I was glad to see Sheldon today back again all right and hope he has seen enough of the "pomp and circumstance of War" for the present he says Mr. Raymond told him he could go to work again at anytime. And he seems to think he will do so tomorrow or Monday. Says Mr. Raymond says he has credited up the $150— it seems there was a months Salary not credited that made the difference in their accts —

The <u>Major</u> General Agent of the N Y Life Ins Co of which Mortimer is Agent at this point is around again he is establishing State Agencies and wants a general Agt for Ohio. Mortimer recommended you for the position and came near sending Mr. Backus (the Agt) to Milan to see you but I told him it was no use you could not stand the travel, if it could be attended to at home you could do it but your health would not admit of it otherwise, it was then suggested that you might take Erie Co. — I dont suppose you would be able to make it an object but you know better than I and can report —

We have got a large comfortable office now on the quiet side of the street, and from the back room get a breeze from the river — have got a new $200— lock on the vault door in the place of one that <u>I wouldnt have anything to do with at first</u>. I am improving in health — tell Ma I <u>cut off my moustache</u> long ago — was sorry to learn by Sheldon that Ma wasnt well this morning — I suppose Sheldon told you he did not write that piece you thought he did from Columbus signed "S" — I understand it was written by Larson Smythe who used to live here — Mrs. Stevens is about the same — Henry Waite is still alive without consciousness ———
I send $5———

Love to all from
Carlos

H. Calton

Milan Aug. 11 1861

Dear Carlos,

      Your letter was duly received yesterday & contents carefully noted, which said contents have become so much a matter of course that it would seem hardly worth while to say more on each successive arrival there that it comes safely though the certainty & frequency by no means lessens the feeling of thankfulness that arises each time on receipt of such favors — not to you & Sheldon particularly except as faithful agents — for y<u>ou</u> <u>cant</u> <u>help</u> <u>it</u> but to the higher power that has preserved <u>such</u> sons to us for the staff & pride of our declining years — & imbued your hearts with a spirit of filial duty, kindness & liberality, our feelings on that subject you cannot <u>now</u> be expected to realize —

      You are right in supposing that I couldnt do justice to business that required much exertion or fatigue, & a home Life Insurance Agency must be a small matter at best in a community like this where a larger proportion of the inhabitants are little better than dead already, & where there isn't even the ghost of a "Free Press" left to advertise in, It would involve the necessity of keeping a "place of <u>business</u>" down Town & I dont know of anything that could be connected with it to make it an object for me to emerge from my present <u>status</u> of dignified retirement & exclusiveness — Still I would be exceedingly glad of some profitable employment, & if the <u>Major</u> General should offer such terms for an Agency for this county, or for this & Huron combined as you may think could possibly be made to pay anything for the trouble, I would use my best endeavor to make it do so —

      I would like to have you & Sheldon do what I have done today viz. read Mr. Beechers last & best published in the Independent of the 8th, last Thursday.

48

H. Culton

There is also on the first page of the same paper a letter from Washington signed B. & written by him no doubt — which among other things explains what had puzzled me in regard to the battle three weeks ago to day — I have queried a good deal within myself why after the partial repulse of Thursday, Sunday should have been selected for a renewal of the fight. ——

It seems to have been understood there that that day was selected solely to give idle Congressmen a chance to see the fight, men that had forced on the imprudent movement by taking up the Tribune — cry of "On to Richmond" — It is a great pity that Old Secesh had not nabbed every whelp of them, if he could make them useful in throwing up intrenchments. —

Your mother is highly pleased to learn from your letter, that you have removed the outward & visible sign, of an inward & martial spirit, that had begun to manifest itself on your upper lip — & hopes Sheldon may be induced to follow the good example — now that his value cannot be questioned since by his forced march from Toledo to Graften he closed up the war in that region so gloriously

She hopes you may both be satisfied with civil life & peaceful pursuits, till the country needs your services, which time we trust may be distant — Your Mother is recovering from the severe attack she had when Sheldon was here — she has been sitting up mostly to day — & has just been informed that Mrs. Carter has been guilty of a slight break of the Sabbath this P.M. — excusable under the circumstances — result a ten pounder of the female persuasion ——

Yours Affectionately

Shelden Seton

Toledo, O. Aug. 19 — 1861.

Dear Mother:

I have gone to work again as you know, for Raymond and Jones, but cannot tell how long the arrangements may last, as business is not exceedingly lively. They do not say anything about not wanting me but their partnership year is out the first of next month, and though their time was not limited, they may think it a good time to place their matters in a different shape if desireable. I do not know how such a change would affect me, and in fact do not know that there will be any change made, only if there is to be one, that would be the proper time to do it. We will find out in time probably.

I called on the Mrs Stevens yesterday, and found her pretty weak. She seems to be failing slowly. She cannot lie down any now, and gets but very little sleep. Not more than a half an hour each night she says. She is very nervous too, and easily affected by anything disturbing. She said if she had a fortune she would spend it for nothing so quick as a good nights rest. Jane Norton has gone home but Mrs Ryan is here yet. The rest of our acquaintances are well yet I believe.

I am boarding at Mrs Eldridge's, where I was before I went away. Her oldest daughter is away visiting, but Mary is here, and a Music teacher — Miss Page — is boarding there also, so we have some sport occasionally. Miss Page is an Irish girl I think, at any rate she has an old country style of conversation that is quite amusing at times. She is very fond of chess playing also, but I have played but one evening with her, and then we were about even, though by strict rules I won both games.

When I was at home I discovered that you was buying flour in small quantities, and upon suggesting the propriety of buying a

barrel at a time I was informed that there was seldom a sufficient amount of cash on hand for that purpose. I have sent two barrels by Rail Road today, but it did not come convenient to pay the freight on them which will be forty cents, to Norwalk. I presume you can raise a sum large enough to get them home if I sent you three dollars in this as I expect to do. I got the flour for ten dollars, and you can send up a receipt for that amount to be placed to my credit in the final balancing of all things.

I would like to have Father see what the chance is for getting the cash for five or ten brls. of flour of this quality — and it was sold to me as the best, and what amount of cash could be got for it, delivered in Milan. I think I can get flour from Mr. Raymond's brother at anytime, on favorable terms. I do not care about his taking any particular trouble in the matter, but just make the inquiry casually when he has an opportunity, perhaps I will not send any more at all, certainly not unless I think it will pay pretty well, and no trouble.

I met Grandmother and Lucinda at the depot a day or two ago, on their way to Perrysburgh, and sent Myra's letter up there for them to read. I presume they will not go to Milan this time.

They have commenced recruiting again for the Fourteenth Regiment, but it will probably take them some little time to fill up. I believe they are to have an encampment for several regiments a little distance out from town.

Enclosed find $3.00 —

Love to all — especially Lottie and family — It does not come so hard to be Uncle now as it did at first. Honors set easy on me now.

Yours truly —
Sheldon Colton
— cold again —

The Dream Car

O'er my writing desk wearily bending,
    'Neath the summer day's sultry heat,
In the heart of the busy city,
    I long for a cool retreat.
No zephyrs, with perfume laden
    From the rose, or the lily, come there;
Nor sound of the murmuring brooklet,
    To gladden the hot, stifling air.

The iron limbed giant is toiling
    All day close by in the mill;
Little recks he of the sunshine;
    His food, it is hotter still.
The monotone sound of his breathing
    Falls dreamily on my ear,
Till the endless columns of figures
    Commingle and disappear.

In the "Dreamer's Car" I am riding
    Back to my boyhood's home,
Leaving "Debtor and Credit"
    To care for themselves while I roam;
And soon again I am standing
    'Neath the spreading chestnut trees,
While the sound of the toiling engine
    Is the voice of the evening breeze.

I stroll again through the valley
    Beside the winding stream,
Where in by-gone days I wandered,
    When life was a golden dream;
Where I lured the bright-scaled fishes
    From the limpid depths below,
And the sound of the toiling engine
    Is the rippling brooklet's flow.

Again through the leafy forest
　　With my rifle, I wander now,
To bring down the cunning squirrel
　　From his seat on the lofty bough.
On a mossy bank I am sitting
　　And low, sweet tones are heard,
And the sound of the toiling engine
　　Is the voice of the warbling bird.

Then homeward my steps are turning
　　As the setting sun goes down,
And shadows are slowly creeping
　　To the eastward along the ground.
The air is cool and fragrant,
　　As through the fields I come,
And the sound of the toiling engine
　　Is the wild bee's busy hum.

'Tis night, and the stars are gleaming
　　In the boundless space above;
While the firelight now is falling
　　On the faces of those I love.
All of the happy circle
　　Have knelt in worship there,
While the sound of the toiling engine
　　Is my mother's murmured prayer.

The sweet goodnights are spoken
　　With a blessing on each head;
The rest to sleep retiring,
　　But I to wake instead;
For the Dream Car's flight is ended,
　　My desk I am bending o'er
And the sound of the toiling engine
　　Is fancy's theme no more.

Sheldon Colton

Relative

Trenton August 27th, 1861.

Dear Melinda

Think not from my delay in answering your kind letter, that it was received with indifference. I will not attempt to excuse myself, for what you may consider negligence, but merely add that it may be in part, not wholly, I think of you every hour in the day, and truly sympathise with you in this your just grief, parting with your dear son, Sheldon, let us hope and pray that it is not a final separation, should it prove to be, we can only say Gods will be done, it is He alone that can heal the broken heart and dry the mourners tears. O Melinda in this distracted state of the country how little we know of the fate that awaits us, when will this terrible war close! not until hundreds and thousands of valuable lives are sacrificed.

Your Mother and Lucinda left here about ten days ago for Perrysburg after spending about a week there they expected to make a visit in Toledo, your Mother will then go to Milan and Lucinda returns home at least that was her calculation, when she left I have just received Linas letter informing me that Lottie has another daughter, give her my love and tell her if she is troubled to find a name I propose the name of its great-Aunty, with a slight abbreviation, for instance Clarie Bill

The photograph of Sheldon I prise very highly, we all think it an excellent likeness, his letters to the Editor of the Blade are very interesting. I hope Hamilton will continue to think of me whenever there is a letter published, from him, intelligence from him by any source will be interesting to me as well as the rest of his friends. Since receiving Linas letter, I have concluded to be the more brief with you and write a few lines to her and hope you will both excuse me for enclosing in one envelope, stamps and change are both scarce. Tell Hamilton I receive my Independent regularly, also Harper, to Clarinda
Love to all

Yours Truly
C. Bill.

Toledo O. Sept. 29th 1861

Dear Delia:

I received a letter from you a few days before I went to Milan, and think I will answer it now.

You can tell Father that I sent a copy of that item which he enclosed to me, a day or so before his letter was received to Genl Hill with a request to do what he could for me but have heard nothing from him since.

I have got something going that will bring me out all right however, I think. It is generally understood that there is to be a new regiment formed here, and Hon. Richard Mott, M.R. Waite Esq. Mr. Hathaway, and Mr. Raymond, as I understand it, are all going to Columbus tomorrow to make the necessary arrangements. They have all said that I could have a commission as Lieutenant and go to work to raise a Company. So I presume there is no doubt about my getting it this time, and if you know of any good boys who would like to be soldiers you can tell them to wait two or three days and I will give them a chance.

If I get the commission as I expect to I shall be in Milan by Thursday I think. I do not know as I can get any recruits there but think I can somewhere around in the country.

Tell Mother that I have just been to see Mrs. Stevens and she is looking very weak. She says "tell your Mother that I am not able to walk across the floor without almost fainting." She says she has almost lost her faith in homeopathy, at least as far as curing the dropsy is concerned; but I do not think she will change treatments now.

She talks pretty strongly of going to Milan if she can to place herself under Dr. Gibsen's care, as she has heard that he was very successful in treating the dropsy. She would like to see Mother again, she says.

The war fever is pretty strong here now, and I think that this new regiment will be composed of good men. I should not wonder at all if Mr. Raymond would be one of the field officers. He seems to take a good deal of interest in it this time. I would like to go to war under him, as I think he would be kind to his men, and careful of their welfare if he was an officer. He says he is going to raise a company at any rate. I think I have a pretty fair chance of raising a company myself and if so, I presume I can be Captain if I wish to, but I do not exactly like to take the responsibility of doing so, until I am better acquainted with the duties of the place. I would take it though under some circumstances.

Give my love to all of the folks.
Enclosed find three dollars.
Yours truly,
Sheldon Colton.
I heard that John Turner wanted to go to war if he does I can give him a chance I think. Tell him so if you see him.

H. Colton

Milan Oct 1 1861

Dear Carlos,

Your letter was rec'd Saturday evening & Sheldons about the same time — The girls soon brought in each a recruit from the Normal scholars. One of them whose name I mentioned in a recent letter to Sheldon, will go as "Orderly" in case Arthur should want the place of 2 Lieut under his commission, if not he will take that poor.

Sheldon has seen the old sarge that he relies on as 1 Lieut & is pleased with him & his prospects in the way of raising men — I shouldnt be surprised if his Company should claim the post of honor by being the first one filled for the Regt. notwithstanding two companies have been recruited in Ohio neighbourhood recently. The Cavalry company left for Camp at Monroeville Saturday & Shipman Company is about full ——— I telegraphed you this morning in hopes that a word by way of puff might come back in the Blade this evening for the reason that Victor of Sandusky opened a recruiting office here on Friday & it is desirable to scatter information as early as possible — we do not of course fear him if Sheldon can get about an equal start — Banks is to hang out the banner this morning & Sheldon to prospect in the vicinity today & address a Union meeting on Packer Brush this evening. He intends to go to Toledo tomorrow when he can report more fully as to prospects than I can at this writing —   I enclose an Advertisement for the Blade, any proper amendment before insertion will be in order ———

Yours affectionately
H. Colton

H. Colton

Milan Octr. 3rd 1861

Dear Carlos

      We recd. some "Pencilings by the way" from Sheldon yesterday advising of his change of employment — There seemed to be some objection to his attempting a military life & I have till recently discouraged his doing so, though I was glad of course to see that he was not insensible to the call of duty, & he will doubtless discharge it to the best of his ability —

      We hope from the applause that Nelias composition recd in school yesterday that he may be able to raise a few recruits from the Normal. I enclose it for your perusal without her knowledge & you can return it at some convenient time, she would'nt like to have it seen in its present shape, she says she "just scribbled it off in a hurry", an incorrigible way she has of doing things — but her disposition is so kind & gentle that it will cover a multitude of sins.

      I wrote to Sheldon yesterday, which of course did not find him — you might open the letter & if the composition it contains can be of service to any young man aspiring to military honors, let him have it ——

                Yours affectionately
                H. Colton

Sheldon Colton [signature]

Milan O. Nov. 8th 1861

Dear Brother,

Your letter containing the $5. was rec'd in due time today and also the bugles and the $3. some days ago, but I forgot to acknowledge the receipt of them at the time.

I have more trouble than the law allows with the Germans connected with the band, and am not certain of starting them all now. They are very much afraid of having some trick played on them, and I hope they will get sworn in to stay when they go up tomorrow.

I do not much expect to get thirty men by next Thursday, though I shall work the best I know how. I have eleven sworn in now and several have promised to come in tomorrow and more on Monday.

I have had hard work here, and not a particle of assistance from the source from which it should have come. The men who have enlisted with me have done what they could but they were no more able than I was. I could make a good report for the benefit of this district Committee.

There is to be a scholars gathering at the Seminary this evening, and I hope to be able to do something there. One needs all of the patience of which a man was ever possessed to keep his temper and listen to the excuses of able bodied young men who are asked to enlist, for instance: one young man who is perfectly able to go, told me that he thought he could make a little more money by teaching school at twenty five dollars a month this winter — didn't know but he would enlist in the spring. I felt as if I would like to meet him down South.

Buck sent down my Uniform a day or two ago, but the blouse was not at all what he agreed to send. I will see him when I come up. You can tell him so and that if he wants the blouse before Thursday, he can let me know.

All well here —

Yours truly
Sheldon Colton

Sheldon Colton (signature)

Milan O. Nov. 12 1861

Dear Brother:

I was surprised as well as pleased today at receiving a notice of my appointment as Second Lieut. in Haskins' Company, just the place I wanted to get and one which I shall endeavor to fill to the best of my ability.

I would like to have Buck make me a regular coat now like the first one he made only be sure to get it large enough this time, and I would like to have it here by Saturday if possible.

I have enlisted two more men, and that makes thirteen, and one boy has just gone for his mother to give her written consent, so that he can enlist, if she does I will have fourteen men, and I hope to swell the number some tonight but do not know yet how that will be.

It is about time for me to go after Mr. Brown and I will close. You will hear from me again in a day or two. Ask Haskins if it is sure enough about the Commission to get a uniform if you happen to see him, if not it is no matter. All well here,

Yours truly

Sheldon Colton

Relative

Mutual Insurance Company of Toledo

Toledo, Ohio, Novem 27 1861

D Brother

The enclosed are from the Golden Aid Society

The Milan Teachers and your young Ladies would be very much astonished to see a document which Alphy brought Home a day or two since being the Autographs of Miss T Brown Supt. & R Dickinson Principal certify, that for the whole term then expressed he had not been absent 1/2 a day or tardy once   I intend to have it framed for the benifit of posterity

So far as I can judge Sheldons prospects are fair, for his Commission and pay, during the progress of things I have sometimes almost regretted that I had not tendered his services to Genl Anderson in Kentucky — who was some years since _my_ Superior Officer, it may however be as well as it is

Yours
C

The Money that Sheldon will need
will be ready for him whenever he wants it

H Calton

Milan Dec. 24 1861

Dear Carlos,

Your unquestionably sincere wish for a Merry Christmas — because accompanied by the essential to make one — is received, & the motive that prompted it duly appreciated, which would seem to be all that need be said on that point, as you seem to pay no regard to my recent previous remonstrance against your backing such wishes for us with too much liberality —

We can only return the <u>wish,</u> so extended as to cover many future festive seasons with abundant <u>wherewithat</u> to make them merry — And if perchance in the dim distant future, Bairns, bairns shall kindly cuddle your "auld grey hair" — may they be <u>like</u> <u>ours,</u> then you be blessed indeed

We were rather glad that the 67th took the other route as it could have been rather hard to let them pass Norwalk without seeing some of us — & considering the few minutes they would have stopped there & the probability that Sheldon will come home from Columbus, it would have been hardly worth while to merely take a look at them there — at the expense of a tedious ride over the rough roads ——

Sheldon has received some pretty severe lessons in human nature during the last three months, which I hope may be useful to him hereafter, he needed just such schooling, we encouraged him as much as possible, but he seemed sometimes almost inclined to think that there was a good deal of bogus patriotism & dishonesty among the representatives of "Young America." — hope his future military experience may be less perplexing.

H Colton

With regard to the "splendid fellow" Annie spoke of — he had attended school here a term or two & I had heard the young ones speak of him frequently but had never seen him till shortly before Sheldon came, learning that he intended to enlist I directed the girls to detain if possible for Sheldon, & it was lucky they did for without him S. could hardly have made a start.— Your Mother & I were much pleased with his active & prompt appearance as we noticed him casually passing in & out — but were exceedingly surprised in a more intimate acquaintance to find him quite illiterate & that he had evidently come up from somewhere without any early training — but he seems to be strong, healthy & ambitious, of good ideas as to morals & habits & inclined to look up for associates — which are very commendable points in a young mans character —

This will perhaps explain an allusion to him in a previous letter. I judged that you would not like to have company from home while the subject remained at Toledo

I presume from appearances that he has a right to carry the Ambrotype as nigh his heart as he pleases, though nothing has been said on the subject —

A womans heart is a very mysterious article perhaps I might moralize on the subject as you and experience give me a right to do but fortunately for you it is getting dark & the folks will mail this on the way to church provided it is close, which it is & will merely observe that Lina will superscribe it as a small name will best suit a small envelope which is the only one we happen to have   Yours H Colton

1862

General Ulysses S. Grant, with a force of 15,000 men, captures Fort Henry, February 6. Fort Donelson surrenders, February 16.

An indecisive battle between the two ironclad vessels, the "Monitor" and the "Merrimac", is waged on March 9.

General N.P. Banks occupies Winchester on March 12, causing General T.J. "Stonewall" Jackson to retreat up the Shenandoah Valley.

General James Shields is attacked at Kernstown, south of Winchester, on March 22. When wounded during this battle, Shields turns over his command to Colonel Kimball. On March 24, the Federal artillery posted on Pritchard's Hill causes the Confederates to retreat from Sandy Ridge. Confederate losses at Kernstown — 718 from a force of 3,000 infantry, 290 cavalry and 27 guns; Federal losses — 590 from a force of 6,000 infantry, 750 cavalry and 24 guns.

Federal troops are defeated at the First Battle of Winchester, where General Nathaniel P. Banks loses 3,000 men (most of whom are captured).

From June 25 to July 1 (the "Seven Days"), Generals Robert E. Lee and McCLellan engage in the battle for possession of Richmond. Although the Confederates retreat, McLellan fails to occupy the city.

President Lincoln issues his Emancipation Proclamation in September, effective January 1, 1863.

Grant moves against Vicksburg, but retires back when his supply depot at Holly Springs is destroyed, December 20.

On December 29, General William Tecumseh Sherman is defeated at Chickasaw Bluffs, six miles north of Vicksburg.

Sheldon is wounded at the Battle of Kernstown, then captured by the Confederates when Winchester is re-taken. On May 27, Sheldon and his Sergeant James Banks, despite their injuries, manage to escape and return home. While recovering from his wounds, Sheldon works as Muster Roll clerk in the Adjutant General's Office in Columbus.

Carlos and his cousin Hammie enlist for three months in the 84th Ohio. They are sent to Camp Lawrence in Cumberland, Md., where Hammie unexpectedly dies of typhoid fever.

Nelia teaches school and boards in Milan.

Carlos

Toledo Jany 15th 1862

Dear Sister Delia

        I received your letter written the 12th and was very glad to hear from you after so long silence — I read along some distance before I looked at the signature, and thought it was from Nelia. You have improved very much indeed in your writing and composing. I have just been writing to Sheldon — got a letter from him today. You saw by the Blade I suppose that the Regiment had orders to march and then the orders were countermanded — he says he will not have a chance to go home. Revd Anson Smyth and daughter called on him and invited him to go home with them and stay over night, but he couldnt get away — he seems to be in good health and spirits. Hattie Lockwood is visiting at J D Smiths — I think some of calling on her this evening —— We had some skating yesterday but today the sleighs are running

I must close and go to tea — We are all well and trust you are — Love to all — I send a note to father ——
Please write again soon to your brother
                Carlos

Carlos

Toledo Jany 20th/62

Dear Mother

As J Norton is here and going home today I will probably send this by him — with the slip I send a little package from Annie for Lottie's baby, which she intended to send some time ago — about christmas I think. Also enclose some Secession Whittling — which Sheldon sent by a member of the 67th a few days ago — and some traps he left with me to be sent home, when he went away — the picture is for Lina. I suppose he has gone from Columbus as telegrams were recd here by two or three officers of 67th Friday that hurried them away. We have reports this morning of a big fight in Kentucky resulting in the defeat of the rebels and the death of "Zollicoffer" — <u>good</u> if <u>true!</u> In two or three letters from home recently there have been objections raised to my boarding at a public house, but I dont think with sufficient cause. It is more of a boarding house than a public hotel they dont keep any <u>bar</u>, and have some pleasant boarders. A gentleman (a business man here) and wife, named <u>Sheldon</u>, who I have known a long time have a suite of rooms with a piano and a collection of books, and both have cordially asked me to make their apartment my home to come and go when I choose. Sheldon is, like <u>our</u> Sheldon, a man who neither drinks smokes nor chews —
I dont know how long I shall board there but certainly dont know of a better place now —— Sleighing is still good, and well improved by the use of fast teams — We are all well as usual if not more so — In last letter from Sheldon he spoke of a cane which he was going to send to father by express if he found no other way — Love to all —
From your affectionate son
Carlos

I trust this cloth is dyed the right color and style — if not please let me know ——

H Colton

Milan Jany 31 — 1862

Dear Carlos,

Your letter of yesterday is received all right & contents noted.

I have sometimes made complaint of your liberality in remitting, fearing that you must of course deprive yourself in such cases of some necessary matters of comfort or enjoyment to which you are certainly entitled. — Still I have usually been obliged to admit to myself that you knew best what was needed, for instance when you sent $10— week before last I had hardly got it fobbed when Mr. Tax Collector called with a claim that used it up within a few cents — A recent law has changed the time of payment & I had forgotten that it was due in Dec. instead February as heretofore — I was figuring this morning to see how far a prospective five dollars could be spread over an empty Barn cellar & cupboard & will not at this time complain that it was more than could be used comfortably, though the mystery is in this case, as it has been a good many times heretofore, <u>how</u> <u>did</u> <u>you</u> <u>know</u> what amount would be particularly useful.

Lina also recd. a letter from Sheldon of the 24th enclosing a Photograph which I take to be merely a fancy picture of the <u>way</u> <u>he</u> <u>expects</u> <u>to</u> <u>look</u> to outsiders in case he should bring up in a Secesh dungeon, — As a likeness of him <u>in</u> <u>the</u> <u>bod</u>y I dont think it amounts to much.

Lottie received a letter from him two days later, though nothing important additional. — Every time we have heard from Sheldon lately he has been engaged <u>making</u> <u>out</u> <u>pay</u> <u>rolls,</u> — it is to be hoped he will get them finished soon & draw some pay which might relieve you a little, as well as him — He writes that he didnt get his Livery bills, while recruiting allowed, which was the principal item of expense. I hardly thought he would, it would have made no difference in the amount of them with him whether he or the Govt. had to foot them, but I take it some of the recruiting officers would spread themselves if Uncle Sam was soft enough to foot their livery bills ——

Lina says that her last letter to you was superscribed by Agnes Ingersoll, who teaches writing at the Normal — She thinks you may have been disappointed on opening it to find the signature different from the superscription. — Lina & Nelia have hopes of getting rather pleasant county schools in the Spring, they intend to go tomorrow to make personal application.

All well & nothing new ——
Yours affectionately
H Colton

Sheldon Morton.
Lieut 67" Regt O.V.I.

Carlos

Toledo Feby 7th 1862

Dear Father

I have deferred writing for two or three days in hope of receiving a letter from Sheldon and got it this noon, dated "Camp Sanders New Creek Va Feby 4th" — He does not say anything in regard to the Colonels trouble which you have of course heard of partially through the papers, it seems to be almost a fact that he is to be superceded by Genl Hill. Hill was asked if he would accept the Command and replied in the affirmation. Sheldon writes that he has received his Camp Chest and as his valise is only in the way is going to send it home via Toledo — He says "you can keep my valise or send it home just as you choose" — unless you need the valise at home I will keep it — He says the 53rd Reg. came there the previous night and encamped close by them and he saw quite a number of Milan boys — Aunt Sophia has just recvd from New York a $35 Sewing Machine which she is greatly charmed with — and says "tell your Mother when she comes in the Spring she must bring along all her work" ——Am invited to a party at Lucien Fitches tonight and think I will go — Sheldon says has not got his pay yet and probably wouldnt till last of month — will send your draft sometime this month for Insurance —

Love to all

Send enclosed $5—

Carlos

Pawpaw Tunnel, Va. Feb. 12th 1862

Dear Father:

Your letter of the 5th Inst. came duly to hand. We did not stay at New Creek as long as you thought we would, and when we left there it was in a hurry with a pretty fair prospect of a fight.

I have had a pretty rough time for about a week. On the 5" Inst. we left New Creek and came down to French's Store — about a mile and a half below the junction of the North and South branches of the Potomac, arriving there early the next morning. There was hardly room in the two cars for the Company, and the one that I was in was so crowded that the only place I could find to lie down was across the feet and legs of two or three of the men, and my sleep that night was not of much account. We did not pitch our tents that next day, and that night I slept in the car where our baggage was, across some tents the poles of which I found to be in unpleasant proximity to my ribs, and from various causes my rest was little and broken. The next morning I was put on duty as "officer of the guard" and got between one and two hours sleep during the night. I was relieved just before noon and after dinner sat down to write a letter home to Mother which I had hardly finished when the "long roll" sounded in an adjoining regiment. We all started up to see what was going on, when a messenger came into camp and we received an order to march immediately without knapsacks, carrying our blankets and three day's provisions. The report was that our forces at this place were engaging the enemy, and needed our assistance. We were soon on the move and made a forced march to this place, about ten miles without any rest of any consequence. When we arrived we found no enemy here, and our march unnecessary. This was somewhat provoking but we are getting used to such things, and do not mind it much. When we arrived it was about seven o clock in the evening, and

we were marched down to a cornfield which had been cleared off, and halted for the night. There was some snow on the ground at the time, and it was rather muddy too, but the men got some rails and started fires and then found a few boards and some cornstalks on which we made our bed for the night. I was pretty tired that night on account of loss of rest and the march and my feet got cold and wet. I got them partly dried before I went to sleep but had to get up before morning again and warm them as they got so cold that I could not sleep. I had taken some cold a few nights before, and got a little addition to it that night so that for a day or two I have done some barking. I am getting pretty well along with it however and think it will not trouble me much. The next morning, Sunday — we moved down to our present position, near the tunnel, and sent back some men after our tents and baggage, expecting that we could easily get them transported to us. We did not much expect them back that night and so went to work building a shelter which you would have smiled to look at. We drove sticks into the ground about four feet high and placed a rail across, on which we placed other rails resting the ends on the ground. We then covered the rails with boughs of evergreen which we got from the mountain close by, and also strewed some of the branches on the ground beneath to lie on, and so we passed Sunday night. The next day a part of our men came back, and said that no cars could be got yet, and it was not certain when our tents would be along, so we extended our shelter to accommodate the rest of the Company, and Monday was passed in the same way. Tuesday a train stopped a few moments near our baggage, and our orderly Sergeant threw on all but one of our tents and came along without saying a word to the conductor about it. We got them pitched and slept pretty comfortably last night.

I exchanged my enamelled blanket for a rubber one, which is in reality a piano cover. I had to pay some difference but it is a much better one as it will stand coldweather without cracking and the others will not. It is much heavier to carry though. I had this and my woolen

blanket a full haversack, and canteen besides sword and pistol to carry on that march which was made right on the railroad track over the ties, the spaces between which were filled with small stones, which made it more tiresome than if we had been on a good road. I am feeling pretty well tonight and think we will get along much better for a while now, as I presume our next movement will be on Winchester and we will not be compelled to make any forced marches. We can easily reach it now in two days march and when we move it will be in a large body so that we cannot move as fast as a single regiment if we wished to. I do not care how tired I get if I can only keep my health so as to retain my place in the line when the order comes to move on again.

I have no fears of the 67th disgracing the state if we are led by some one in whom the men have confidence, and I am particularly satisfied with the majority of our Company. They agree together well and get along among themselves finely. I have never had a word of trouble with any of them.

We are now in Col. Kimball's brigade under General Lander, awaiting further orders.

I have seen quite a number of acquaintances within a few days, James Vansicc, Mack Townsend and several others in the 7th, some in the 8th and some Toledo boys in the artillery. All are well and seem to be enjoying soldier's life well.

I cannot send this tonight and will leave it open a while. The Express Agent told me that it would cost about fifty cents to send that cane home. You can do as you like about paying any more than that, the cane is of no particular value. I sent it for your benefit.

Just got Marching Orders — probably for Winchester — You will hear from me again soon.

> Yours Truly
> Sheldon Colton

Carlos

Toledo Feby 20th 1862

Dear Mother

Aunt Sophia has had two or three letters recently from Mrs Shepard of Northampton speaking of the sickness of Mrs Monroe — a general failing of her health — the letters were sent to Trenton and Detroit and I dont know that I have made any mention of them. I did not see them but heard Aunt speak of her illness. Yesterday she said tiding was received that she was no more —— I give a copy of Mrs Shepards letter

"Northampton Feby 17th/62

Dear Aunt Colton

My beloved Mother and your dear Sister fell asleep in Jesus at 20 m past 9 oclock this morning. She passed away very quietly and without suffering — When able will try and write you the particulars. I cannot now I am overwhelmed with grief —— Funeral Thursday at 3 oclock P.M.

Your sorrow stricken and duly afflicted Niece Susan"

When she writes again will tell you the particulars. The shirt and letter sent by Ella Stevens were recvd and am duly grateful my supply now is good —— We dont know of any way to get word to Myra — just at present but think there will be a way opened in a <u>very short time</u>. We knew that Mr. Blinn was raising a Co for the war and I was much surprised that you didnt know he had gone.

SUNDAY APRIL **2**

MONDAY APRIL **3**

TUESDAY APRIL **4**

WEDNESDAY APRIL **5**

THURSDAY APRIL **6**

FRIDAY APRIL **7**

SATURDAY APRIL **8**

Carlos

I received a letter today from Sheldon at "Camp Pawpaw" near Pawpaw Tunnel Va Feby 13th" — he speaks of their receiving intelligence of the Capture of Roanoke Island and that "we were drawn up in line to have it read to us by Maj Bond The news was received with loud and frequent cheers by the Regiment but we regretted that we could not have had a hand in the work — We hope soon to be led to attack Winchester however —— Speaks of their forced march from their last camp expecting to meet the enemy but found none. When they started on the march he "Never saw a happier set of men than our Co was when we marched out of Camp singing and laughing" — and "if I never feel any worse in going into battle than I did then when we thought a fight was certain before night I shall be satisfied" — closes with a pencil memo and "Just got orders to leave — probably for Winchester all right"

If father will send up his broken pen will get it repointed — saw Ben & Jim Stevens today — Aunt has been doing without help since her servant Mary married but expects to get a girl as soon as can find a good one as Annie has commenced studying French again. Thinking you might wish to preserve Sheldons letter to Pa I return it. I also enclose $5 for <u>whoever</u> <u>needs</u> it <u>most</u> - I have not sent any illustrated papers to Sheldon yet — have any been sent from home?

    Yours affectionately

                Carlos

Carlos

Toledo Feby 25th 62

Dear Father

I enclose herewith dft N.Y. $39.41 being amt less exchange 20 cents of your premium 32.11 & mine 7.50. I also send bank note $10 —— Did Sheldon attend to his for last November? I send your pen repointed — it dont suit in any particular return and will have it attend. That fragrant geranium leaf from Mother was very acceptable. Got a letter from Nelia today — hope the School she is to take soon may prove a pleasant one — Abram recvd a letter from Arthur today written "on board Steamer Northern on Mississippi River" Said he didnt know whether he was going to fort Donelson or Columbus — he had left the Missouri Department and was with Capt Swain of Genl Popes Division — letter was written 20th — said Genl Pope & Staff were on board, that the Genl was going to take the field in a few days and march into "Dixie". Have not heard from Sheldon since I wrote you last — I sent him a copy of the Blade with his letter —— Uncle said he was going to send you the "Continental Monthly" — Am invited to night to a large party at H L Walbridges (produce merchant) think I will go — weather has been cold again two or three days.

Love to all from
Carlos

Camp Chase,
Pawpaw Va. March 1st 1862

Dear Mother:

I owe letters to Lina, Delia and Carlos I think, but will hardly have time to answer them now, as I expect we will be on the move again in about an hour or so.

We are now in the second Brigade under Col Kimball.

I have had a pretty hard cold for a few days but am about well again now, have not been off duty yet on account of sickness, and do not expect to be.

I enclose the lock of hair for which you sent by father's letter I believe — I suppose I receive all, or nearly all of the letters and papers that you send to me, but forget to speak of them singly when I write. I also receive many papers from Father and Carlos, which are very welcome.

Nothing new to speak of now, only that I expect we will see some fighting before many days, perhaps before I get a chance to write again.

Do not borrow any trouble about it however — if anything serious happens to us you will know it. If I should be hurt or dangerously sick so as to require assistance I will let you know it, but our force is so strong that I do not apprehend much resistance wherever we may march.

Your flower letter was received, and I send you in return the lock of hair —

Yours truly
Sheldon Colton.

You cannot do too much for the Cumberland Hospital —

"Camp Chase"
Pawpaw Va. March 3rd 1862

Dear Delia:

I received a letter from you a few days ago telling me all about what a good time you had at the party at the Normal School building. You must have enjoyed it very much, and I am presume I should if I had been there, but I do not wish I was there for I intend to stay in the army and not go home till I am no longer needed here, and our country is all right again.

I wrote to Mother, Saturday night saying that we expected to march the next morning, but Genl. Lander was taken sick very suddenly and died yesterday afternoon. This is a hard blow for the army as he was a good man and very brave. He seemed to have no idea of fear but would go right into battle without any hesitation.

His remains were conducted to the cars this morning by the Seventh Ohio Regiment, and some Massachusetts Riflemen. The Soldiers encamped here were formed into lines on each side of the road from his headquarters to where the cars stood by.

The Infantry were in four ranks on both sides of the road and the Artillery there on one side and the cavalry behind them on the other. It was a most splendid sight to see so many men in uniform and armed. There must have been over ten thousand at least.

We hear that Genl. Sheilds is to take command here now, and we are much pleased at that for he was a good general in the Mexican War.

I presume we will move on tomorrow, perhaps not till next day, and cannot tell where we shall go, so I cannot say anything about where to direct any letters to reach me sooner than by Cumberland as you have been sending.

There is nothing new to write about besides what I have been telling you.

Love to all

Yours truly
Sheldon Colton

"Camp Chase."
Pawpaw Va. March 3rd 1862

Dear Carlos,

Your letter is received, and contents noted — Haskins understands the Camp Chest business, as McKee wrote to him about it. If you get a chance to send Capt. Lewis' trunk to Waterville, care of Morehouse and Brigham, without too much trouble you might pay the express charges and do so.

We should have moved from here I think, yesterday if it had not been for the death of Genl. Lander who was taken suddenly with congestion of the brain and died yesterday afternoon. His loss will be severely felt as he was a good man and a daring soldier.

His remains were conducted to the cars this morning, and I think that more than ten thousand soldiers participated in the ceremonies. It was a grand sight, so many men armed and in uniform. Battery H. stood right behind us in the line — I presume we will all be off now very soon perhaps tomorrow, as Genl. Sheilds takes command of this division, immediately, I understand.

I will write to you again soon, when I find out what mail arrangements are to be made — if any different from the present ones. I would like to have you send a few postage stamps occasionally, as they cannot be bought in this part of the country and I am getting nearly out. Our payrolls are made out again up to the first of March but the cash does not arrive yet. Our venerable Uncle Samuel owes me over five hundred dollars now and I would like to see some of it and send a part to my venerable Uncle Carlos and pay up some other small items before I take any pay in rebel lead.

Give my respects to all of the family and inquiring friends.

Yours truly
Sheldon Colton

The bridge was made of four ropes of iron wire and these were covered with planks... It was about fifty feet above the water, & would vibrate back and forth as we crossed it... We could have but three or four on at a time, and when I got halfway across the men in front of me began to run and the bridge would spring up and down about a foot every step.

Martinsburg Va. March 8 1862

Dear Mother:

We left Pawpaw at four o clock Wednesday afternoon and rode by cars to Back Creek that night. There we had to wait till a suspension bridge could be made across the creek where the rebels had blown up the railroad bridge. At one o clock we moved on and crossed the creek. The bridge was made of four ropes of iron wire and these were covered with planks so as to make a foot bridge about eight feet wide and about one hundred feet long. It was about fifty feet above the water, and would vibrate back and forth as we crossed it in a manner not very consoling to weak nerves. We could have but three or four on at a time, and when I got half way across the men in front of me began to run and the bridge would spring up and down about a foot every step. We got across without any accident however, and moved on about four miles when we halted and ahead of us on the march and while we were halted the 5 Ohio, and 84 Penn. came up and passed us. We all moved on about five o clock and marched to Martinsburg, passing through Hedgesville on the route. We arrived here about one o clock Friday morning and our Company with two or three others were quartered in the Catholic Church. We slept soundly till about daylight when we got up and ate our breakfast and I went out with one of our Corporals and found a house where we quartered the Company, and in which I am now writing. It is a pretty good brick house two stories and a basement, and is the property of a Union man who had to go to Maryland while the town was in possession of the rebels.

The rebels destroyed a large amount of railroad property here last summer. One bridge about three hundred and fifty feet long, and there are now on the track here about sixty locomotives which they burned. The railroad track has been torn up for miles between this place and Bath one way and between here and Harpers Ferry the other. They also destroyed the Machine shops and other buildings belonging to the company. They left this place two weeks ago on the approach of our forces. They all seem glad to see us, that is the Union parties — some of them look rather sour but do not say much.

When we were on the road we passed two negroes, who stood by the side of the track bowing and grinning with their hats off as Company after Company marched past. I said to him "Well! Old fellow how do you like this?" He showed his ivory extensively and replied "O! I'se been looking for you dese five months." We were the first Union troops who had been through on that route. Our march was a pretty hard one for

some of the men, but I came out all right after a few hours sleep. I got a new pair of heavy boots two or three days before we started, and they made my feet sore, so I got a pair of shoes yesterday and think I shall make my next march in them. I presume we will leave here for Winchester today or tomorrow, but it is of no use for me to say anything about our movements as you know by the papers and by Telegraph long before you can hear from me by mail. I presume our mail facilities will not be as good as they have been and will be worse the farther south we go, but at the same time I have an idea that we will be back where you can hear from us pretty often and see us too before a great while. The people around here have an idea that the war cannot last much longer, but think we will have some hard fighting to do yet.

They have some pretty good Union men and women here. They tell of one here who had the stars and stripes flying when the rebel Cavalry rode into town. They came up to capture the flag and she got hold of it and would not let them have it, and they could not get it by threats or any other way. When they rode off to leave her she ran out into the road and waved the flag at them. Another woman kept a kettle of hot water on her stove ready to baptize the first one who attempted to enter her house. Some of the people in the houses near us are very kind to us, and help us all they can, so that we get along pretty well. We may be left out in the cold when we leave here as our tents are all back at Back Creek where we left the cars. We have blankets enough though, and can sleep out doors as well as not, and without catching cold.

This place has about five thousand inhabitants I should think, and is a rather pretty place. You can tell the location of it on the map. We are thirty miles from Harpers Ferry and twenty two miles from Winchester. I believe we have a pretty good road to travel on from here — I hope it is better than some that we have been on. We are now in Genl. Sheilds' division and under the command of Col. Sullivan who is acting as Brigadier Genl. for the present.

We are getting along very well. John Turner says "tell them I am well if my father inquires after me I have no time to write".

Tell our friends that we are well and will have possession of Winchester in a few days and Richmond as soon as our commanders will let us.

You can let Carlos know where and how I am. I cannot write another letter today.

Love to all

Yours truly
Sheldon Colton

... He showed his ivory extensively... We were the first Union troops who had been through on that route.

They came up to capture the flag and she got hold of it and would not let them have it, and they could not get it by threats or any other way.

83

Martinsburg Va. March 10th 1862

Dear Brother:

I received a paper from you and a letter from Father today. In his letter to me he said he had spoken to you about something I had said in regard to the hospital at Cumberland. I do not remember what I wrote to him, but I think I did not tell him half that I knew about it. One thing is certain, there cannot be too much done for the institution to improve the condition of those who are so unfortunate as to be compelled to go there. Many of our brave boys who have gone there with diseases that would have been of but little consequence at home have never come out alive, and I fear many more will die there. We have lost four from our company since leaving Ohio. Old Hoover who used to saw wood at Uncle's died at Columbus, after we left there — Hugh McMullen died at Benwood, Fred Miller a German boy from Toledo, and Frank Stewart, one of my men from Milan, died in the Cumberland Hospital. Banks, Baird, Bartow, Akers and McFall are all there from my detachment, but are getting well, and better off than they would be with the company just now. Banks is able to run all over town and take care of the others — none of them are dangerously sick. Do not let any of the Milan folks know any of my men are there. I only mention it to you to let you see the necessity of something being done for the hospital. I do not know where the fault is but there is a great lack of proper medical attendance there.

We left Camp Chase Va. last Wednesday afternoon and rode that night to Back Creek, crossed the stream on a suspension bridge the next day and marched to this place reaching here about one o clock Friday morning, when our Company and two or three others were quartered in the Catholic Church. The next morning we moved out to a brick house which we now occupy. It is the property of a Union man who was obliged to leave on the approach of the secession forces, and is now in Maryland.

I must wind up my letter as the room is scarce and time also. We are ordered to be prepared to leave at a moment's notice, and to have three days rations in our haversacks.

I presume we will move in the direction of Winchester soon, and hope we will occupy it within a day or two, though I hardly think we will have to fight for it. In my last letter to you I spoke of sending me some postage stamps. I am not quite out yet but they cannot be had in this part of the country.

U.S. does not say anything about pay yet, and I am afraid that I shall not be able to send anything to Uncle for a while.

My writing desk is the stock of a gun; this will account for the style of penmanship.

      Love to all,   Yours truly
                                  Sheldon Colton

My writing desk is the stock of a gun; this will account for the style of penmanship.

Carlos

Toledo Mch 12th 1862

Dear Father

I recvd yours of 7th duly — the box from Milan came yesterday and will be shipped this evening via Cumberland Md. We have heard that the Regt has gone to Martinsburg. Mrs. Osborn wrote to Sheldon last night telling him the things were to be sent to him. The box from Milan has lain in the express office without opening — they concluded the things for the 7th Regt could be sent by Sheldon as well as from here. In the box prepared here they sent a lot of pop corn with a patent wire "popper" in which was a card with the writing —

"Sheldon Colton

When this you see

Remember me — Soldier's Aid Society"

Mrs. Raymond requested me to send the enclosed scrap to Mother to show the way they have usually sent their stores giving the full direction on the box, and tacking on a card directed to Geo B Wright etc Columbus and that if the Milan ladies should send anything more it would be just as well to send in that way. They had to pay express chg from Norwalk — They say they want the box for the 55th as they will have some things here to put in it.

Aunt Sophia & Alpha went to Trenton last Saturday to be gone a couple of weeks I think — they have a good servant girl at the house. I have just been writing to Sheldon and directed to Cumberland Md <u>to follow</u> <u>Regt</u> —I like my new boarding place very much. Hope the rebels will run from Winchester before the <u>Sicksty</u> Seventh get there. I send $10 and much love to all

Carlos

Abram intends leaving Strong in a few days to a propeller agency — also an insurance agency

By Telegraph, from Fairfield June 24, 1868.

1861.

To H Ella

Midas telegraph from Fairfield, Aus
recalled in hip, Ball extracted
doing well

Carly

12 X 39 p

Carlos

Toledo March 27th/62

Dear Father

I send with this one of Sheldons letters brought back by Clarinda. Also enclose $10 — Dont get any thing farther from Sheldon as yet — hope to tomorrow — if not by mail will probably learn something from the escort of the remains of Capt Ford — expected tomorrow — Annie got your letter today — that was an awful word of Gibbs' lower jaw shot away. Would much prefer being shot through the heart. Uncle wrote to Sheldon yesterday and sent a couple of Illustrated papers — The Blade reports tonight 24 wounded of 67th exclusive of killed. I send a copy of the Blade

Love to all
Carlos

Toledo March 31st 1862

Dear Brother
      You will see in this evenings Blade a letter from Dr. Forbes in which he reports Sheldon doing well, also that the wounded are to be removed to Winchester on 25th which may account for there being no letter from him as yet.
      There is a letter in town this morning from Col Roustenbruden who being under arrest was not in the action (he ought to have been with a Gun in my opinion which could have silenced his enemies batteries) he says "Lt Colton slightly wounded in the right hip, a <u>pair of scissors</u> in his waistcoat pocket saved his life".
      The children say he always carried a pair of scissors in his vest pocket, they did him yeomans service this time if never before

Yours
C Colton

Carlos

Toledo April 3rd 1862

Dear Father

One of our citizens (Mr. Platt) who went down to Winchester before the fight to attend to a sick brother, and was on the field at the battle, got back last night. I saw him for only a few minutes on the corner of the street this morning. He did not bring any letters from Sheldon said he didnt think he was able to write then — he left there the Wednesday after the fight — but that he was getting along well and in first-rate spirits. Said he saw him on the field and in the hospital. I asked him if he "whimpered" any. He laughed and said "You wouldnt know he was wounded by the way he talks". Says he has all the care he needs now and if he should want to come home by and by and needs help will let me know. Says he saw the ball that struck him it was of large size and broke the scissors in pieces glancing into the hip. Says "that one of his men stooped to pick him up, and while in a stooping position a bomb shell came along and <u>ripped open the back of his coat</u>". <u>Oh! Scissors!</u> I think that letters from that region have been detained by authority in some instances, but think we must get something now very soon. Suppose we neednt feel any anxiety about him now and only wish he was at home. About the only trouble that I see any reason to fear now, is, that he may get sick by confinement in hospital. Mr. Chase came in the office few minutes since and brought me a bouquet from Mother which is very sweet and acceptable. I send $5. — Love for all

Carlos

H Colton

Dear Carlos,

Your letter of yesterday is received. We are glad to hear so favorable an account from Sheldon.

We get nothing here direct yet, though a letter is in town today from Banks written at Strasbourg 26th.

He knew but little about Sheldon, seems to be under the impression that he is or soon will be at home. Thinks he himself got through the scrimmage pretty comfortably, all the hurt he got was when at one time he had occasion to dodge a shell he fell with his face a few inches from the ground, it passed so nigh that the concussion bumped his head on the ground violently and stunned him for a time.

It is strange that nothing is heard from Gibbs, he was to telegraph on his arrival at Winchester —

We are in hopes Sheldon may be able to return with him, it is probable that he will be able to travel as soon as the wounded Gibbs is —

At this point I asked your Mother what there was in particular to write about. She says "write about Sheldon, & tell him we cant think about anything else" —

That is pretty nigh the truth. I have been trying all the time to make her believe what I didnt more than half credit myself about his condition & hoping from day to day to hear something more definite. I have told her that our sympathies ought to be with the poor friendless & nameless privates, who would be left to suffer while he would have every attention & comfort that men could give him under the circumstances.

Sheldon could always bear pain & sickness with a good deal of philosophy & he will doubtless be proud of his present position rather than complain, though he may feel some chagrin at being counted out so early in the action.

It is gratifying to see that it is being found out that there is a 67th Regiment, which didnt seem to be known by some of the first narrators of the battle —

It was a fight that they may well be proud of, if they should never see another.

From all accounts every man seems to have felt his responsibility & resolved to win or die — Secesh must be beginning to mistrust that when he proposed to fight five to one it was offering rather too much odds.

In acknowledging receipt of a letter from your Uncle the other day I neglected to say that the "Continental" came also.

Yours Affectionately
H Colton

Winchester Va. April 17th 1862

Dear Brother:

You will probably be surprised at the post mark on this letter, but I have a chance to send it as far as Cleveland by a gentleman who is going this morning.

Frank McCord arrived last night bringing some packages for me from Toledo and a letter from you. The enclosed photograph is an excellent one and I am much pleased with it. He brought a box from Miss Leull and also one from Miss Taylor. Tell them I am much obliged and will make the proper acknowledgement of my indebtedness under my own hand and seal soon.

As to myself, I am getting along slowly but surely and am able to sit up some now, but do not expect to be ready to take the cars for home for about two weeks yet. I have not got my leave of absence yet, though I applied for it some time ago. It passed through the proper hands and Genl Shields signed it: from him it had to go to Genl Banks and from there I have lost track of it. I hope I shall receive it soon for I do not wish to be kept here any longer than is necessary.

I was removed from the hospital yesterday to the residence of Mrs Jackson, a Quaker lady whose husband was carried off by the rebels when they retreated.

I have excellent treatment here, and have formed the acquaintance of several young ladies who come to see me in my affliction, so you see I am doing pretty well in consideration of being so far from home and among strangers. I never had any trouble in finding friends anywhere for some reason.

Banks is not well enough to be with the regiment and so he stays here and takes care of me which is a very convenient arrangement as far as I am concerned.

For some time after I was first brought here we could not send any letters away, now we have a post office and yesterday I got five letters, but it is poorly arranged and I do not expect to get more than half that are sent to me — and do not know as half that I write will reach their destination. I shall keep on trying however and hope my friends will do likewise.

I have nothing special to write this time and will close as I have no time to write a descriptive letter, and that is the only kind that would be interesting from here. Say to Aunt that I am much obliged for the fruit & etc. and will try to make use of them in the proper manner. I may be able to eat a few dinners in her house in a month or so.

When you see Mrs J.R. Osborn tell her that I received her letter announcing the shipment of more donations for our regiment, that the first have not been received yet, but when they are will be properly acknowledged — also thank her for her kind wishes in my behalf.

Love to all the family and best respects to inquiring friends.

Yours truly
Sheldon Colton

Dear Mother
     Yours and fathers letters of 17th were recvd — as you spoke of the unfavorable reports recvd then about Sheldons condition I know this will be good news to you as it is to me — I enclose a letter from Lucy —
     Carlos

... I concluded to see if my revolver would reach the enemy and had drawn it and was stooping forward slightly to get a look through a rail fence... when a ball struck... penetrating my body about two inches forward of the joint of the hip bone...

Sheldon Upton

Winchester Va. April 19th 1862

Dear Mother:

I have received several letters from home since I was wounded but have been able to write but two or three, and do not know that they were all received.

I am sorry to hear that you worry so much about me for I am in a pleasant place and well cared for, nearly as well off as I should be if at home.

I am now at the house of Mrs Jackson, a worthy Quaker lady, whose husband was taken and carried off by the rebels when they left this place on the approach of our army. She has three grown up daughters, and they have several relatives of about their own ages in town who are here almost every day, so I have no chance to get lonesome.

Banks stays with me all of the time so that I do not lack attendance. He is not well enough to be with the regiment just now, though he is not much sick.

My wound, though severe, is not dangerous nor very painful either. I am able to sit up a good deal of the time but it will be some days, perhaps two weeks, before I shall be able to stand the jar of railroad travelling. My leave of absence has not reached me yet, though I applied for it some time ago. I am in hopes of getting it soon.

I should not be surprised if I made you quite a visit when I do come home for I shall be lame for a long time I think on account of the balls striking the hip bone as it went around.

I cannot give a description of the battle just now as it is hard work for me to write. During the action the Lt. Col. came along and ordered our company to be moved a little to the left. In the meantime Capt. Lewis had got hold of a rifle and was fighting on his own hook so I took command and executed the movement. Just after this I concluded to see if my revolver would reach the enemy and had drawn it and was stooping forward slightly to get a look through a rail fence behind which we were standing when a ball struck the pair of scissors I have carried so long in my vest pocket breaking one point and bending the other. The force of the ball was partially broken by my pocket diary. It then glanced down penetrating my body about two inches forward of the joint of the hip bone, passing around the bone in a semicircular direction, grazing it as it went along and lodging about two inches around the joint of the bone.

I had the ball extracted the next day, and intend to keep it carefully as a memento of the battle of Winchester. The wound keeps running constantly and I think will begin to heal soon, but I shall have to wait for it to get well healed before I attempt to go home and then I cannot make the journey alone. If I do not find some one going I must send home for some one to come after me and I would like to have Carter get all necessary information from Gibbs in regard to the route, where he would find one & etc.

We have not been paid off yet but are expecting to be soon, if we are whoever came for me would not need to bring much money, if not, about fifty dollars would be necessary which I could easily repay I think, as I could call on some paymaster on the way home and get some money. I think I shall not be ready to go home for at least two weeks yet.

I would rather have Carter come after me than any one else, but if it is not convenient for him you could find some other good man. I will telegraph if I want anyone and then you can do the best you can about it.

Once more I ask you not to worry about me. I am in good hands and doing well. There are no kinder people that I know of than the ones where I am staying. They seem to think they are not doing enough for me, and exert themselves for my welfare all of the time. Banks is with me constantly and I do not lack attention. I pass the time here very pleasantly, under the circumstances. My wound does not pain me much and I am not sick. Day before yesterday I received the box which you sent to me directed to Cumberland. The packages for Vancise and Hopkins were sent by Mrs. Townsend. You can tell Mrs. Townsend that Mack called on me the other day and is looking well and hearty. The regiments are all on the advance along the road.

Give my love to all of the family and respects to inquiring friends.
Yours truly
Sheldon Colton

April 23rd/62

Dear Aunt Fannie
This is just recd. Ma sends it for you all to read and would like to have it returned.
Delia

Carlos

Toledo April 20th 1862

Dear Father

Yours of yesterday enclosing one from Sheldon was recvd this noon. I saw Mrs Blinn and delivered the message from Mrs Butman. I do not think she will go to Milan. She intended to go to Perrysburg yesterday but was too unwell, and will go up today. She said she did not want to take her things to Milan to furnish a room and will try to make arrangements to stay in Perrysburg. I think she did not want to go any where but to our house in Milan at first. We found it would be too noisy for you with her children when it was first suggested but she seemed to feel very much disappointed when she learned by Lina's letter that she could not go there. Was glad to learn that Sheldon is still in good spirits and improving. I don't believe he will be able to join his regiment to do active duty until this Rebellion is brought a good deal nearer to a close than it now is. And am inclined to say I am glad of it — he has nobly done his duty as a soldier and can afford to retire now on the honors he has won — he can particularly afford to if he continues to receive a credit of $100 per month while the wound is healing <u>and ever gets it</u> — Mr. Chase has recvd word from Edward in hospital at Cairo saying he is slightly wounded in knee — done at Pittsburg Landing — he is with the 7th Illinois — I hope Carter may be able to go after Sheldon when he is ready to come as he has requested. We will of course see that he is supplied with the necessary funds —

I enclose $10—

Carlos

You need be in no especial hurry to answer this — letters seem to always go right between Milan & Toledo now adays

Winchester Va. April 25th 1862

Dear Carlos:

I have nothing interesting in regard to myself to write about this morning, but as I have an opportunity to send this letter directly to you by a member of our regiment I will write a few words.

I am gaining slowly, and can sit up a little while at a time quite frequently: but you must not be in too much of a hurry about expecting me home.

I am not able to get on my feet yet, and I wish to be in pretty good condition before I attempt to travel by railroad. I think I may be here two or three weeks yet. I have got a leave of absence which gives me till the tenth of July to rejoin the regiment. If I am not well by that time I might as well conclude to resign.

Mr. Jackson, the gentleman at whose house I am staying, arrived here yesterday, he and the others taken from here having been released by the rebels. You may well believe that it was a day of rejoicing for the family here, who had thought they might never see him alive again. He is sick now, but I think a few days rest is all that he requires to make him well again.

You at the North in your quiet homes know nothing of the horrors of this Civil War. When I get home I can tell you of things you never had an idea of, which I have known to occur.

I send you some specimens of the money which has been in circulation here and is now to some extent. I have not been able to get hold of any Confederate Scrip yet, but hope I shall before I leave here. I saw one bill but the owner did not wish to sell it at much less than the face and I do not regard it as being very valuable. If you wish to know the value of this scrip which I send you look at your detector and find what Virginia money is worth and then guess at the value of the scrip — that is the only way I can get at it.

I received about a dozen papers all in a pile the other day, two from you and the rest from Uncle and Hammie I judged. Tell them I am much obliged, and also tell Hammie that I received his letter a few days ago. I have not been able to answer all of the letters received by me since I have been here. I have not got the strength to do it, and presuming that my correspondents are well aware of that fact I have said but little about it. I shall be able to commence writing soon however.

I have just been paid off up to the first of March and will send you some money by express in a short time with directions what to do with it. I was very glad to get the cash, and think I can find use for some of it.

I have nothing further to write about just now and it is time for the letter to be closed.

Best respects to all inquiring friends and love to Uncle's family.
Yours truly
Sheldon Colton.

Dear Mother

This was brought to me by one of the 67th who left Winchester Sunday night. He speaks in praise of Sheldon as every one else does — he was wounded and lay in the Hospital with Sheldon. He says Sheldon is in good hands and thought he would be ready to leave next week — but I think not and think he ought not to try to travel till it is perfectly safe to do so. Lucy is in Trenton, has made arrangements to board in Perrysburg. She sent Aunt a copy of portions of a letter recd from John, he was before Corinth expecting daily to be ordered forward — and thought there would be a big fight.
Carlos

Nelia.

Milan April 1862

Dear Brother Carl

Well! I am "school ma'arm" at last and as it is too stormy for me to go to my boarding place this noon, I have seated myself at the desk and am trying to write a few lines to you amidst the "music" of half a dozen mischievous children. But they are only melancholorous, never ugly, and I get along very well indeed, and I think I have the pleasantest school house and neighborhood for teaching that any one ever had. I like teaching full as well as I did attending school and that was so well that I never liked to stay out a day! I believe I would teach just because I liked it if they would only give me my board.

We have had very rainy weather for a day or two past, and I have almost waded to school but still I am not homesick much or lonesome for you know I "take no heed of time save when the sun is shining", and I am not so far away from home but that I can go just when I choose.

There is to be a concert in town tomorrow night given by a Mr.Grannis of the Amphion troop. Half the proceeds are to be given to the Soldiers' Aid Society.

I have no news to tell you as I am in a place where the news is scarce and there is so much for me to attend to now that I must close my very short letter and send it up to Pa that he can add more if he chooses.

I should like to hear from you soon and when I can will write a longer letter.

Love to all the folks and very much to yourself from

your sister
Nelia.

Winchester Va. April 27th 1862

Dear Carlos:

I send you with this a part of the pay I got for being shot at so many times five weeks ago today, and finally brought down.

I wish to have you pay Uncle the hundred dollars which he so kindly lent to me when I left Toledo. And send Father one hundred dollars with the enclosed letter which contains directions for its disposal.

The balance you can deposit in the bank, in your own name, or in my name subject to your order or else put it away in some safe place till I return just as you may think best. I should like to have that bill of Buck's settled whenever he presents his claim.

I cannot form any idea yet as to when I shall be able to leave here: my hip bone is broken, how badly I cannot tell, and the wounds are still running freely. I am able to sit up about half an hour at a time several times a day but I cannot rise nor even turn over in bed without help. I suffer but very little pain however. There is nothing new for me to write about this time. I am getting along the same as usual, slowly but surely I think, and hope to see you all soon.

Give my love to Uncle's family, and best respects to all who inquire after me.

Yours truly

Sheldon Colton

Continue to direct to the "Seminary Hospital" or my letters may go past to the regiment.

May 3rd 1862	Paid C Colton Ser.	100—
"	Sent H Colton "Milan"	100—
"	Pd C H Buck	45.25
"	Placed to Credit in Bank	104.75
		$350.00

Carlos

Toledo May 3rd 1862

Dear Father

I send herewith one Hundred Dollars— $100— received from Sheldon, this morning—

I have paid Uncle $100, Buck 44.25 and send you 100— leaving a balance of $104.75 which is placed to the credit of "Lieut Sheldon Colton" in the "Bank of Toledo". I suppose the most of the 100 for you will have to be expended in payment of bills contracted while recruiting last fall. I think Sheldon ought to be urged to stay where he is until perfectly able to travel without any possible chance of further injury by so doing. Since I commenced writing Sheldons Dutch 2nd Lieut called on me about half drunk, of course. A brick building owned by him — used as a bakery — burned down a few weeks since he says he came home on that account, though he is charged with cowardice by members of the regiment who say he ran and hid behind a bank during the battle. He says he helped carry Sheldon off the field. Says he has got in his trunk which he expects today, Sheldons Scissors — which he will bring up to me this afternoon — if I get them in time will send them with this. He says, in broken English "Your brother is a good fellow, he is a good friend of mine, I like him better than any one in the regiment, <u>he</u> <u>is</u> <u>smart</u>, <u>he</u> <u>has</u> <u>no</u> <u>fault</u>" & etc. I got this noon a letter from Lina. In speaking of teaching she says "the usual price in district schools is "two dollars per week and <u>board</u> <u>vowed</u>" — I hope she will not take any such if offered, in the first place the pay is not a fair equivalent for the labor then the <u>boarding</u> <u>vowed</u> arrangement won't <u>go</u> <u>down</u>, unless she is offered a good pleasant place, and above all a first class pleasant <u>home</u> I shall object to her accepting a School. We can live without resorting to any such means. Lina speaks of a photograph Mrs. Draper had of Henry Chase & myself. We had four printed he took two & I the others. I sent one to Sheldon and left one at the house. I did not think they were good <u>of</u> <u>me</u> but others think they are. I will get another and send down next week. Draper is in the office now and I will close to send this by him, he knows this is an important package, and expects some money I believe for livery hire.

Carlos

Carlos

May 8th/62

Dear Father

I send herewith $5— You dont say how much of Sheldons remittance will be consumed in paying those <u>few</u> <u>bills</u>, though I suppose considerable more than half of it, as Halsey Draper said his bill was over $40.

Col. Hathaway who figured so conspicuously here at the time of the organization of the 67th regt. is about "played out". He was arrested here on some old business scrape and taken to Cleveland. He refused to answer some questions propounded by the Court and was placed in Jail — by some means he got "loose" and fled to Canada. Genl Hill is in Columbus acting as Adjutant Genl. The Semi Annual dividend of the Bank has been declared, without making any provision for the book keeper. My "assistant" still stays in the office — and takes away a great deal of my labor. His pay is not yet decided upon — Carlos

According to family records, I was yesterday 25 years old

Carlos

Toledo May 8th 1862

Dear Lina

I send enclosed the wonderful Scissors that saved Sheldons life. I suppose he has the points that were broken off as they were not returned — they have been examined by a great many here and all think it was a most miraculous escape from death — I havent heard anything further from Sheldon since. Halsey Draper was here — I send you a photograph of Henry Chase and myself — it is most too small size to look very natural. The Chases have moved from Uncle's neighborhood nearer the business part of the City — They have been cleaning house at Uncles but have got through now. Annie is not in very good health, the rest are all as well as usual. Ella Stevens is getting around again. Dont know as to her separation from Tom Page — but guess if there has been any trouble they will "Come around" again — I think rather better of Tom than I used to — although he is not a remarkably brilliant young man — yet he seems industrious and attends to his business ——

I called on Mrs Raymond last night to see if I could learn anything about the boxes that were sent here from Milan and forwarded by the Aid Society. Mr Wright was written to once about them and said they left Columbus all right and Mrs Raymond has heard of their being at Martinsburg where they were placed with the Government supplies <u>under</u> <u>guard</u> to be forwarded and then they are lost trace of. The first boxes were marked to Sheldon to Martinsburg to follow regiment — the last box which was detained here was marked to Sheldon at "<u>Union</u> <u>Hospital</u> <u>Winchester</u>" — She fears they have been stolen or taken to some other Hospital — though we may yet hear of their safe arrival. I recvd a letter from Nelia a short time since. I intend to write to her soon. Am glad she is so pleasantly situated. I hope you will not accept any of those poor paying "boarding around" schools if offered, but wait patiently till you are offered a pleasant agreeable place ——

Give my love to Delia, and all the rest of the family — Lucy has not come back from Trenton yet. Aunt thought some of writing to her and if she did would send your letter to her. Remember me to Bell Anna Gordon <u>and</u> <u>everybody</u> ——

Your brother
Carlos

Monroe May 12th 1862

Dear Brother

Can you throw any light upon that dried fruit — we hear nothing of it.

Going down to the Pier the other day to see Mr. Davis off I found the Schr. Essex Capt. Richardson loading with wheat there for Bronson & Crocker, and as usual we had to wait nearly a day for a Steam Boat, and should have starved but for Capt. Richardson furnishing us with some of Mr Bronsons corned Beef however to balance the account I brought him up to town and gave him his Supper. I wrote by him a severe letter to Mr. Brace about their keeping Mother there so long, and recommended her to get along back here as quickly as possible.

It is true enough what Sophia says on the other side that one half the town is clearing out — what few are left are to have a meeting tomorrow to see what can be done towards opening the Ship Canal — it is the last desperate effort and we hope something may come out of it.

My count is drawing nigh but the prospect is slim enough Gov Ellis and his family made out to get away to Detroit, a few days since. I hope they may get something "better than pumpkins" to eat there — they have had hard times enough here since the Governor discovered that he was a big man.

I shall send you a shilling novel that I have the promise of — reading is very cheap now a days.

Some good Whig friend of mine is sending me the daily NY <u>Tribune</u> — receipted for a year. I presume it is one of Mr. Davis favors.

It is very strange that we hear nothing from Mother

C.

Sheldon Colton (signature)

Winchester Va. May 19 1862

Dear Father:

I wrote a few lines home the other day and sent by Serg. Ramsey. I presume you have received the letter and probably have seen him by this time as he told me he would call on you if he had time.

I do not know of anything in particular to write about and write more because I have a good opportunity than from any other reason. I am getting along finely now and think I will be able to travel some after the first of June. Such is the opinion of my attending Physician also.

I had a large abscess form just below the wound which gave me a great deal of trouble for a week or so but after it was lanced I improved rapidly, and am now able to sit up for two or three hours at a time, and have an excellent appetite, and rest well at night, so you see I stand a good chance for a speedy recovery as far as the wounds are concerned, but expect to be lame for some time. I am pretty confident that my warrior days are ended, and that I must now retire on whatever little reputation I may have gained, having at the same time the satisfaction of knowing that I did my duty as far as I was able, in the camp and in the battle.

I presume that I shall send for Carter soon after the first of June, as I shall be ready to go then unless something unforseen occurs to set me back again. Such is not likely to be the case however, for the bones are becoming well united in my hip, the place where it was lanced is closing up and the wound made by extracting the ball is about healed. I am anxious to get home once more now that I can be of no further service in the army. I have been in this place full long enough to satisfy me. I would like to look around the country here for a day or two before I leave, especially in the neighborhood of the battlefield. It is not safe to venture out many miles in some directions from here on account of the guerrilla bands which infest the valley. I hope this mode of warfare will be summarily put out of

the way by the powers that be. These bands are a great nuisance to soldiers who are returning to their regiments and are liable to be fired at any time from the woods along the road. This valley of the Shenandoah is a splendid part of the country to live in, the land is exceedingly fertile, and the scenery some of the finest I ever saw. It is a very different place from Western Virginia among the mountains.

The weather has been beautiful for a few days, and summer will soon be fairly upon us. Such weather fairly makes me homesick. I want to be sitting where I can see the garden or look across the hills: it will not be long however I hope before I shall be doing so.

I received papers from you and from Toledo every few days but the letters are extremely scarce lately for some unknown reason.

I hope the women folks have contrived to make themselves happier with the remittance which I sent, it was not a very large sum to go around among so many but still it would do some good. I may have some left when I get back, hope it will hardly be necessary for Carter to bring much with him when he comes, as I think I shall have enough left to pay all expenses.

Give my love to both families and respects to all inquiring friends.

Yours truly,
Sheldon Colton

Rev. Mr. Freeman formerly of Sandusky, now chaplain of the 8th Reg. O.V.I. has called upon me several times and wishes to be remembered to you.

S.C.

I am writing to Carlos today also

Friend

Toledo May 19th/62

H. Colton Esqr

      Allow me to express my regret at having unintentionally said anything, in my communication to the Blade, which could convey a feeling of uneasiness or displeasure to the friends of Lieutenent Colton. I did not intend to say anything disrespectful of Lieutenant Colton, but on the contrary, I regret, that I did not give him that tribute of respect, which he deserved. He was, and is my favorite officer in the Regt. He is a man whose courage "in the Field" was only equalled by his gentlemanly conduct in the Camp. He was wounded whilst bravely leading his Compy. I was sorry for it. I used a strong word "Implore" to which verb I applied the meaning of <u>request</u> and seeing Lieutenant Seiter behave afraid I was anxious to exonerate Seiter from the charge. — Lieutenant Colton knows this I hope he has seen the letters you seem to complain of — he knows I esteem and love him!

      And here, I assert, in the presence of God I would follow him to the mouth of the Waring Cannons, he is a favorite officer, of all the Regt. and of mine in <u>particular</u>, my Dear Sir, pardon me for having omitted to speak of Lieutenant Colton in the terms I should in my article to the "Blade" and
          Allow me to remain
          Yours, very sincerely

          F.I. OSullivan
          First Srgt. Co. D
          67 Regt.

Carlos

Toledo May 23rd 1862

Dear Mother

I wrote to father and sent by Ed Chase yesterday. I got a letter today from Sheldon written 19th brought by some soldier and mailed at Wellsville, O. He wrote in good spirits. In a postscript he says "I take the present opportunity to write home also" — so I suppose you may have got something by this time from him. He says he is getting along finely now — that an abcess formed just below the wound which had been quite troublesome and painful — but it had been opened and discharged a large quantity of bloody matter since then he had been getting well very fast — the bones in his hip were becoming well united and he felt very much encouraged to hope for a speedy recovery — his physician said he could go home in about two weeks — he says "I don't know how serious my wound is yet, or how much it may lame me, but am pretty certain that I shall not be able to do any more military duty for a long time yet, and probably shall never rejoin the 67th — says he has "the best of medical attendance and excellent care" — he notices and chafes a little about a statement that appeared in the Blade of 14th from a wounded Irish soldier refuting the charge of cowardice against Sheldon's 2nd Lieut "Seiter". The substance of the statement was that when Sheldon fell the men rushed on without heeding him — and Sheldon "implored Seiter not to leave him but to take him off the field" — It was an Irish "hifalutin" composition & of course Sheldons friends would place no importance to the statement. In speaking of it Sheldon says "It is highly drawn and not strictly correct — he represents me as <u>imploring</u> aid of Seiter. When I fell the men were all standing still instead of "rushing toward the enemy" and Seiter was standing within twenty feet of me.

Carlos

I raised myself partly up and said to him as cooly as I ever said anything "Seiter I wish you would send me one or two men" & etc Sheldon modestly says "you need not say much about this but if any of my friends should make any remarks in your hearing about it you can tell them how it was" — We are all getting along in the usual way here and have nothing important to write — havent heard from Lucy lately. I believe she is still in Trenton.

Your affectionate Son
Carlos

Since writing this I have been up to the house and learn that Lucy has been here today with her children and gone to Perrysburg. Grandma is staying at Lucindas and is quite feeble with rheumatism. Lucinda has been quite sick but is pretty well again. Fanny has got her house fixed for the summer. So she does not intend to break up ———

Saturday 24th

   I neglected to mail this last night and suppose it will not go till Monday morning. I recvd fathers letter this noon. I dont attach any importance to that letter from the Irish Soldier, it was a highfalutin thing and any of Sheldons acquaintances if they noticed it at all would think nothing of it. We all hope Sheldon will not resign while he is crippled, and I believe he does not think seriously of it. When his "leave of absence" expires in July he can of course get it extended. Uncle says he will write to him about it ———

C

Relative

OFFICE OF THE
MUTUAL INSURANCE COMPANY OF TOLEDO

DIRECTORS

M.R. Waite.	H. M'Culloch.
F.J. King.	E. Walbridge.
T.H. Hoag.	Matthew Brown
W.W. Griffith	H.D. Walbridge
H.S. Walbridge	Fred'K Bissell.
John Stevens.	

M.R. Waite.........President.
E. Walbridge..Vice President.
Carlos Colton......Secretary.

Toledo, O May 26 1862

My dear Brother

The news we get to day is astounding Sheldon is unquestionably in the hands of the Rebels, for even if he had been able to be removed I have no idea that Gen Banks had any time to attend to wounded — We can only hope for the best and trust that the same Providence which has so far protected him will continue to guard him

Our town has been all excitement to day in consequence of a call from Gov Todd for 500 men immediately to proceed to Columbus where those who did not want to go to Washington would be detailed for Guard duty at Camp Chase in place of the Regiment now there. Hammie goes with them. I found that Carlos had made up his mind before asking my advice and consequently said nothing. So they will probably both go tomorrow — when I will write more fully

Yours
Carlos Colton

Carlos

Toledo May 26th 1862

Dear Father

I suppose you must have heard 'ere this the exciting news that Genl Banks' forces (or a portion of them) have been repulsed and driven back this side of Winchester, so that the Rebels probably occupy the latter place. This of course is startling and sad news to us, leaving us in suspense with regard to Sheldons fate. The logic that I use is this — if Sheldon is able to be moved he <u>has been</u> moved to a place of safety on the approach of the rebels, by his friends, and we will hear from him as soon as he can possibly send word If he is not able to help himself (as we believe) the Secesh will not molest him, for, as a prisoner he would only be a burden to them. It seems very sad to think he and we should be subjected to this disheartening occurance when he was getting along so nicely with every prospect of an early return. I say disheartening because we <u>don't know</u> more about him. I hope we may turn the tide right speedily and find new Joy in his entire safety — you will see by the "Blade" that this community is agitated by the news today. The old "Light Guard" Co have a meeting tonight in response to a call from Genl Hill for 3 years <u>or for</u> 3 <u>months</u> if they go it will be for 3 months and in that case I shall go. It will do me good to go and I couldnt stand it to stay — if I lose my situation I think I can do something else when I return — and in the meantime I know you can get along with what you now have and what will be due Sheldon. Don't think too seriously of this however, for we may not really be wanted after organizing. Hoping that all may yet turn out for the best and with much love to all the family I remain, Your Son

Carlos

Will write you tomorrow

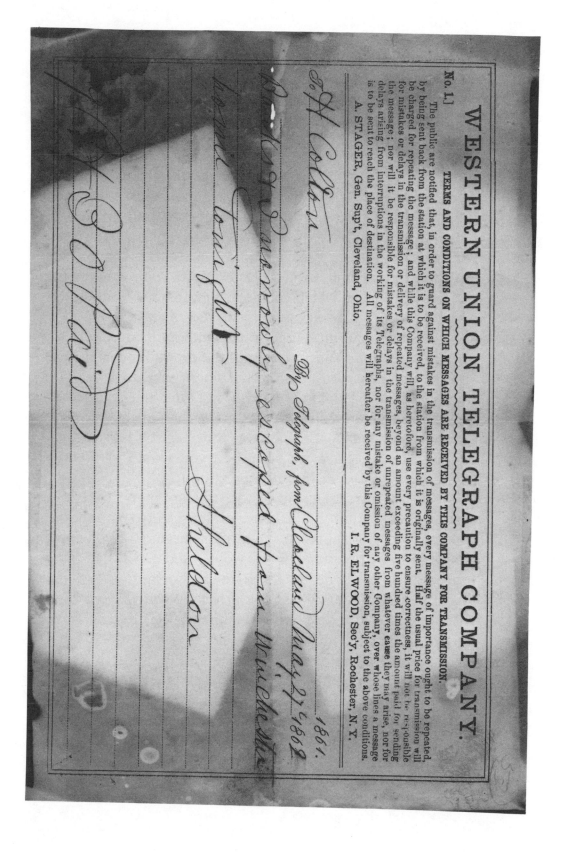

Banks & I narrowly escaped from Winchester   home tonight

J H Calton

Milan May 27 1862

Dear Carlos,

In replying to your letter of yesterday — if the Telegraph hadnt in the meantime removed doubts, I should have said it expressed the conclusions we had arrived at exactly, that is, if removal was possible he had been removed, if not, the rebels would not cumber themselves with the like of him, & if molested at all they would only require his parole, which could do him no harm & them no good.

But we had little time to think about it after rect. of your letter when Wiles brought in the despatch which read "Banks & I narrowly escaped from Winchester, will be home tonight". Thinking he might not have telegraphed to Toledo I directed Wiles to pass along the substance of it.

When I saw the call for the "Light Guards" last evening in the Blade we supposed you would go if they should reorganize, & had no objection to offer.

It is no time now for young men to shirk responsibility, that make any pretension to manhood, though I do not think the need of a large body of extra troops is so pressing as it would seem to be from movements of Federal & State authorities — some additions are necessary & could not be readily obtained without some little excitement. But whether events show hereafter that all the noise was necessary or not, it will have a good effect, people were generally falling into the belief that the rebels were as good as conquered already & some were turning to their farms & others to their merchandize leaving matters to be adjusted or quarreled over by partizan demagogues.

Patriotism needed a poke in the ribs by way of reminder that there is something to be done yet — that needs attention from <u>the</u> <u>people</u>.   But aside from other considerations you are entitled to three months vacation from Office work, & though we are sorry for the reasons that seem to require it, hope the change may be beneficial to you.

I recd. a letter from your Uncle at the same time, he says that Sheldon is undoubtedly in the hands of the rebels as it is not probable that Genl Banks had time to look after the wounded.

He seems to have forgotten that there are two of that name, one of whom is Sheldons body guard, & would move Heaven & Earth if necessary to get him out of danger.

But I have already said perhaps more than is necessary as we shall rather look for you home tonight — Carter will go after Nelia & I should not be at all surprised if our Rev Uncle should come on the same train with Sheldon — as it is about time for him to return.

The news of Sheldons escape & expected arrival seems to give pretty general satisfaction as far as it has spread in town. Capt. Shipman returned Saturday bringing a young Contraband, but no one seems to know or care anything about it.

It is a little singular how often Sheldons name has been brought before the people in one way & another while of four other commissioned officers from here nothing has been heard since they left by the public. Yours affectionately

H Colton

Carlos

Camp Chase Columbus O
May 30th 1862

Dear Sheldon

One of the boys is about starting for Toledo and I take the opportunity to write you — our Co was mustered into the service of the United States for the term of three months, this morning. What that service will be I cannot yet say — but hope it will not be to guard Camp Chase prison — think we will be sent somewhere soon. We have a splendid Co. of 84 men or more now expecting more. We had an election of officers this morning resulting in the choice of Richard Waite Capt. Joe Lannsbury 1st Lieut. and H. C. Colton 2nd Lieut. — some of the boys yesterday signified their intention to vote for me for 2nd Lieut. and I told them I didnt want it but as Hammie had been talked of would like to have them go for him — this morning on voting, two other Candidates received each 7 votes. I got between 20 & 30 Hammie between 30 & 40. A new election was necessary and I withdrew my name with a short speech to the boys, telling them that between the two Colton Candidates Hammie was the man. At the next vote Hammie went in all over! — Dont know who the non commissioned officers will be — think Frank Braisted — formerly a Toledo Merchant. One of the 2nd Lieut. Candidates will be Orderly Sergeant — I talked with Genl Hill today — he was gratified to think Hammie was elected. Said he had expressed the opinion to his wife that he would be — he inquired particularly about you as did his wife yesterday. I am with a tip top mess such as Henry Waite — Joe Johnson — Charley Swift Foster Wilder & etc too much confusion to write more.

Give much love to all the family.
Your brother
Carlos

Relative

Detroit June, 1st/62

Dear Melinda

Have you got tired of looking for myself or a letter? I intended to visit you before this time according to your request — but Harry has not been very well — he has a rash on his chin — which I am told is caused by teething — I have been giving medicine and supposed it would disappear in time for me to go to Milan before Sheldon returned, but it is not much better and I now give up in despair and write to let you know that I cant come as this is the first day of June. I hope that Sheldon will now soon be at home — you will then be relieved of so much anxiety Write me as soon as he comes. Mother has been at Trenton about two weeks on a visit — she was well when I heard last from her — perhaps you know that Lucy has gone to Perrysburg to board — she has a nice place there and I think will be happier there than at Trenton.

I am sorry that Uncle Hamilton has so much headache — I saw a recipe for the sick headache the other day which is said to be excellent — "Mix two teaspoonsfull of <u>powdered</u> <u>charcole</u> in a little water and take when you feel the headache coming on" — try it — may relieve if not cure. I am afraid that Uncle Hamilton will not be very sorry that I cant come — but I assure you that Harry would not trouble him at all — for all he wants is to be out of doors, making bouquets of grass and dandelion and sell them for a dollar as he says. I am afraid he would walk into your strawberry bed — for the way he devoured that <u>Vegitable</u> is a caution to all babies. I have had a short letter from Myra I do not think she wrote in very good spirits — Mrs Bill and family are very well — Give my love to Lottie and family also to the school marms — I hope they will succeed to your satisfaction and I know they will for trying to help themselves. If I should be left now without a protector and poor I would work my way along by myself — some way — you would see a different person from the one who lived round where they would keep her awhile until she found her husband and home. I hope such a thing will never happen — but if it does I shall be prepared

I have written Myra a long letter this morning and must write to Mother — therefore will say good bye — write soon
Your sister
Fannie Hyde.

Relative

Detroit June 4th 1862

My Dear Brother

I am rejoiced to learn that Sheldon, has arrived, safe (if not sound) to the home of his childhood, it seems almost a miracle that he lived to reach the end of his journey. We have all felt very anxious about him from the first of his being wounded, and now that he is at home, his mind will be more at ease and his recovery more speedy, although it will doubtly be some time before he will be the same in health as when he left you a few months ago, I should think it highly necessary for him to be kept perfectly quiet, and see but very little company, for some time. I wish very much that I lived near you so that I could render Melinda some assistance.

I infer from what you say in your letter that Carlos is going to the war it is the first we had heard of it. I am sorry to hear it and can truly say that no one can sympathise more deeply with you and yours than I do. Melinda doubtly recollect Mrs Burrow of Grooseish formerly a Miss McComb Niece of Mrs. Buchus, her oldest son was Lieutenant in one of the companies in Col Brodheads regiment of Cavalry, he is reported to have been killed, in this last battle at Winchester, shot through the heart, it is a terrible blow to his widowed Mother, when we look around us and see so many that are called to mourn the loss of friends who are slain on the battle field we have reason to be thankful, that our afflictions are no greater.

The same mail that brought your last letter brought me one from Mary, which I intend sending to Milan after Melindas Mother has seen it she is now in Trenton. Mary says Hiram wrote to you about a month before her letter was mailed the 1st of May they were all well, living on a beautiful farm six miles from a small Village called Lakeport. Hiram owns the farm. I have heard nothing from our Rev. Uncle since he left your house I am afraid I shall miss of seeing him he must have taken some other rout or I think he would have been here before this.

The paper containing an account of Sheldons arrival, I received and sent to Fanny Hyde she had just closed a letter to Melinda.

On taking this to the office I hope to find the paper you spoke of in your letter We are all well Phin has gone to Saginaw will probably be home the latter part of this week. Hatty has been intending to visit you this month, but on Sheldons account she will probably defer it for the present, I shall hope to hear from you often, as we shall all be anxious to know how Sheldon gets along.

Love to all particularly Sheldon

Your Affectionate
Sister
C Bill

Sheldon Colton

Milan O. June 8" 1862

Dear Carlos,

Yours of the 3" was received in due time and I will endeavor to make some kind of a reply to it though I do not feel a great deal like writing letters.

I am improving in health and strength all of the time, but, still have no control over the muscles of my right leg and am entirely helpless. I cannot turn over, get up nor lie down without assistance, and cannot move my foot from the floor at all. By strapping up my foot so that it would not touch the ground I managed to get out as far as the gate this morning but it was all I wanted to do. I expect to be lame for a long time. I presume it will not be long before I can do some travelling on crutches, but it will be some time before I can do any walking especially such as I used to do when I was in Virginia. One time I walked twenty miles without sitting down to rest. I never supposed that I was capable of doing it till I tried it.

Presuming that you know about my escape from Winchester by this time I will only say that I got very tired and it has taken some time to bring my strength up to what it was when I left there. Forty miles travel by wagon and over four hundred by railroad is pretty good exercise for a wounded man. I had no choice however but to take the ride or fall into the hands of the rebels, and I did not feel much like being taken prisoner by them for I did not admire their style of treatment of wounded men.

I am sorry that circumstances have made it necessary for you and so many others to enlist, but hope you may get through it all safely, and reach home alive and well when your term of enlistment expires. I may be able to take the field again by that time but it looks very doubtful now, indeed I may never be in marching condition again. I am glad to hear that your Co. letter is "A" for several reasons, but especially for this: when you come to march you will find that yours will be much the easiest place in the regiment. If the ground over which you are passing is at all rough and difficult, you will be moving at an easy pace while Co's G and B will be on the double quick half of the time, on account of the uneven marching of the intervening companies especially for the first few times.

Several prisoners captured by the rebels at Cross Lanes, belonging to the 7" Reg. have returned but I have not seen any of them yet. I know of nothing in the way of news for I do not get around any now days. We are all as well as usual here.

Give my respects to Waite, Wilder, Johnson and others of my acquaintances in Camp. Remember me especially to your worthy officers.

If you see Sarah Smyth, tell her how I am getting along and that I wrote to her a few days ago. Remember me to Genl. Hill also if you see him.

Yours truly, Sheldon Colton

OFFICE OF THE

MUTUAL INSURANCE COMPANY OF TOLEDO

Toledo O June 13 1862

My Dear Brother

You will have seen of course that the 8th Regiment is at Cumberland ere this. Should like to hear from Sheldon what kind of a place it is as to size etc. I cannot learn what the object is in their going there, presume it is however to take the place of some older troops — have received a letter from Annie this evening. She says they were about as dirty and tired a set of Boys as one would wish to see of a summers evening after their March in the baking afternoon sun from Camp Chase. Carlos with his Hair cut <u>Fighting</u> <u>Fashion</u> and tanned as black as a genuine Contraband, they were well provided for in every respect however. Annie says naively that none of the Privates or Non Commsd. Officers came out to Town to see her as they were ashamed of their Uniforms, but she saw them all at the Depot and Mrs. Raymond kissed them all round before starting. Was glad to hear from E. Walbridge that Sheldon is improving and hope he will soon report himself here, has he ever heard from his Winchester Friends. Do you need to anticipate any on his pay. If so, and you cant do it in Milan Wallfield may perhaps be able to aid you here to something. I am tired but try to work out my sentence at Hard Labour — the time will soon expire however.

C Colton

(Delia)

Milan June 15th/62

Dear Carl,

I wrote to you last Sunday I believe, and sent by Dr. Cornell. Alphy copied a letter from Hammie and sent here for us to read. In it he said you had had your hair shaved close to your head. Dr. Cornell wrote home that he saw you and said your hair was shaved so close you could not take hold of it with a pair of pincers. I think that is pretty close.

I suppose you are at Cumberland by this time.

I expect Mr. Carter and family will be up here to spend the afternoon and I must hurry and finish this before they come for there is no peace for me when 'Carrie Belle is around. If she cant find me when she comes she runs round calling "Aunt Dedele" until she finds me then I have to hunt the cat for her before she will be quiet and then if I leave the room she is after me again.

Sheldon is gaining fast now and we are in hopes that he will soon have the use of his limb again.

Last Wednesday seventeen of us young girls & boys had a grand picnic out to Enterprise. Us girls furnished the eatables and the boys the team, we took the Bandwagon and it was crowded full. We had a grand old time you may imagine what it was to get seventeen of us young ones to gather in the woods where no one could hear us, and we were at liberty to make all the noise we wanted to. The boys say they are going again. I hope they will.

The majority of this household are getting along very well though Mother is not feeling as well as usual to day or she would have written you herself. She hopes you will write just as often as you can, for she is anxious to know how you are getting along. She sends you this bud of the Sweet scented Shrub for you to carry in your vest pocket (in the place of a letter) and it will keep sweet a long time.

Lottie and family have arrived and I must close now. Write soon and often. Has Morton Raymond enlisted with you? If so give him my "best respects"
From your Sister
    Delia

    In addition to the Carter family Capt Orris Smith & family have just come in so that there will be no chance for anyone to write more today even if there was anything to be said. There has been no day — since Sheldons return that he has not had more or less company — to which there is no objection now, as he has improved very much during the past week, & can entertain his friends without injury to himself. Banks intends to start on his return a week from tomorrow & will try to see you on his way
    Yours affectionately
    H.C.

Toledo Market Review.

TOLEDO, Monday, June 16th, 1862, 2 P. M.

FLOUR—Receipts, past 40 hours, 9,888 bbls. Shipments to Buffalo, 9,047 bbls.; to Dunkirk, 8,080 bbls. Sales 50 bbls. XXX from white wheat at $5. We quote dull and nominal, shipping brands R. H. Ohio $4 20 to 4 30; superior grades $4½ to 5.

WHEAT—Receipts, past 48 hours, 58.664 bu. Shipments to Buffalo, 2.422 bu.; to Dunkirk, 546 bu. Sales, on Saturday, were restricted by want of vessels, and the delay in transmission of the steamer *China's* news from Cape Race. The only transactions were 3,000 bu. Mich. red at $1 01; 1,300 bu. choice Canal red at 97c.; 5,000 bu. white Wabash at $1. To-day, before report, sales 2,000 bu. Mich. red at $1; 2,500 bu. white Wabash at 98c. Since New York report, holders are firm at our quotations.

White Michigan	$1 06@	1 07
Red do.	@	1 00
White Wabash	@	98
Red do	95@	96
Red Illinois	@	93

CORN—Receipts, past 48 hours, 27,068 bu. Shipments to Oswego, 10,040 bu.; to Algonac, 1,000 bu. Sales, on Saturday, 3,000 bu. damaged at 27c.; 5,000 bu. new at 32c. At close buyers could not be found at over 31c. To-day there were sales before New York report, 6,000 bu. new at 32c.; 6,000 bu. on terms not made public, and 2,000 bu. warm at 25c. Since report holders are asking 32c, but we hear of no transactions.

OATS—Last sales reported were at 29c.

RYE—Held at 46c.

SALT—No coarse on market, fine $1 50 per bbl.

FREIGHTS—Lake—To Buffalo: Wheat 3¾c.; Corn 3¼c.
　　　　　　　　　To Oswego:　"　7½c.;　"　7c.
　　　Canal—Buffalo to New York: Wheat 12½c.; Corn 10½c.
　　　　　　　Oswego　　"　　　"　8½c.;　"　7¾c.

Through rates, Toledo to New York, Steam and Rail: Flour 70c. per bbl.; 4th class 35c. per 100 lbs. To Boston: Flour 80c. per bbl.; 4th class 40c. per 100 lbs.; Corn 24c. per bu.

OCEAN FREIGHTS—New York to Liverpool—Advancing, Wheat 10d. (20c.); Corn 9½d. (19c.)

RECEIPTS OF FLOUR, WHEAT AND CORN AT TOLEDO,

For week ending June 14, 1862.	Flour, bbls.	Wheat, bu.	Corn, bu.
By Michigan Southern Railroad	21,039	49,133	1,614
By Toledo & Wabash "	6,506	43,520	50,870
By Dayton & Michigan "	3,650	15,140	7,430
By Canal	8,900	51,679	8,059
Total for week	40,095	159,472	62,473
For preceding week	36,716	133,267	39,954
For corresponding week, 1861	27,171	144,361	94,299
Total since January 1, 1862	497,916	1,346,483	1,205,638
Same time, 1861	354,603	936,863	1,584,906

SHIPMENTS FROM TOLEDO,

Week ending June 14, 1862,	Flour, bbls.	Wheat, bu.	Corn, bu.
To Buffalo	30,312	14,960	17,680
To Dunkirk	14,423	846	......
To Oswego	800	12,000	10,000
To Ogdensburg	2,480	......	2,000
To St. Clair	......	......	2,000
Total for week	48,015	27,806	31,720
Total shipments by Lake since opening	359,216	791,002	876,427

RECEIPTS AT NEW YORK.

Week ending June 11, 1862	149,138 bbls. Flour.	537,926 bu. Wheat.	500,673 bu. Corn.
Preceding week	117,100	1,425,400	690,100
Since January 1, 1862	1,763,479 "	4,646,592 "	2,521,267 "
Same time 1861	998,414 "	6,377,902 "	4,162,270 "

EXPORTS FROM NEW YORK.

Week ending June 11, 1862	46,254 bbls. Flour.	817,176 bu. Wheat.	212,409 bu. Corn.
Preceding week	67,668	1,023,571 "	333,545 "
Total since January 1, 1862	1,171,271 "	4,813,291 "	5,223,792 "
Same time 1861	998,414 "	6,377,902 "	4,162,270 "

New York, June 14th, 7 P. M.—Flour, market 5c. lower with a very moderate business. The further advance in freights materially checking the export demand. Wheat—Market opened a shade firmer, but with a further advance in ocean freights closed quiet at about yesterday's prices. Chicago Spring 92c. to $1 08; Winter red Western $1 11 to 1 15; Amber Michigan $1 17½; white Western $1 23 to 1 26. Corn—Shade easier, with a moderate business doing for export and home consumption; 44 to 46c. for damaged; 47 to 50c. for new mixed western; 51 to 52c. for old.

New York, June 14th, 7 P. M.—Liverpool, June 7th, ex steamer *China*—Breadstuffs generally dull and steady. Wheat steady but dull. Corn steady. Provisions, generally, heavy with a declining tendency.

New York, June 16th, 1862.

Flour unsettled, favors buyers. Wheat scarce, one cent better, fair export demand. Corn, one cent better, fair demand.

Yours respectfully,

Relative

TOLEDO MARKET REVIEW
Toledo, Monday, June 16th, 1862, 2 P.M.)

Sheldons letter received, let him come here as soon as he is able Genl Hill will do any thing he can for him when the right time comes, the 84th are I presume under Fremont's control. I had been in hopes that the latest fighting would have been over before the 84th would have a chance but it does not look much like it just now. The African question must be disposed of for all time before we can have Peace.

Should you have any Berries out at any time I presume that Sophia would gladly pay the charges, by the way she is now a most diligent student of Geography and is making considerable progress therein —

Jane Colton writes me that Haight Louise Coltons Husband was killed at the great Fire at Troy — and that they have buried the children with Diptheria within the past year — there had been in Haights case I fear a moral death before, and the same is true with Sherman Marys Husband. I am told when these two girls were Married the World thought they had done remarkably well.

James, one of Marys sons is a private in the 36th N.Y. Regt. Seymour the other one is in the 21st New York but on duty at [illegible] (Genl McDowell and Jane think doing better than he did [remainder of sentence partially scorched]

What has become of our Rev. Uncle — it takes him a long time to get round his Circuit

I have just got through the Press 1400 copies of the annexed and Alphy is distributing them — it is more trouble than one would think to reconcile the news of 23 Produce Houses — and get quotations that suit all
So far to my own astonishment I have succeeded — my Issue ranges from 12 to 1400 copies tri weekly and aid the Post Office Department if no one else —

I enclose some Blank Checks and am happy to hear that Sheldon has use for them
                    Yours
                    C Colton

I stop the Press to say that there is a report in Town that the 84th have been, are, or will be, ordered to Annapolis for a course of instruction — but — I cannot tree the reliable gentleman that brought the intelligence
                    C

Carlos

Camp Lawrence
Cumberland Md
Thursday June 19th 1862

Dear Sister Delia

I got a letter from you yesterday written the 15th. As I know you are all anxious to hear from me as often as you can I will reply now, tell Mother that Sweet Scented Shrub was <u>very</u> sweet and I was pleased to get it. She was not well the day you wrote I hope she has recovered before now. I wrote to Sheldon two or three days ago. Since then there has not been any great changes in our life and not much to write about, tell Sheldon we were reviewed by Genl Kelly day before yesterday. Major Frothingham is on his Staff. The Genl is a very severe looking man. Lieut Colton thinks our regiment is as well drilled now as a good many that are in the field. John Hicks is with us he is now a Corporal. I told Morton Raymond that you sent your respects to him and he wished to be remembered to you, he was sick a day or two but is around again. We have a Darkey now from Toledo who cooks for the Captain, Lieutenants and we Non Commissioned officers. Which makes it much pleasanter than when we were doing the "kitchen work" ourselves, this is a quite uncivilized kind of life we are leading but Sheldon has seen it all and he can tell you better than I can write the way we pass the time, they are pretty strict about letting the boys pass outside of the camp so we dont have much chance to explore the Country. I have only been in town once since we came here tell Sheldon the town is under martial law. Hammie has been officer of the Guard in town once. I have not acted as Sergeant of the Guard since we came here but expect to be called on in a day or two. I have no idea yet what will be done with us but think we will stay here sometime. Genl Mulligan formerly Colonel is in Cumberland or was yesterday with a part of his Brigade. We have had considerable rain for two or three days which makes the air seem purer. We have been having very warm days and cold nights. We dont receive many visits from the Citizens of Cumberland so I cannot tell you much about the girls and boys. Hammie has received two or three boquets — one of our boys said the other day he thought Lieut Colton the finest looking officer in the regiment. I will close now and write again soon. Have got two or three papers from father. Hammie and I are well, love to all

Your brother   Carlos

Carlos

Camp Lawrence
Cumberland Md
Sunday June 22nd 1862

Dear Sister Nelia

    I got a letter from you with Mothers yesterday also received one from father <u>written</u> <u>13</u>th commencing "we suppose you are now on your winding way for B & O RR" & etc. it was marked "missent"　I receive papers quite often and think I have got the other letters regularly — before leaving Columbus　I wrote a short letter to father and Mother in the missent letter father says "a letter from you was recvd yesterday" which I suppose is that one.　The extracts from Col Varis letter with regard to Sheldons conduct on the field are good.　While in Camp Chase Genl Hill said he had written to Col Varis about Sheldon but had not then recvd a reply.　I am glad to hear that Sheldon is improving so fast.　We are still passing away time in Camp as soldiers usually do or rather as new regiments do — drilling most of the time.　With rumors from day to day that we are about to be called into the field <u>some</u> <u>where</u> to strengthen forces which are being overpowered but still our future is uncertain.　I hope and think we will be able to serve our Country in some way other than lying in Camp, before our term of enlistment expires.　Referring to your letter I see it was written one week ago today Sunday — finished Tuesday and sent with Mothers.　I wanted to go to church in town today but we had a regimental inspection this morning which kept us till church time, then I was so warm and dirty I did not feel like going.　Hammie went with two or three others.　He is getting along as usual — the same dignified gentlemanly officer commanding the respect and admiration of officers and men, old and young.

Carlos

I trust no harm may happen him during this three months experience. We have had cold nights and warm days for the most part here and the boys have got shivering each morning at reveille, but last night was quite mild and comfortable. Joe Johnson of Toledo sleeps next to me in our tent and furnishes me with a portion of his rubber blanket which we spread on the ground and wrap ourselves in our army blankets — last night I was awakened by a tickling sensation under my left arm and an examination found a large brown colored <u>worm</u> which had caught me napping and crawled down my neck. I suppose the thing thought I had surrendered when I laid down to sleep and must have been somewhat surprised at the suddeness with which I took up arms when I felt his touch. It was not a very pleasant circumstance but "there is nothing like getting used to it" — I am in much better health than when I left Toledo and if my life is spared I hope to be in much better physical condition than I have been of late, at the close of this campaign. John Hicks says he does not hear from home often and when you write he would like to hear about his sick sister.

Since writing the above we have recvd orders to march between four and five oclock tomorrow morning into the Shenandoah Valley to Fremont's headquarters, from here to Harpers Ferry then to Martinsburg from there to Winchester then to Mount Jackson and since then the orders are countermanded but we are to hold ourselves in readiness to go <u>at a moments notice</u>. Such is a soldiers life. Well, we have had an excitement and the boys were all jubilant. Much love to all

Carlos

Lina

Milan June 23rd 1862

My Dear Brother,

If it is raining as hard in Cumberland, as here, this morning, you surely must have a "foretaste sweet" of Soldiering. It must be very disagreeable camping out in such stormy weather. Well, how do you like a Soldiers life? You must know something about it by this time.

Sergt. Banks started this morning to report himself at Columbus. He does not feel fit to join the Regiment at present, but may possibly, and if so, expects to meet the 84th somewhere on the route. We did not send letters by him, as it was rather uncertain when you might meet.

Sheldon is gaining, slowly, but cannot use his limb at all. He thinks now he can, after the wounds are healed. They discharge yet, and have to be dressed three times a day.

Now that he is able to move around on crutches, he wants to be moving all the time, but finds he cannot go but a few steps without resting. He has had calls every day, but one, since his return, Sundays not excepted.

We expect visits from our relatives during the Summer. Myra is on her way, Cousin Hattie is in Toledo, suppose she will come here. Aunt Lucinda writes that she is coming.

Father received a letter from Uncle Brace Friday, with photographs enclosed of himself and his <u>intended</u>, said they would be here on their way home.

Ella Stevens was here last week, is looking badly, and feels miserable most of the time. I think you ought to have your picture taken for us now in your military clothes — <u>minus</u> the cap. Am quite anxious to see how you look.

Delia has received your letter since I commenced writing we were all glad to hear from you, and hope you will write often.

John Hicks sister — Carrie Hastings, was buried yesterday, she suffered greatly in dying. I believe Sheldon intends writing to you to day.

Accept much love from all.

Lina.

June 25 1862

Sir

My nephew Lieut. Sheldon Colton of the 67th Ohio, severely wounded at the Battle of Winchester and also suffering from the hasty removal on the retreat of Genl. Banks Div., is now at home slowly recovering but still unable to walk, he has applied to the Adjutant General for an extension of his leave of absence till he is sufficiently recovered to be able to rejoin his Regiment. May I ask your favorable endorsement of his application.

Respectfully
Your Obdt. Servant
Carlos Colton

(Delia)

Milan July 3rd 1862

Dear Brother Carl

I believe I have not answered your last letter yet so I will endeavour to do so now, although I do not feel much like writing to day. Hattie Ballard arrived here Monday morning I do not know how long she intends remaining

Banks recd a discharge and returned home last Sunday He has just gone off with Sheldon to take him a ride This is a very warm day although I have seen warmer ones

I expect Nelia will be home tonight she intends having a holiday on the Fourth. We both intended going to a picnic down to the lake shore but concluded we would spend the "Fourth" at home. The folks are all well here at home except me. I have been ailing for a day or two.

How do y<u>ou</u> <u>all</u> like Camp life? I <u>do</u> <u>wish</u> you would send us your picture, if you do not care to have it please send it to <u>me</u> and if you do not want <u>me</u> to have send it to the <u>folks</u>, any one only so I can see how you look with your hair cut so close. But I do not think that <u>old</u> picture of you is a very bad one at least I should not want to think so for everyone that looks at it says, <u>How</u> <u>much</u> <u>Delia</u> <u>looks</u> <u>like</u> <u>Carlos</u>.

Now Carl I cannot make out which one they mean the compliment for, and they say <u>If</u> <u>Delia</u> <u>was</u> <u>only</u> <u>a</u> <u>boy</u> <u>she</u> <u>would</u> <u>be</u> <u>a</u> <u>second</u> <u>Carlos</u>. Others say "<u>I</u> <u>think</u> <u>Delia</u> <u>looks</u> <u>so</u> <u>much</u> <u>like</u> <u>Lina</u>". So I have come to the conclusion that if I <u>look</u> like <u>Lina</u> and <u>act</u> like <u>Carlos</u> <u>I</u> <u>must</u> <u>be</u> <u>perfect</u>. What is your opinion on the subject?How do you intend spending the Fourth this time?

(Delia)

I wish you could be here to help us 'celebrate' although there is nothing going on in town But never mind <u>there</u> <u>will</u> <u>be</u> <u>a</u>
<u>"glorious"</u> <u>Fourth</u> <u>to</u> <u>celebrate</u> <u>when</u> <u>the</u> <u>war</u> <u>is</u> <u>over</u>!
========== ====== == =========
But how many homes will be chilled!
How many chairs empty!
How many <u>thousands</u> less to celebrate <u>that</u> Fourth.
But I am getting tired, (<u>and</u> <u>of</u> <u>course</u> <u>you</u> <u>are</u>) so I will close now with much love I am as I always have been your sister

       'Delia.

  Dear Carlos,
   I see that Delia has left a blank page but hardly know of anything interesting to fill it. I think Sheldon mentioned that Banks went no farther than Columbus being there condemned by the examining surgeons as unfit for further service. He says he cannot reenlist but can & will go down to Virginia & do a little something on his own hook if he would be needed.
  It is a little singular that Sheldon bore the exposure & fatigue of the winter campaign better than many such stout appearing fellows as the Sergt. — Capt. Shipman has just returned from Columbus being declared unfit for service — Banks says there were over 500 men & officers awaiting their turn to be examined when he left there a week ago — Sheldon has got an extension of his furlough from the Adjutant General at Washington, which puts him in a more favorable position — Your letter to Lina was recd yesterday
    H.C.

130

Relative

Mr H. Colton —
     My Dear Nephew —
     I have returned from my western tour as far as to this Ohio City of 3500 inhabitants. I am lodged on the banks of "the Great Miami" at the pleasant & hospitable mansion of the <u>Widow Fish</u> — a very int<u>ell</u>igent & sprightly lady of 60 — suitable in all respects to become my wife — but as I much prefer the <u>daughter</u> of 33 — I have contended to let the Mother remain in her <u>widowhood</u>. And this note is to advise you Sir — that we expect to be made <u>one</u> in <u>interests</u> as we are now one in <u>heart</u> on the Morning of Saturday next (the 19th) & to leave immediately for Toledo where we shall expect to spend the Sabbath & probably — Monday — & taking an early train — shall hope to be at your house on Tuesday (22) in season to dine with you — On the evening of that day I shall hope to introduce <u>all</u> your children to their <u>new</u> <u>Aunt</u> — & with them to spend a <u>social</u> pleasant evening —
     With kind regards, to Mrs. C. — & others of your family with you — I remain very
          Affly your Uncle
          S. W. Brace

P.S. Let no high expectations be raised respecting the personal appearance of my <u>intended</u> She is not a <u>beauty</u> except in <u>mental</u> & <u>moral</u> qualities — She is a native of N.Y. City of the very best Antecedents — highly educated & promises all that I can expect in a wife at my period of life — much more than I deserve —
     She has been in Ohio but a few years — & is willing to exchange it for "the Empire State" again — & especially or by the exchange she expects to get <u>A Good Old Husband.</u>
     She is the one only sister of Rev Mrs. Hubbard of Whitesboro Oneida County (2 miles from me) where I became acquainted with her more than two years ago & have seen her there on visits a number of times since — She had become quite intimate with my Niece Emma at my house — & had been <u>at</u> my house in a number of instances — previous to my first visit here in May last.
     From this showing, you will perceive that we are quite well acquainted with each other & not acting a hasty part in celebrating as we contemplate the banns of Matrimony the present week —   Yours & etc S.W.B.

H Colton

Milan July 18 1862

Dear Carlos,

Some one advised you the other day that some cans of fruit had been sent to Toledo to be forwarded to you. We learn that a box will be packed tomorrow & as Addie intends to go to Toledo in the morning your Mother is preparing some more to send to you & Hammie — by his pardon I mean Lieut. Colton ——

I mentioned the matter to Mrs. Hicks & she will send a couple of cans to John who she tells me is sick —

Hattie Ballard, Mrs. Capt. Poe & child, Mrs. Carter & two children are here, while your Mother & the girls are exceedingly busy in the kitchen & adjoining room, where I am trying to write a few lines to you — preparing fruit & making household arrangements generally — it is late in the day & you may naturally infer that I am somewhat confused & perplexed & should in fact omit writing today only that it would insure a delay till Monday & by that time you may be chasing "Stonewall Jackson" down the valley & thereby lessen the chance of a letter reaching you.

For reasons above stated my <u>think</u> is out of gear, so that this will be disjointed if not short, perhaps both.

As there will be three cans for you in the box that are now unsealed your Mother has just concluded to send but one more to each of you at this time together with some small packages of dried cherries & dried currants — all which she hopes may reach you before you have to strap your knapsacks on your backs & be "marching along".

My mind has been a good deal exercised about getting some small amt. of money to you & should have risked some by mail long ago if there had been any certainty of your remaining in Camp long enough for it to reach you.

Unless we could know that it was needed did not think best to incur the probable risk of a letter following you into Virginia, and have hoped you would profit by my suggestion to draw on Toledo as there must be persons going, or wanting to send some often who would willingly cash a small draft.

We want you to feel that you have a deposit at Toledo not needed by anyone else, & make yourself comfortable with it. We dont expect you to make much out of your present wages even if the pay was prompt, & should be sorry indeed if you lacked anything for comfort or Independence in your new position ———

Sheldon advised you that he had about a hundred dollars left. Samuel also owes him five hundred, on which he can get advances if needed, on that you must have no hesitation about helping yourself at anytime & in any manner that may be necessary as convenient. Genl Hill has written two friendly letters to Sheldon since he came home & I have no doubt, if he was sound, that some position would be offered him in the new Military arrangements. Men of even his small experience are needed now ———

Your Mother has a couple of white havelocks on hand that were made for Sheldon last summer — we suppose they are pretty much out of fashion but she will send them with the fruit thinking they may serve some purpose for you or the Lieutenant — for night caps if nothing else. I noticed a letter in the Commercial the other day & have hoped there might be "a few more of the same kind on hand" — it is said the "Spoke" of that "reverberated" some in Toledo — but I would suggest some more distinctive nom de guerre there was another letter published in the same column from some other Mr. "C"

Yours affectionately

Toledo, O. July 27th 1862

Dear Father:

Supposing you would see my "distinguished arrival" in the Blade, I did not write to you Friday.

Mother has gone to Trenton and may go on to Detroit.

I find enough to busy myself about here, plenty of friends to visit, and all seem glad to see me. I met Mr. J. M. Ashley on the street yesterday, and he seemed glad to see me, and said he thought I was gone sure at the time of Banks retreat.

I went down to Mr Raymond's Friday evening, found the family all well. Aunt has just got a letter from Carlos, in which he says that Hammie has been taken to the house of Mr Boehm, a Union man in Cumberland where he has good nursing and homeopathic treatment. Carlos is with him. His is not very sick.

No further news in particular. Send my sword up here. I can get the sheath repaired here, send belt also, by express if you like.

Love to all.

Yours Truly

Sheldon Colton.

Please return Parson Browlow's Book and "Mt Vernon" to Mrs Bates with my respects and thanks.

M. S. Cotton

Toledo August 1st 1862

Dear Husband,

      I know you must have wondered, a good many times, why I have not written home sooner, but if you could realize, or even imagine what a time we have had in Trenton visiting, with from thirteen to seventeen, all in one house going to & fro, the older ones, trying to keep the eight little ones (between the ages of four months & ten years) from getting into mischief or runing over each other — then you would wonder more at my being able to write even now — Addie & I arrived here yesterday, & she has just left on the cars, for Perrysburg. — It will be a week or two yet, before Myra comes here, so it will be a month or more before she gets as far as Milan —

      Tuesday I went to Detroit with George Truax in his Carriage, & I have <u>never</u> had <u>so good</u> a visit with <u>him</u> before, as I have had this time, from first to last of my stay, there are but few men, I think, that could have got along with such a houseful of women & children, more patiently & kindly than he has done this time — I spent the day with Mrs Bill, Clarinda & Hattie. Fannie went up with us, & I only went to her house about half an hour before we left the City —

      Charles Brace left Mrs Bill's but a few minutes — before I got there, was very sorry we could not have been a little earlier, so as to have met there, they were all very much pleased with him.

      Alphy has just rec'd a letter from Carlos, says Hammie is some better — says the family all insist upon his still staying with Hammie at their house.

      It is a great comfort to them here, that Carlos is with him — I shall try to get a chance to write to Carlos in a day or two cannot tell
[following portion of letter is scorched]

      We have heard enough about War, for the present, & have declined an invitation to go — hope you all keep well, & are enjoying yourselves — would be glad to hear from some of you —
Love to all. As ever — yours
        affectionately
        M.S.C.

Friend

Toledo Aug 2nd 1862

Dear Carlos,

Perhaps, in some of your lonely watchings over Hammie's sick bed, you may feel cheered to read a letter from a <u>woman</u>, even if she <u>is</u> an old married dame! Every soldier is interesting to me, and when they are friends and go out from among us, they are near my heart. I have been at the aid rooms to day, and sewed bed ticks by the side of your mother. She is one of the Spartan women — "<u>with</u> your shield, or <u>on</u> it" — is her feeling. I can't quite reach her attitude, but I can wonder and admire. The Lieut (Sheldon) came in with Lieut Col Varis of the "67th", and the ladies had quite a chat with them. Sheldon looks really handsome — is quite fleshy and in good spirits. We had a look at the murderous ball, and the blessed scissors — what a narrow escape! Thank God, all of you, for it. He goes to Columbus next week to see about his ability to return to the field. Mary is going for a visit, at the same time. She was quite amused at my enthusiasm, about gallanting the Lieut to C. I told her it would be a proud day for me, if <u>I</u> could go with a wounded Soldier to the Capital of the state! The blood stirs rapidly through my veins, every time I see him, and I do not dare to say all I <u>think</u>, even, <u>about</u> him, much less <u>to</u> him. But he is a hero in my eyes, and I render him silent homage every time we meet. He is so bright and cheerful, under it all — his spirit is lovely — uncomplaining and patient in the extreme.

Friend

Hammie's mother bears up under her trial better than one would suppose. I can see that your mother's presence cheers & strengthens her. I hope the "boys" will all be well very soon. They feel more quiet about Hammie, because you are with him. I, too, am glad you are there. But be careful of your own health, for the care of the sick is very wearing these hot days. I called upon the Rev. H. Walbridge and from him learned quite definitely about all of you. The situation must be delightful — and healthy. Your letter was a great comfort to me — and in imagination I ask a thousand pardons of Mr. Ross for having such a wrong impression of him. Every one who speaks or writes of him gives him great praise. How pleasant it is, to be thus agreeably corrected in one's impressions. I shall make my best bow to him when he returns. We count the days now when the "boys will return". How much I wish Hartwell was among you! It will soon be a year since he left us! He is now in Schenck's division, near Gordonsville — in good health and spirits. Don't you think McClellan a fine specimen of "masterly inactivity"? I have always defended him, but although those who are not on the ground, are not competent to judge — still it does seem as if something more ought to be accomplished by the "Grand army of the Potomac". How horrible it all is, and when will the end come? War meetings are numerous, and there is a general "making up" among the people. I suppose you see the "Blade", and know the general news. I wish I had something new to tell you, but it is awfully dull here.

Carlos

Residence of Mr Boehm
Cumberland Md
Monday August 11th 1862

Dear ones at Home

I have never before known such grief as I have experienced yesterday and today. I presume the telegraph has informed you before this that our beloved Hammie died yesterday at 12 oclock on Friday last. We were for the first time during his illness alarmed at his condition as his mind was wandering — the day before all his symptoms were for the better, was stronger had better appetite etc, but this delirium of Friday caused us uneasiness and it was thought best to call in a physician and the leading doctor of the place was sent for. After hearing a full statement of the case and examining him he assured us that there was no cause for alarm, that it was a mild type of typhoid fever which had so far been treated <u>perfectly</u> <u>right</u>. That his delirium was caused only by nervous irritation that a simple restorative and simple remedies were all he required, and recommended a drink of Camphor Water, gave no other prescription and would take no pay for his call. We all felt light hearted. Mrs Boehm expressed her joy by pounding my shoulders — but his delirium instead of abating increased at night, the next forenoon Saturday he had two bloody passages of the bowels. The doctor was called and was then alarmed saying it was a very unusual and aggravated case, at my suggestion he called an other physician for consultation, it was thought that if there was not further movement of the bowels he might yet recover — there was no more — towards evening he fell into sleep, as we supposed but which was really prostration a state of unconsciousness from which he never rallied — but went to his long home on Sunday noon August 10th.

Carlos

We were mustered into service on June 10th, if not summoned before — the balance of the company expect to be mustered out on September 10th, by an Earthly Mustering Officer. He had in his hand while dying a little testament which was sent to him here, on which was printed in gilt letters "from Mother <u>July</u> <u>10th</u>" — In the morning whilst he was sleeping his last sleep Mrs Boehm asked if I would not like to have the prayers of the Church offered for him saying she would send word to the Minister. I of course requested that it should be done, but I had an uneasy feeling and not long afterward asked her if the minister could not come <u>before</u> <u>service</u>, he did come, (the Rev Mr Percival) and offered up a most beautiful prayer. Capt Waite says that when we joined in the Lords prayer Hammies lips moved as if repeating it — Mrs Boehm says that the day before he was unconscious he requested her to pray for him, during his delirious talk he did not utter a word which might not be said in the presence of Angels, he was a pure minded noble boy whom everybody loved — everybody who became acquainted with him here have learned to love him. My grief has been very great, it has made a child of me, but what can it be compared with that of his home circle God help them all — I have not got the heart to write to any of them yet.

Yours affectionately   Carlos

Friend

Toledo Aug 17 1862

My dear Carlos.

Your letter came while I was about and was not opened until my return, the very day, of Hammy's funeral and upon consultation with Abe we thought it advisable not to publish it, a decision with which I presume your own judgment will agree. In any other event the letter would have been most gladly published. — I myself am going to the war soon. We are in hopes to secure to Toledo a battery of artillery, a service which seems to be very popular, and in which I am convinced a large number of our finest fellows will enlist. If that falls through entirely, I shall go in in some other shape. — You have undoubtedly heard from John Johnston all the news. Your cousins death was a sad shock to all of his friends, and caused general mourning throughout the city. Mr Walbridge preached the funeral discourse this morning, and a more appropriate, eloquent, and touching discourse it has never before been my lot to hear. The letter from the lady, at whose home Hammy died to your aunt was read, and the effect it had throughout the whole audience was most touching scarcely a dry eye could be seen.

This war is assuming day after day more & more terrible dimensions. Where will be the end? Nearly every one is getting ready to go. I have thought of all such friends who are scuffling for newspapers and propose to have a hand in in some shape. Shel is now I believe at Columbus. Our Milan folks are mostly well. No news of importance from that quarter. I saw your Mother & sister, and Myra at your aunts the other day.

Let me hear from you. By the way I saw Jim Kilbourne at Columbus the other day. He is quite recovered and has gone into camp with his Company.

Yours as ever
Kent Hamilton

Nelia,

Toledo Aug. 18th

Dear Father,

      Hammic's remains were brought to the city last
night at ten oclock, by John Johnson, the coffin was
opened at the depot, and his body was so much decayed
that Mr. Chase would not allow it to be brought to the
house. So it was sealed up last night and this morning at
ten oclock the hearse with the body were brought before
the door and the services held at the house, as Aunt was
not able to go to the church. It was the longest funeral
procession I ever saw they said it was a mile in length and
all the flags in the city are at half-mast. Every one says
that they never saw so many tributes of respect paid to so
young a person. None of us saw the corpse it was not
brought into the house. We could see through the glass
window of the hearse that the coffin was covered with a
flag & strewn with flowers, and wreaths of flowers were
carried by the pall-bearers & laid in the grave. Aunt went
into one fainting after another & convulsions when
Johnson came last night and told her that the body could
not be brought to the house but she has been very calm all
day, & it is wonderful how calm Annie & Abram are.
Johnson brought a most beautiful and comforting letter
from Mrs. Boehm, in which she says "Carlos has given up
entirely to his grief, and is really heartsick so much so he
wishes me to say for him that "Hammie died with his
mother's testament clasped in his hands and his sister's ring
on his finger." John says Carlos is not sick but tired out.
But he says we need have no fears of his reenlisting, and in
fact none of the company have the heart to do so now that
Carlos is kindly exempted from all duty until he has

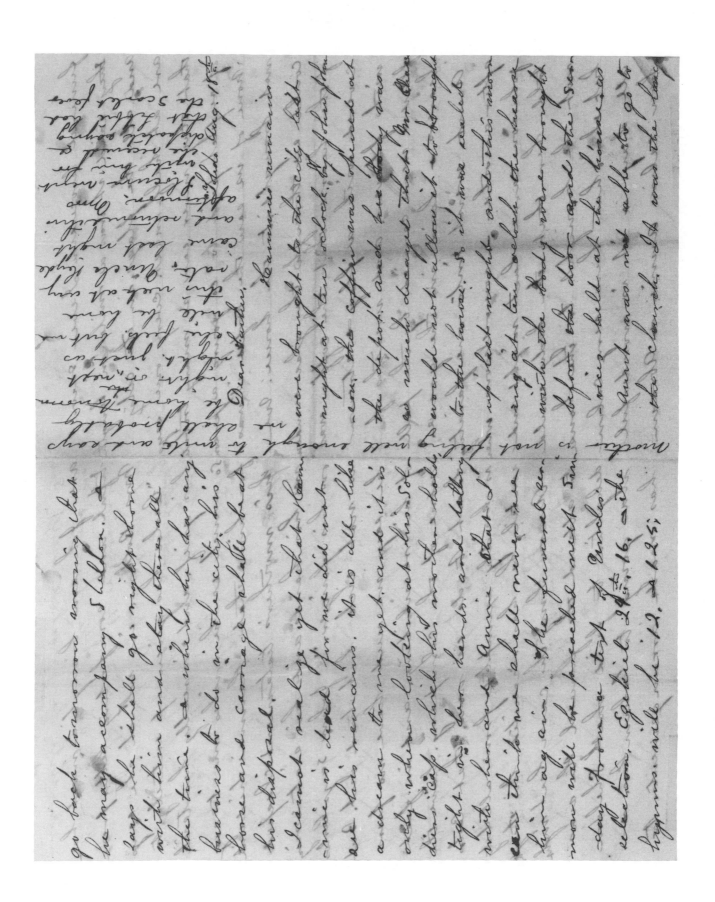

Nelia,

recruited his strength. Anson Smyth came last night to attend the funeral. He was delighted to find that Sheldon was going to Columbus, & has made arrangements, to go back tomorrow morning that he may accompany Sheldon, & says he shall go right home with him and stay there all the time, & when he has any business to do in the city, his horse and carriage shall be at his disposal.

I cannot realize yet that Hammie is dead for we did not see his remains, it is all like a dream to me yet, and it is only when looking at his soldiers cap which his mother holds tight in her hands and talking with her and Annie that I can think we shall never see him again. The funeral sermon will be preached next Sunday from a text of Uncles' selection. Ezekiel 24th , 16. & the hymns will be 12. & 125. Mother is not feeling well enough to write and says we shall probably be home tomorrow night, or the next night, just as she feels, but we will be home this week at any rate. Uncle Hyde came last night and returned this afternoon. Mrs. Slocum went with him for she received a dispatch saying that Libbie had the scarlet fever. Uncle was very much excited yesterday but on the whole he has borne it much better than we expected. But now he walks the floor almost constantly, & tells Annie that Hammie wont have to lie there alone long, he is more calm today and seems to be relieved to think it is all over, and everything passed entirely to Aunt's satisfaction in the arrangement of things.

We will bring a copy of Mrs. Boehms letter home. I cannot write more now, my love to the girls, and a great deal for yourself from your affectionate daughter

Nelia

H. Calton

Milan Aug. 22 1862

Dear Carlos,

I was suspicious that your brief & hasty note of last Sunday to Nelia meant something more than mere haste to go to Camp from Cumberland, (the latter place being East of the former Some distance) — but did not mention my suspicion as it would only lead your Mother to fear that you would get into some danger, a position she is anxious you should avoid as much as possible. "Delta" in the Blade of last evening confirmed my fear that you had been ordered from Camp "some distance" but this morning our suspense was relieved by rect. of your letter announcing your safe return in triumph to Camp Lawrence. We flatter ourselves that the time is approaching when we shall see you at home & free from all military aspirations till your services may again be specially needed, which is not probable as the Government is about to establish the more equitable mode of drafting, which will in a measure relieve the best & bravest young men from taking the field for the benefit of sneaks & cowards. The volunteering system is good to a certain extent to bring out the military spirit of the young when needed, but as a general thing the portion of community that could best be spared are the last to offer themselves as martyrs for their country, & can only be reached by conscription. The first law of nature, self preservation, is being displayed to a considerable extent in individual efforts to reach the Queen's dominions, but that game is pretty effectually blanked now.

H. Culton

You are probably aware that Sheldon is writing in Gen Hill's office we have not heard from him since he commenced & dont know what the effect may be, but were sorry to have him attempt it so soon as he was not in fact able, one serious difficulty is that the use of crutches affects his right shoulder which is somehow out of gear, & causes swelling & lameness of the arm & hand, — which we fear may be troublesome for a time in the way of writing. He writes that he can dress and undress himself without much trouble though we know it must be difficult for him to do so. He will doubtless do all he can without complaining.

He will probably soon have leave to retire from public service on a pension of seventeen dollars per month; his furlough expired yesterday & is not likely to be renewed under a recent order.

I mentioned in a recent letter to you that Mr. Jones had learned that they could run the Bank without your help — whereat your Uncle was exceedingly indignant — probably they are not of the kind that continue half pay to their employees who volunteer & give them their places when they return. In a subsequent letter I sent Lina's photograph — as you have not mentioned either of these letters perhaps they did not reach you.

I didnt like the picture but as there had been delay about getting any better ones, thought she had better send it before you left your present quarters.

You may perhaps be aware that a letter of yours to Kent reached there in his absence & consequently was not published. Your Uncle sent it to me the other day.

The spontaneous & universal tribute paid to Hammie must in some measure mitigate the grief of his parents. It is quite unusual for one so young —

Yours affectionately

Sheldon Colton

Columbus O. Aug. 24 1862

Dear Mother:

Your letter enclosing those from Carlos and Uncle was duly received. I was glad to hear from you all again and to find that you were well. I hope Lina will not have to suffer any more with the toothache, but if she does, tell her if it is from an ulcerated tooth to wet some cotton with Camphor and put it on the gum, and hold it there. I did so for the one that troubled me two years ago and found that it eased the pain a good deal, though the remedy is rather warm itself.

I am getting along very well here, do not have to work hard, and have a good boarding place, though I presume the board bill will be rather high. That does not make much difference when I am earning more than enough to pay it all of the while. There are a number of boarders here, mostly young men, and very pleasant company.

Dr. Cornell has been in to see me two or three times, he has just been appointed an Assistant Surgeon in one of the new regiments and seems highly pleased about it. He could have been a Surgeon if he had wished to, as he passed first class examination and his name was put down as such but he modestly and wisely chose to be an Assistant. I am very glad that he has got the position, and hope he may do well in it. At any rate it will be a help to him in future.

I do not have any trouble about dressing my wounds and think I am gaining strength all of the time, though rather slowly. I use only one of my crutches now, and a cane, but do not like to walk far. I have not heard a word from Washington yet, and cannot tell what disposition will be made of my case. I presume I shall know sometime this week though.

I do not know how long Genl. Hill may want me, but presume not more than three or four weeks if he does as long as that. I do not know how much pay he intends to give me, but it does not concern me much. If I get enough to pay my board I shall be that much ahead, for I should have to stay here at any rate, and I can do all that I have to here as well as not.

Of course I cannot draw any pay till I get some kind of papers from Washington, either a discharge or an extension of leave of absence, and have not much left with me. You had better make an account at some store for a week or so for what you want, and if you have any money on hand use it to buy meat or whatever little articles you may need. I will send you some as soon as I can.

I understand that the three months regiments are to be mustered out of service immediately, if that is the case Carlos will soon be at home.

No more news that I know of to tell you. Love to all,

Yours truly   Sheldon Colton.

Carlos

Cumberland Md
Tuesday Aug 26th 1862

Dear Mother

Your letter was received a few days since enclosing one from Sheldon written at Columbus. I also recvd one from him written 20th he expected to stay with Genl Hill for a short time — am very glad he is able to get around so well now and hope to see him in Columbus soon. We cannot tell yet whether we will return before the 10th or not. Excepting the night we were on picket duty I have spent every night for the past month at Mrs. Boehms. I find it necessary now to keep off the ground and out of the night air as much as possible. I think I should have been attacked with fever if I had not such opportunities to guard against it and that my cough which has now almost ceased would have been much worse but for the doctoring done by my deliverer Mrs. Boehm. I owe the family more than I can hope to repay for their uniform kindness and care. I send this afternoon by express the rest of Hammie's clothing, — with some pictures of Mrs. Boehm and Alice — also some pressed flowers arranged by Mrs. Boehm which were in the room with poor Hammie's remains. Mrs B pressed them and made a frame with ornamental leather work, into which she has arranged it. I think it will be highly prized by Aunt. Mrs. Judge Potter of Toledo has just been at Mrs. Boehms (where I am writing this) She and her husband have been here to see their son who has been quite sick but is now getting well. Henry Waite is boarding down town and getting along nicely. Mrs. B is suffering with headache today, the other members of the family are in usual health. I must close in a hurry to mail this — love to all from

Your affectionate Son
Carlos

"Picket's Last Watch"

All quiet along the Potomac "they say",
Except now and then a stray Picket
Is shot as he walks his beat to and fro,
By a rifleman hid in the thicket.
'Tis nothing - a private or two, now and then
Will not count in the news of a battle:
Not an officer lost, only one of the men
Moaning out all alone the death rattle.

All quiet along the Potomac tonight,
Where the soldiers lie peacefully dreaming;
Their tents in the rays of the clear Autumn moon,
O'er the light of the watch fire are gleaming.
A tremulous sigh as the gentle night wind

etc

There's only the sound of the lone sentry's tread
As he tramps from the rock to the fountain etc
His musket falls slack, his face dark & grim
Grows gentle with memories tender etc

The moon seems to shine just as brightly as then
   That night when the love yet unspoken
Seaped up to his lips - when low-murmured vows
   Were pledged to be ever unbroken
Then drawing his sleeve roughly over his eyes
   He dashes off tears that are welling etc

He passes the fountain - the blasted pine tree
   His footstep is lagging and weary,
Yet onward he goes - thro' the broad belt of light
   Toward the shade of the forest so dreary.
Hark was it the night wind that rustled the leaves
   All quiet along the Potomac tonight etc

[written in pencil, author unidentified]

Why is a hen immortal?
Because its _son_ never _sets._

When did Ruth treat Boaz roughly?
When she pulled his ears and trod on his corn

Carlos

Cumberland Md
Thursday Aug 28th 1862

Dear Father

I wrote to Mother two or three days since — have since then received yours of 22nd in which you speak of two letters that I had not acknowledged the receipt of — one containing Lina's photograph, the other in which you said it was not probable my place would be reserved for me at Bank of Toledo, both of which I <u>did</u> receive duly, and am surprised that I made no mention of Lina's picture. I do not think it a good picture, but there is resemblance enough for the Boehm family to consider her a very pretty girl. As to Mr Jones conclusion that they could run the Banking Institution without me, I am not surprised. I never suspected the friendship of the officers of the Bank to be any thing more than a wish to keep me until they saw a fit opportunity to put in my place some relative or other favorite. Neither am I disappointed for it has been a question with me whether I would ever return to the office if wanted. I think there will always be work for me to do somewhere. I have never had much serious thought of making "Military" a profession and unless I get a clerkship in some Military department think I will not continue in the service after our present Campaign, except in case of great emergency when we are really needed for a short time, to smite our enemies.

The camping ground of the 84th was changed today, by the removal of our tents a few rods from the old place, it was found necessary to do so as every body was getting indignant, the same ground has been used almost constantly for 18 months as an encampment and it is claimed that is the chief reason for so much sickness among the boys — there has been several deaths since our beloved Hammie left us — (only one belonging to our Co) — Am in hopes the change of ground will be benificial to the sick. I have been staying almost constantly at Mr Boehms as I was threatened with fever, which assumed an intermittent form. I have been lounging around the house and taking Homeopathy — also cold sitz baths the past two nights. I think the disease which might have assumed a serious form in Camp, is broken up — and that I will now rapidly regain my usual health. Capt Waite informs me that we will be mustered out and paid off here about the 10th Sept. Will probably go to Columbus as a regiment, and from there be sent to our different starting points. I hope to see you all soon after that time. I got a letter from Sheldon written in the Adjutant Genls office Columbus since the one sent in Mothers letter, he seemed to like his present employment very well. Kent Hamilton wrote me about the unpublished letter saying he would gladly have published it if it had been recvd in time — Love to all   Carlos

Friend

Toledo, Ohio, August 31 1862

Dear Karl

You must not suppose from my silence towards you that I have not often thought of you Delia and myself often talk of you & wish we could do something for you or send something to you that would smooth the "rough & rugged path" you have slected the first good chance I got of sending you what I supposed would suit your taste occurred on Johnson's return & I was pleased to learn that I suited you

About the time you left us business became quite active & as you doubtless are aware the "heft" of the burden fell on my shoulders & it rested heavy enough for a while to make me feel as though I was doing more than my head could well stand but I worried through it until I made a first rate Bookkeeper of our young friend H. — if teaching him had been the only thing that I had to contend with I could have got along well enough but the cussed mistakes & omissions of <u>an old associate of ours</u> I must confess were <u>so numerous</u> as almost to — I was going to say ruffle my <u>quiet</u>, <u>cool</u>, & <u>even temper</u>? You will recognize the old stereotyped phraze — "Did I do that" or "didn't I make a memorandum of this" as emenating from one who in days of yore has often tried men's souls — We are doing an immense business this season Exchange on N.Y. selling at par buying rate 1/2% off — we are ordering about $150,000 — per week in currency from NY city —

I went out to Camp Toledo this afternoon with "Ho" where I am informed there are about 2400 recruits ready to fight, bleed, & die for the good cause — we are trying all we can to avoid a draft in our (First) Ward we only lack about 13 men to fill our quota under both calls —

Poor Hammies death has cast quite a gloom over all his friends & acquaintances. You have no idea how much has been said about it to me at the Bank. Many persons in Toledo labor under the impression that I am related to your family after that reason I presume I have been so often addressed on the subject — Your poor Aunt must feel terribly cut up by this sad event I dared not even look at her on the morning that Mr Walbrige delivered the funeral discourse — God grant her strength to bear up under her affliction —

Mrs M tells me to send you her best love & wishes you may soon be back amongst us — Libby often speaks of you & if she were awake would doubtless send you some message it is now past 11 P M so excuse me if I close without sending you any "gossip" but rest assured of one thing you have my best wishes for your success   Yours truly G Mortimer

Carlos

Cumberland Md
Friday Sept 12th 1862

Dear Father
Our regt was yesterday paid off to 1st Inst today
a vote of the regt was had as to whether they would stay
here any longer — they refuse to stay. I was not at Camp,
had no desire to say one way or another. My wish was to
do as the majority decided. Johnson is writing to the Blade
about it tonight. I think we will leave here tomorrow or
Sunday for Columbus. The Unionists here have been
alarmed for some days at the prospects of a large force
coming this way — of Rebels. Mrs Boehm and daughter,
child and servant leave here early tomorrow morning for
Wheeling, telegram was recvd from Uncle this morning
asking them to go to Toledo — think they will go there
from Wheeling soon. I am in a hurry, to mail this this
evening, hoping to see you all soon. I close with love to all
I suppose you have been somewhat anxious about us for
some days, but it dont look now as if we were going to do
any fighting
Carlos

Head Quarters, Ohio Militia.

ADJUTANT GENERAL'S OFFICE,

Columbus, O., Sept. 17 , 1862.

Dear Father,

Carlos passed through here this morning on his way to Delaware, with the rest of the Regiment, to be paid off and mustered out, which will take three or four days I presume.

I saw him a few minutes at the depot, he is looking pretty well, and seemed glad to get home again. I presume you will see him along Saturday, perhaps not till the fore part of next week.

I have nothing now to tell about myself, have not received any papers from Washington yet, but hope to in a few days. As I wish to have my case disposed of in some way.

I am sorry to hear that Leina and Delia are sick, hope they will soon recover.

I presume that Mr. and Mrs. Boehm will be in Toledo soon, as they left Cumberland on Saturday,

Yours truly, Sheldon Cotton.

Sheldon Colton (signature)

Head Quarters, Ohio Militia

ADJUTANT GENERAL'S OFFICE

Columbus, O., September 22, 1862

Dear Father:

Yours of the 17th is received, am glad to hear that Delia is better, and hope that Lina will soon follow her good example.

The cane was received at the same time the other things were. I am using two canes to walk with now, having laid aside my crutches for a while at least, as long as I have no further to walk than now I can get along pretty well without them.

I do not see why I cannot hear anything from Washington. I am afraid that I cannot get my papers soon enough to answer my purpose, as the Regulations say that "Any officer who is absent from his appropriate duties for more than six months, with or without leave, thereby forfiets all the emoluments to which he would otherwise be entitled," so if I come under this head it will make a difference of nearly three hundred dollars in my pay.

I was wounded six months ago tomorrow, but my first leave of absence dates April 10th and Genl. Hill seems to think that the latter will be the date to reckon from: if so I am comparatively safe.

There is nothing new going on here now, that I know of to interest you and I will begin to wind up. My health is pretty good, as good as I could expect while unable to take any exercise.

I think General Hill intends to keep me here for some time, perhaps as long as I wish to stay.

I enclose three dollars. I would send more but cannot safely do so this time. I may not be able to send any more this month unless I can draw my army pay, but I presume that Carlos has given you some by this time, at any rate you can make a small account at some store till the first of next month and then I will send you enough to pay up. I shall look pretty anxiously for my papers now, for this week, unless they come along sooner — I would not like to lose so much of my pay, just when I want it so much.

Love to all.

Yours truly,

Sheldon Colton.

Milan Sept. 22nd 1862

Dear Carlos,

By some mischance your letter only came to hand this A.M. — if it had arrived a day sooner it would have relieved us in some measure from a state of "Suspended animation", —

Not hearing from you on Monday we felt so certain of your coming that Banks — who was here yesterday — went to Norwalk last evening to escort you home — your not coming last night made it so certain you would be here this morning that we were — a little disappointed, perhaps ——

Your Mother fears that "you have a Beam in your eye, & cannot see clearly" how glad she would be to see you at home.

But we are willing to count your convenience & can appreciate your desire to make the stay of your Maryland friends at Toledo as pleasant as possible. — Your Uncle & Abram both mention your being sick yesterday but seem to think it only a temporary matter we hope it was so.

Lina has been for about ten days, & still is by far the sickest anyone we have had in the house for many years. — Last evening the Doctor, Morrell of Norwalk — thought her symptoms more favorable, & her condition today would seem to justify his opinion, he comes down every evening ——

Doctor Dean joined the army as a Surgeon, perhaps two months ago, much against the wishes of his wife — She is informed to day of his death in some hospital on the Potomac — Another martyr of more value than a thousand rebels. ——

Myra has advanced to Cleveland & seems to be fortifying there with a view to remaining till the way is open to Nashville. —

Tell "Father Abraham" that I shall return his Basket, or a substitute for it — by Express tomorrow morning ——

Yours affectionately
H. Colton

Your Mother corrects my time, she says it is two weeks to day since Lina gave up — Delia was confined a week or more but is now about the house ——

H. Colton

Dear Carlos,

Your two letters were duly recd — we are glad to learn that your prospects are so good for pleasant & profitable employment by & by with Mr Strong. I should think it preferable to either Bank or Railroad it may be hard work at times but there must be more chance for some diversity & out door exercise & also a small chance for ultimate promotion of which there is but little if any in the other branches of business named —

In writing to Sheldon the other day I refered to the fact that you did not then know what you could find to do but I did not think you would be long idle after you got able to work for boys like <u>ours</u> were always wanted somewhere. — We were surprised & astonished with a great astonishment, at a late hour last night by a rap at the door from Sheldon — It seems there is some difference of opinion between him and Father Abraham about the member of Congress to be elected from Toledo

The President — according to several reliable gentlemen who write for the papers — wants Ashley should be reelected, while the Lieutenant prefers Waite, & is now stealing a march on Old Abe — who cant leave home — by marching with his Staff to Toledo, where he intends on Tuesday next to secure by his vote the election of Mr Waite & return to Columbus Wednesday. —

Your Mother will pack some articles for you to send by Sheldon which we intended to send soon in some other way — which fact I refer to for the purpose of saying that I had injured the pen you had pointed for me and intended to have you take & get it straightened — which will be but a small job for anyone that knows how to do it —, you can get it fixed & return it at any convenient time hereafter.—

We all hope that your health may be fully restored by this time & that you may find pleasant employment. I think it will be so with Mr Strong.

Sheldon is in good health & spirits, has heard nothing from Washington —

Yours affectionately
H. Colton

The clothes your Mother intends sending will be in a trunk that I had procured for the purpose before Sheldon came — He intends to proceed on the Tuesday morning train. —

M. S. Cotton

Milan Octr 26th 1862

Dear Carlos,

You will see by the enclosed letter, that Myra's little Fannie, has been, & is still very sick, I rec'd a few lines from her last Thursday, saying that Fannie was very sick with <u>scarlet</u> <u>fever</u>, & they were fearful she could not live, — I sent that letter to Perrysburg — but when Aunt has read this one I wish she would send it there if Mother is still there, or to where ever she may be. — I had a few lines from Addie, last week, written from Perrysburg, she said her Grand Mother wished to return to Detroit in the course of a week or two, & that Lucy had written for Lucinda to come there & return with her — so if Lucinda comes to Toledo, I wish Aunt would let her know how anxious Myra is for her to go there —

I was sorry that I could not have seen Mrs Boehm, before she left Toledo, & I wanted to write to her before now, to let her know that we were pleased that our small present was so kindly rec'd, & that I tried to get a chance to prepare some other kinds of fruit, to send her before she left, but Lina's sickness & my own poor health prevented my doing many things that I would have been glad to have done before it was too late in the season. As I always feel so backward & diffident about writing letters, I do not like to address her now — & if you will mention some of these things in some way when you write, if you think it will answer as well, I should prefer it — I want them to know that <u>we</u> can never hope to <u>repay</u> them for their kindness to you, but we shall ever have a <u>grateful</u> <u>remembrance</u> <u>of it</u>

M. S. Colton

We have not heard from Sheldon since your Father wrote you, but probably shall again in a few days, he seems to be in good spirits & enjoying himself well.

We are glad to hear that your health is improving, & hope you will not have so much night work to do as to impair it again, but hope you may enjoy yourself better, & have better health, than you did while in the Bank —

Lina's health is improving so that she can now help me some about the light kinds of house work, which is a help now in these busy times, of house cleaning & Fall work, generally — Nelia is counting the days & weeks to the time when her <u>happy</u> <u>school days</u> will commence again, — there will now be only three weeks more of school this Term, — & she expect to commence with the next Term.

I wonder if you have been having such a snow storm there, as we have here — it snowed some all day yesterday, but partly melted as it fell — but this morning we found the ground was covered to the depth of several inches, & the trees & shrubs bent down, some of them to the ground, & some with the limbs broken off, with the great weight of snow, which lodged upon them, while all their leaves were on, some of them, as fresh & green as ever. It was a sight that I had never seen before, it will injure many fruit trees, by breaking off so many limbs.

Much love from all, for yourself, & Uncles family —

Yours affectionately

M. S. Colton

Sheldon Colton (signature)

Columbus O. Oct 26th 1862

Dear Delia:

Your letter of the 19th came along in due time and now I will send you an answer, not so much for the reason of having any important news to tell you as for the purpose of letting you know, that, in the language of the immortal Webster "I still live".

One bad thing connected with this letter is the fact that you will not find any "good notes" in it for the simple reason that I am out of cash but will have some in a few days and will then send enough to make up for last time. I have got the necessary certificate from the Regiment. It came this morning, and I think I can get my pay this week. I am pretty certain.

The clerk of the weather made a sudden change in the programme last night. The weather for the last few days had been particularly pleasant and this morning I woke up to find a pretty good covering of snow on the ground: and by the way that puts me in mind of a joke that one of the clerks, Mr. Hume, perpetrated this morning. I was over to the office to see if there was anything necessary to be done, and while sitting there up came Mr. Hume and said, "What color is a grass plot covered with snow?" I asked him for his idea on the subject and he said he would call it "<u>invisible</u> <u>green</u>". I smiled grimly, and turned away sadly to meditate.

I am inclined to think that if Lina had any such hopes as you insinuate, she must have been sadly disappointed for I had a letter dated at Plaster Bed, Oct. 23. The young man was well, but I judged from his letter that he had not been at Milan since I was there.

I presume he will stay there for this winter at any rate and perhaps longer. I think the business suits him very well, not so confining as a store would be.

I presume that General Hill will be here tomorrow again, and then I shall know soon whether I am to stay here any longer than this month or not: though I am inclined to think that I shall. I have nothing new and interesting to mention that I know of and will draw to a close.

Love to all,   Yours truly
                              Sheldon Colton

X Lieut 67th Regt O.V.I.
and Muster Roll Clerk for the
Adjutant General of the State
of Ohio

P.S. I wish you would take that ring off from my camp chest key and send it me by letter.

159

Friend

"Home" Sunday aft' Nov 2nd 1862

My own dear friend,
"Delia"

Thank you ever so much for that dear, good letter, that I received from you nearly — three weeks ago. — I am really ashamed of myself for not answering it before, but really, and truly, I have hardly had one half hour to myself, for the last four weeks, until today. I have a few leisure moments and have resolved to devote them all to my friend — Delia —.

I closed my school one week ago last Friday, and indeed I was very sorry to give it up. I had become very much attached to the little flock placed under my care, and, — without the least desire to brag, I flatter myself that they all — every one — thought "considerable" of their "little" "school ma'am". As one of my scholars said, on being asked why he liked me so much, "Why she is such a wee tawny thing." Oh, Delia I like it so much. It is such fun to be permitted to dictate to others, — to use my own authority — I think I shall try it again "next summer" "perhaps" this coming winter. Oh, of all things, Delia, is'nt it the funniest thing that ever happened, Wild Eddy "married" My I can hardly believe my senses. I only heard it today at church, Mate House told me, but I guess every body in Perkins knows it by this time. It seems to be the "all-absorbing" topic of conversation.

Oh, dear, what an unpleasant afternoon it is so rainy, and dreary, it makes one feel so dull, and stupid. I actually feel miserable — I wish you were here Delia, with "the one you love," perhaps, Oh I know it would make me feel as bright as a dollar. Why don't you come and see me Delia? I wish you would come in vacation and stay a week. I should like so much to have you. Oh, When does the "Reunion" come off? I suppose pretty soon does'nt it? I should like very much to attend it, and perhaps may.

I was over to "Johnson's, or "rebel" Island", last Wednesday, for the first time, and a fine time I had too. I saw lots of "secesh" and such a miserable, degraded, looking set taking them all together — for there were a few that looked quite respectable. — I think I never before saw.

Friend

I saw all of those "three" that I told you about in a previous letter, and several others. Frank Wheeler took me all through the hospital — he is "hospital steward." — Eugene Bates has recovered and looks as healthy as ever, he is just as full of fun "as of old," my "cousin" Eugene Mitchell" has not got very well acquainted with me yet, and as he is a very bashful youth, he was rather shy of me, and consequently I did not have much conversation with him. It is such a pleasant place over there, indeed. I don't know but I should like to live there myself. Davis Taylor took us into the bakery, which, I can tell you, is something worth seeing, they bake up 9 barrels of flour every day, at the time we were there they had 364 loaves of bread in the oven, and it was very nice looking bread, so light, and spongy. The Perkins folks are mostly well now, I believe although there has been a good deal of sickness this fall, for myself, I am enjoying very good health at present. I think it agrees with me to teach school. How are all the Milan folks? Geo & Hann Parker, Geo Prouty. Mary Gaston & Clara Prouty were over to Perkins to church a week ago today but I did not see them, for I was not at church. Tell Hann. I should love, very dearly to hear from her but if she does not write soon I shall not wait for her. I wish she would write next week it has been so long since she wrote me, tell her I want her to and may-be she will. Oh Delia does G.P. wait on Mary yet? perhaps he would think we very inquisitive concerning his affairs if he should see that, but you know dear that I want to hear "all the news" ha, ha. I often take paritcular pains to inquire about George, & I should feel bad indeed if I thought he did not take pains "sometimes", to inquire about me. Delia I have not said one word about "Willie" or Mary B— but I guess I shall have to close now, with lots of love to all the girls & boys too that I know & a good big share yourself.

I remain your Mary, and here's a kiss and a heap of love from Wild Mate

1863

Severe winter weather and floods prevent Grant from transporting his army across the Mississippi to the high ground around Vicksburg.

At the Second Battle of Winchester, June 13-15, the Confederates rout the Federal troops who are without artillery, their guns having been left in abandoned forts.

After a three day battle, with tremendous losses on both sides, Lee is defeated at Gettysburg. On July 4, he begins his orderly retreat back to Virginia.

In July, after a long campaign, Grant captures Vicksburg and Port Hudson, thus gaining complete control of the Mississippi.

September 19-20, General William S. Rosecrans is defeated by General Braxton Bragg at Chickamauga valley, and driven back to Chattanooga. Federal troops are in danger of starvation.

November 19, President Lincoln delivers his stirring address, honoring those who sacrificed their lives on the battlefield at Gettysburg.

Sherman is dispatched to Knoxville, and succeeds in controlling the greater part of eastern Tennessee.

Sheldon continues to serve in the Adjutant General's office. He becomes engaged to Mary Whiting.

Carlos works for the shipbroker, A.W. Colton, in Toledo.

Lina has an extensive visit in Detroit among numerous relatives, and acts as companion to her cousin Hattie.

Nelia, on Sheldon's invitation, takes room and board in Columbus. She receives piano instruction, and tours the city's Camp Chase, State House, Lunatic Asylum and Blind Asylum.

Delia remains in Milan, providing care for her parents, and taking an active role in Sunday School and social activities.

Lina

Trenton Jan. 11th 1863

Dear Delia.

Well, according to promise, I seat myself, the first Sunday in Trenton, to write to your ladyship. Not having much to say I use a small sheet so as not to waste paper, and another reason is, my trunk has not been brought from the Station yet.

My visit in Toledo was a very pleasant one, after I wrote to Mother I spent an afternoon with Mrs Chase, Aunt and Annie went with me and Uncle came to tea. Friday I spent the day with Lizzie Minuse at her boarding place, and enjoyed it very much. John Page boards there too. Lizzie is going to Milan in a short time if you see her, ask her, for my sake, to tell you about <u>my</u> <u>friend</u> Mr Sylvester. It is too long a story to write. Carlos was very attentive to my wants, and spent every evening with me either at Uncles or elsewhere.

Mrs Boylan met me at the cars, I was very glad to have such good company. Before she got to the cars, Carlos had placed me under the "protecting care" of a "<u>Toledo</u> <u>exquisite</u>" who was going to Detroit. He discharged his <u>duty</u> <u>faithfully</u>. Got off the cars and made the acquaintance of Uncle George, when we arrived at Trenton. All things considered, any trip yesterday was a very pleasant one. Do not wonder if my letter is somewhat mixed. Irene sits here writing to you and wants me to spell out "every letter as she goes" along. Uncle and Aunt have gone out to a funeral. I went to church and was warmly welcomed back to Trenton by old friends. I told Libbie you had sent her a cushion, she seemed much pleased and is coming up tomorrow to get it.

Lina

Alice is very sick today, with what they call flying Rheumatism. Her mother is fearful of its going to her heart. Elliott is in Washington trying, I believe, to get some situation in the army. Ben is with the Regt. in Coldwater. They do not know whether he will be back this winter or not. I want to write to some of the girls this afternoon, and as Aunt has brought in some <u>small</u> <u>paper</u> think I will do so. How goes the gay world with the Milan people. Suppose you have not had Skating since I came away, nor much sleigh riding.

I was sorry to hear that Father was sick yet but hope he is better by this time: Is Myra with you yet? She wrote to Aunt that they were going to Milan as soon as they heard something more definite from Wm Standard. Am afraid I shall miss, again, visiting with her, as the scarlet fever is here yet. There is a child to be buried this afternoon.

Write soon and tell all the news. When I write to Nelia shall send her Alphas picture for her album.

How does kitchen work prosper? Hope you will learn to <u>love</u> it, for I shall not want to <u>soil</u> my <u>hands</u> again, when I come home. But no telling when that time will be for Uncle has a Gent., in readiness for one <u>so</u> <u>quick</u>. It is not <u>Mr</u> <u>Hanchett</u> but Mr <u>Hentig</u>. I will keep you posted of how we progress Let me write nonsense if I want to! There is nothing else to talk about.

Love to all, write soon.
Lina

Tell Mother that Carlos paid my fare to Trenton, so I have enough on hand to supply my wants. I spent a dollar for a Veil in Toledo.

Sheldon Colton [signature]

Columbus O.
Feby. 1st 1863

Dear Delia:

       Yours of last Sunday is received, and as the cash came safe to you that time I shall repeat the experiment again today and see if I can send you some more for family use.

       The world moves on as usual here, plenty to do to keep me busy, but not enough to drive me very hard. I think I am gaining a little over my lameness, though it is not very perceptibly diminishing. Of course I have to stick with my cane yet, and make it my constant companion.

       I had a letter from Annie Jackson a few days ago which was dated Jany 21st. I was pained to learn from her that Sarah Jackson died on the 2nd of September last. She was the second daughter, and was a lively, interesting girl, the finest looking of the three, but apparently the weakest. Annie says she "was called from works to rewards". A meaningful expression. She died quite suddenly. I hope and believe that she is much happier now than when on this earth.

       Annie says that the rest of the family are well. They were not much troubled by the rebels while Winchester was in their possession, but, of course were subjected to some inconveniences. They had their house searched twice and the Rebels threatened to carry off Mr. Jackson, but they did not do the family any injury.

Annie wants to know when I am coming to make them a visit. She says that I will be very welcome. She mentions having received a letter from Lina a short while ago.

       I have had several letters from the 67th Regiment lately, the first one was from Dr. Westfall, the Post Surgeon, dated Jany 24th. The Regiment was starting on another expedition, and the Dr. wrote his letter on the vessel. He thinks they are going to Wilmington N.C. but of course does not know for certain.

       Capt. Lewis has been dismissed from the service without trial or any chance to defend himself. I do not know the charges against him. I presume he will be restored if he cares to be, for he is a good officer and generally liked.

       Not having any special news to communicate I will close this brief epistle.

Please hand the enclosed notes to Father
               Yours truly
               Sheldon Colton

Lina

Trenton Feb. 2nd 1863

Dear Nelia

In my drawer of unanswered letters, I find one from you, and concluded to devote a short time to writing this morning, as I have <u>nothing</u> <u>very</u> <u>particular</u> to do.

It is so tedious today that I am obliged, as usual, to stay in the house. Charley went down to try the ice, but soon thought he had rather go to school. Uncle went to Detroit last Tuesday morning saying he would return on the late train the same evening! Well, Aunt and I sat up until twelve oclock <u>that</u> night and every one after, the rest of the week. But, no Uncle made his appearance, until, Saturday at midnight.

The report he gave of himself was, that he was having two houses built, one for his own use, which would be completed the first of June. Then they could go right into it. He will change his mind, I know he will, before the week is ended. Keep me from every marrying a man minus — <u>decision</u> of <u>character</u>! Miss Delia was quite "ahead of the time" in accusing me of "mourning for blighted hopes or Plaster Bed" either, and another fact, I am not the happy possessor of any large sheets of paper. Listen to an explanation. I was sitting in the parlor with a music book for a writing desk, when my "camp inkstand" very suddenly excited the curiosity of master Charles, and of course he must try to shut it, <u>just</u> <u>to</u> <u>see</u> how it <u>would</u> <u>go</u>. It did go — <u>over</u>. Fortunate for me it only touched my quantity of writing paper lodging upon the book and my calico dress.

So Dr. Alling has come to Milan? Oh! charming & almost might I be induced to have my "Typhoid fever" over again, why couln't he have come last Fall? Neither did it seem to me that you are <u>eighteen</u> <u>years</u> <u>old</u>. No, indeed! I cannot realize it. I thought of it and wondered how you was celebrating the birthday. I know how mine have been spent for the last five years.

Monday night. I put by my letter this morning expecting John Ballard here to dinner. But he "passed on" to Toledo. Uncle engaged my company to go on to the ice tonight. He has just come in thoroughly convinced that he feels more comfortable by the fire.

I shall be obliged to learn to skate in the Summer time.

Had two letters from Milan tonight. Lottie writes that Mother is not at all well. If you need me, do not hesitate to send word, any time. Is it Our Charles Penfield that is wounded? and <u>our</u> Mr Mead that is a prisoner? I saw their names in the paper.

Libbie Ransom and Caddie Hollister were expected Saturday afternoon. I do think they are <u>lovely</u> girls. Wish they could visit at our house sometime.

Columbus O.
Feby 8th 1863

Dear Delia:

Your letter of the 1st came along in due time, being less time on the way than it took you to write it I should judge from the letter.

I am sorry to learn that your nose is so much trouble that it keeps you "blowing around", all of the time. You knows, I knows, I am sorry your nose gets froze, and it flows till you blows, and Oh's and Oh's — 'taint fun — no, nos, I really suppose.

I am flourishing about as usual here, nothing very exciting going on. I keep on with my work as usual, not being overworked but still enough to do to keep me busy. I have been sending off the Annual Reports of the Adjutant General, for the past year. I sent one to Father last week. I do not know whether it would be very interesting to him or not, but as it contains my humble name I sent it along, that it may be kept to show to future generations that I have served my country with the pen as well as sword.

The amount of service done with either has not been very large however.

I have been intending every few days to send home my valise containing my uniform, Commissions etc. and think I will do so some time this week, as I have no use for the articles here. I expect to send home my crutches also.

I am still travelling with a cane, and expect to be for some time to come. I cannot do any walking without one. I can travel pretty fast however when the walking is good, but to day the sidewalks are covered with snow which is thawing, and that makes them a little too slippery for comfort. We have just had another snow storm here. On Thursday the snow fell to the depth of nine inches, and the sleighing was pretty good. I did not get a chance to try any of it however. I had time enough but I do not like to take a strange horse and go sleighriding with a lady — and of course I could not think of going alone — when I should not be able to get around fast enough to do any good in case of a disaster.

I have been out to church this morning with one of the young ladies, and heard a very good sermon, at the Baptist Church.

I have no recollection "of you sending me any poetry", either, but I have a distinct recollection of receiving some from Milan a short time ago which you were said to have written.

As I have no news to speak of I will <u>evaporate</u> or vulgarly speaking — dry up.

Give my love to all of the family, and hand the enclosed to Father.

Yours truly
Sheldon Colton

Lina

Clarinda's House
Detroit Feb. 10th 1863

Dear Delia

I received a letter from you sometime ago, but have had neither time nor inclination for answering it. There may be letters for me in Trenton but I am <u>here</u> yet, and do not know how long I shall stay until seeing Uncle George again! It is laughable to see the "p<u>ulling</u> and <u>hauling</u>" for me among the different families. I never know from one day where the next will be spent, but am submissive as possible and go where they send me. Hattie is going to Trenton with me when I do return. It may be this week, perhaps not until the latter part of next. I spent the day with Fanny last Saturday, and was over there again yesterday morning. Grandma seemed to be feeling quite smart but worries all the time because she does not get letters from Myra, Lucy and the rest of her family. I begin to feel quite at home "about the streets" here. Can visit all my relatives with out a guide. It did seem at one time as though I never could learn anything about the different streets.

You probably have seen my letter to Lottie and know by this time that I have tried skating at last. The folks here <u>encouraged</u> me a good deal more than <u>you</u> did last winter, and would not laugh at me either, if I skated on my <u>head</u> instead of my heels, for the very reason that I would manage every time to have <u>them</u> assume the <u>same</u> position? John Edwards says "Girls half the battle is won when you learn to fall <u>gracefully</u>." They expect to have another grand "Illuminiskatetorial" to night if the park is in a fit condition. You know I met <u>Dr D.</u> on the ice, and, you remember, he married a widow with two little boys — but,within a few weeks past, has a <u>little</u> <u>daughter</u> of his own, now, allow me to relate an <u>incident</u>, yesterday, Hattie

Lina

and I met his little boy in the street. She opened a
conversation with him by talking about his little sister and
finally asked "what is her name?" He looked up and
answered very promptly ———Carrie! —————
Oh, dear! You can only imagine how I am tormented now.
Clarinda says they have not heard from California since Pa
wrote and wants me to tell him "She thinks Uncle Hiram
could not have finished reading it yet." I have unanswered
letters from Julia and Delight, will write to them soon.
John Ballard met somebody on the cars that sent their
respects "to me." He could not remember the name. I
judge from description that it was Dr. Cornell. If so, tell
him that they were received.
You ask if I have heard from James yet. Well, yes, I have,
and was obliged to exclaim in the words of our immortal
George Phillips — Oh! my grief how chilly!
Do you still sew for the Soldiers? They are not doing
anything for them in Trenton. So you will confess to being
lonesome. I thought you might have some misgivings of
conscience after I got away, and may have still more before
I return. For when that happy period will be no one
knows. If you write to me Sunday or before direct care of
Phin 253 Drawer. Every one sends love to both the
families. Henry & Alice came running in this morning to
tell me of somethings they were going to get to send to
Carrie Bell and Libbie.
Love to all my friends and relatives.
                                        Lina
Phin sent a paper to you for me, but seems to think he
directed it to Toledo. How is it? was it received?

Carlos

A. W. COLTON,
SHIP BROKER & INSURANCE AGENT
Water Street, Between Jefferson & Madison

TOLEDO, OHIO   March 2nd 1863

Miss Delia Colton   Milan O
    Dear Sister

      I got a letter from you a few days ago and I expect you will get one from me about tomorrow noon March 3rd. I will at first speak of the "Harpers Monthly" which Father wrote about. I called Mr Prinn the newsman and he said Sheldon only paid for the year 1862 that the January number was sent by mistake. I then paid him <u>for the</u> <u>mistake</u> — also paid him for a February and March number — he expected to receive some more February numbers the next day & would send one. I took the March number and will send it soon. Now I will pay for the balance of the year and have them sent as before or if any other magazine is preferred I will send some other in place of Harpers — I think you did finely at the exhibition judging from the account you gave — You asked me if I received any Valentines. No I did not deal in the article at all this year. I think I'm getting too old for the business — We have had all sorts of weather lately but I suppose you know all about that as the state of weather is not generally much different between this place and Milan. Miss Gertie Manning came from Monroe Saturday to make a visit with Aunt. Annie is going East Wednesday with her Father, he will come back soon but she intends to make a long visit — in Buffalo and Utica. I got a letter from Lina a few days since written at Trenton. I do not have to work hard now — though I expect to be quite busy when navigation opens. I think I shall like my new place much better than I did the Bank — Please hand the enclosed bill to Father <u>if</u> <u>you</u> <u>dont</u> <u>want</u> <u>it</u>. Love to all from   Carlos

Nelia,

Stray Thoughts.

Did you ever sit down with the soft twilight weaving its web all around you, and the light of the departing day casting dim shadows on the wall and calling up odd fancies or a faint remembrance of some long-forgotten subject. Did you ever I say at such a time sit down and think? Yes, I know you have unless you belong to that class of persons who never have any time to think, whose life is one great hurry and bustle, all absorbed in the pursuit of some unattainable object. If you never find time for one of these twilight self-communings, I pity you, you lose a pleasure which is to me invaluable. If you are a deep thinker and delight to search out sudden mysteries which others have failed to do your thoughts at such a time will perhaps take a Theological turn, and strive to solve some knotty questions which have hither to puzzled you. But if like me you never try to look into things which are hard and disagreeable, but catch the light from the surface your thoughts will take a different turn. Perhaps bring up old memories of times gone by and recall the pleasures of some past friendships, or build castles in the air for future use to be too soon torn down by present realities. I have been thinking as I sit here tonight, how many privileges we enjoy which we never realize until we are deprived of them. Did you ever think of it? Let persons enjoy good health. They never know the little pains and sorrows and troubles which attend the life of an invalid, and yet they never consider what an uncalculable blessing they possess until they are deprived of it. Then indeed they begin to

Nelia,

sigh for their former free and light spirits and realize what they ought to have been thankful for in the past. Persons who enjoy great riches, revel in their wealth, use it for their own gratifications and selfish purposes. But when their wealth takes wings and flies away then they know what they have lost and long for their former prosperity once more. We, as a nation, for many long and happy years enjoyed the privileges which attend peace & prosperity. We have become so used to all that was pleasant and agreeable, that many of our privileges were abused. But now when we are involved in the horrors of civil war, and obliged to make any, and every sacrifice even of the very heart's blood of our nearest & dearest ones, Now, we can realize what we have lost, and when once again our fields shall smile in peace and plenty we shall know how to appreciate more fully our blessings. We have around us many kind and dear friends, who are constantly doing all in their power to make us happy. But how often are these privileges slighted. How often is a cold return made for such kindnesses, and it will only be in later days when the treasures of love are spent, and the dear hand cold which ministered, that we will remember how tender it was how soft to soothe, how eager to shield how ready to support & caress. Then alas the ear will no longer hear which would have received our thanks so delightedly. And if we were only half as lenient toward the living as we are to the dead, how much remorse might we be spared when the grave the all-atoning grave has closed over them forever. Cornelia Colton to Delia

Milan March 25th 1863

Lina

Detroit April 12th 1863

Dear Sister,

I received your letter and enclosure last Monday night. Am sorry to hear you <u>watched</u> for me all that week. Suppose you think, by this time, that I am an uncertain person. When I wrote from Trenton, I did expect to start for home very soon. But on coming to Detroit, changed my plans and concluded to stay with Clarinda awhile — provided I was not wanted at home. My last letter was to find out whether or not I <u>was</u> wanted. Your reply contained precious little satisfaction on that point, but left me more in the dark than ever. Received a few lines from Lottie last week. Wanting to know what was the matter with me? why I did not write? If I was sick? etc. etc. Said Ma was worrying about me for fear of sickness. Could she see me, most certainly she would have cause for anxiety. Delicate creature that I am? With such a <u>poor</u> appetite, and <u>wasted</u> <u>look</u>. Only weigh 132 lbs now. Still am in hopes that Michigan air will benefit me, if I stay <u>long</u> <u>enough</u>. Girls all getting married are they? No! I do <u>not</u> think of doing so before returning home. There are no young men here. They have all gone to war.

Clarinda and I went over to Fannys yesterday morning, and there sat Uncle George Allen. He looks well and much younger than usual. Emelines husband has rented the farm for five years, and Uncle is on his way to Adrian expecting to find employment in a Rail road machine shop. He went to Trenton last night. Sends much love to all our family.

Aunt Lucinda was up here Friday says Irene is improving slowly. Addie is there now with her baby. Grandma is there, and Myra's family are going back there Tuesday.

What could I have written that made you think I was going to send for Bell? Please do not say any thing more to her about it. When it is convenient for any one to have her come, I will write for her. It would not be pleasant for her with any of our relatives at present. Cousin Phin came in

174

the other evening, quite elated over the news that
"Charleston was taken" He thought the report too good to
be true! and said if it was so, we should each have a <u>new</u>
<u>dress</u>. Well, it was not <u>captured</u>, but the <u>dresses</u> were. I
send a sample. They will be very pretty when finished.
Libbie Slocum is having some photographs finished here.
Says she will send one to you when they are done. I have
not had any taken. Was into Randall's Gallery to see
Libbie's and think they will be very good.

Thursday morning Hattie and I attended the consecration
of Christs church on Jefferson Avenue. We went again in
the evening to a Missionary meeting. Bishop Bedell
addressed the people. He is to preach tonight at St. John's
church. Last Sunday afternoon we went over to Sunday
School. They have 550 pupils enrolled. The most of them
not larger than Henry. Carlos wrote that Aunt Sophia
wanted me to visit her on my return. If I could content
myself without Annie. John Ballard writes that they are
<u>doing</u> <u>something</u> to the house now. Hattie has not gone to
the Island yet. Do not know when she will. The men have
commenced work at their place. John bought the lot
adjoining — and will build in the center of the two lots,
leaving them garden room on each side. I will send you
word when to expect me if you do not want me <u>before</u> I
<u>start</u>. All unite in sending love to all.

Write when ever you can and tell all the news. Have not
heard from Sheldon in a long time. How is he? When is
Mrs Rankin going? How delightful to have Ms Croft for
a neighbor —

    Love to all. Lina

Is Em Perry married yet! Where has she gone to. <u>Can</u> Mr
Butman find her? Aunt Clarinda just said, she wanted very
much to go to Milan, but does not expect to this Spring.
Aunt Fanny has been quite sick since I wrote, and is
without a girl.

Carlos

Toledo Tuesday May 5th 1863

Dear Father

Miss Mary Chase arrived yesterday and brought me a letter from Nelia enclosing 12 Coupons 1.50 each Cashier Jones has advanced me the face of them — $18.00 Will send them to New York for collection and when he gets returns will pay me the premium without making any charge for his services. I venture to enclose $23.00 (one 20 and one 3 dollar bill) which of course includes $5. from myself. There may be too much risk in making such a remittance by mail, but as every remittance heretofore has gone all right I trust this will — if not, I hope whoever steals it will be one who is poor enough to appreciate its value — and will use it judiciously. If the gallant "fighting Joe" Hooker keeps the ball moving at the rate he has started it I am inclined to think gold will not command its present prices much longer — and perhaps those Coupons will not bring so large a premium when sold as they would recently but I say perish premiums and principal and premium and principal to come if we can but make the Southern Devils feel our power and end this Slaughter soon. After getting word the first of last week that Lina was quite sick and no better when the letter was finished I was very anxious and looked daily for further news from her, and was very agreeably surprised to learn by the letter Mary Chase brought yesterday that she had recovered. Abram has been just able to be around for the past week from effects of a cold. I am troubled at this time with a severe cold and cough which I think is loosening somewhat this afternoon. We have been visited with a heavy rain storm since yesterday.

Much love for all
Carlos

Office of the
MUTUAL INSURANCE COMPANY OF TOLEDO,

Toledo, May 22nd 1863

Dear Brother

There was a time when "Potatoes they grew small on Manner" your Father in Law of blessed memory used in those days to obtain from my Brother in Law his seed for a consideration, which in the lapse of time I have forgotten, it did not however exceed one Bushel for each individual Potato sent, payable after the crop was gathered (I scout the idea that he ever extorted more than what Old Trassbois would have deemed a fair consideration and still more do I disbelicve and utterly deny that a certain Methodist in that section used to add a Postscript to his petitions on Sundays that Truax' heart might be softened so as not to charge more than an even Dollar for Bushel for the article in the ensuing Spring.) so much by way of introduction and now for business. I shall deliver at the Express office in the morning a Bul of <u>Chili Potatoes</u> upon which Express charges to the end of the route will be paid and shall be content to receive next fall whatever Melinda will upon her honor say were the terms of the contract in the olden time. I need not hint to you that for the purpose of testing them the <u>eyes</u> will answer a tolerable purpose for seed

Annie returned last night bringing Linnie (Harry Coltons Daughter with her) I presume Carlos will describe the latter to you We are in hopes the trip has done Annie good she has certainly gained in flesh

When East I was sadly scrimped for time and was not able to make the research I otherwise should have been glad to have done, so that at present I cannot answer your enquiries as to the Alcaldo. I made arrangements to have the receipts transcribed and when I get them may be able to shed more light on the subject.

The Potatoes you will find really valuable I send you all received and hope you may be in receipt of something handsome for the product from your Farmer for seed

Yours   Carlos Colton

Columbus O.
May 30th 1863

Dear Delia:

Your letter of the 27th came along in due time and I was much pleased to hear from you again as usual.

I dont think that my style of digging post holes would have been of much assistance to Father, all I could do in that way would be to look on and see how well he could dig them.

I would have enjoyed being at your reunion party very much I think, I have not been to anything like that for some time. I have been out to some of the Presbyterian sociables since I have been here with my young lady friends, but I have not got very extensively acquainted with the young folks in town here.

Do you get very impatient over the War matters in the vicinity of Vicksburg? I have been keeping as cool as possible but I get a little impatient at times. I hope to hear of its fall before long in an official way.

I attended a meeting a few evenings ago which was addressed by a Prof. McCoy. He spoke of the rebellion and the causes of it, and I think he was the best speaker I ever heard. He commenced about eight oclock and spoke until after ten, and then proposed to stop but the audience called out "go on, go on", and he spoke for an hour or so longer. He used up the "Copperheads" most effectually, any who were in the house must have been in an uneasy position. He used them very sarcastically and showed them what they were, and how they appeared in the eyes of other men.

Things are moving on almost as usual in the office here. The General has returned but will be off again in a few days I think.

I saw some strawberries in the market this morning and they put me in mind of going home pretty strongly but I suppose yours are not quite ripe yet. I hope I shall be able to see you and get some of them when they are, but if General is going to be gone so much I may not. Not having any more news to tell you about I will bring my letter to a close.

Ask Mother to let me know how much I have got left of the pile that Carlos sent to her, as I wish to make some calculation on my cash account.

Enclosed find $5. for Father to distribute.

Love to all.
Yours truly
Sheldon Colton

Carlos

Toledo July 16th 1863

Dear Father

I intended to send you a barrel of flour this week, but our drays are very busy carting salt, so instead I enclose $5— Will send Bl of flour next week if you want it <u>at</u> <u>our</u> <u>prices</u>! Our best family flour a brand that we keep on hand constantly I can get for 5.50 which will make it 7.00 Norwalk — The picture you sent is good. So all your acquaintances pronounce it. I would exchange if I had any, but havent. I have no idea what "full length" one you refer to, unless it is the one in which I was seated in a chair — if the girls or Lottie have one that you want you might take it and I will sometime give another instead. I return one as requested when in Milan — is it necessary for me to say who it belongs to? Sheldon had said nothing about his recent good fortune as to pay. I am glad he is getting his reward for his gallant conduct in the field and noble determination to keep moving, even though it be on one leg — I regretted it was not possible without inconvenience to my employer for me to meet him in Milan. I think that trip to Columbus just the thing. What bloody times they are having in New York. I think it would have been a merciful thing had the mob been shot down when it made the first demonstration — or still better if the Copperhead Leaders had been <u>hung</u> before the mob had an existence.

All well as usual
Love to all
Carlos

Carlos

Toledo July 20th 63

Dear Delia

I received your letter a day or two since and will write a few lines in answer though I havent much to say — Yesterday and today the weather has been extremely warm but at the present writing we are getting a little shower accompanied by mutterings of thunder, which cools the air a good deal.

There was quite a crowd in the city to hear and see the next Governor of Ohio John Brough. I did not get away to hear him, but I did see him, and a Jolly fat man he is — looks like a plain old farmer — there is a great deal of talk here about resistance to the draft, but they have now got three military companies organized and I guess the Copperheads will not be able to do much. I have been urged several times by one of our dock merchants to help him raise another company — but I tell him it takes time and money — more than I have got. I dont think I will "go in" this time. We are all well as usual here, and I dont think of anything in particular to write about — give my love to all, and find enclosed $5— which please mention receipt of when some one next writes from home. Your brother, Carlos

Friend

Friday July 31st 1863

My <u>dear</u> <u>friend</u> Delia:

I have seated myself this morning to have a <u>nice</u> <u>little</u> <u>chat</u> with you after so long silence on <u>my</u> part, and now I suppose you would like me to give an account of myself, of where I have been, and what doing since I last wrote you. Well! I know I have been a <u>naughty</u> <u>negligent</u> <u>little</u> <u>girl</u>, to neglect writing to you <u>so</u> long, but I <u>know</u> you will forgive me when I tell you that quite a serious accident has happened to myself, no I am not going to enter into a lengthy recital of my various aches & pains suffice it to say that just the week after my school was out I sprained my ancle very badly and broke one of the small bones directly above the ancle joint so that for nearly <u>4</u> weary weeks I have not once stepped on my foot, but have had to sit in my chair "day in & day out" unable to walk the least bit except with the aid of my crutches, & during that time it has pained me so that I have not felt like doing any thing scarcely, but the doctor was here a day or two ago, and he says it is doing finely and if I am very careful he thinks I will be able to walk again in at least two weeks, but <u>dear</u> <u>me</u> it is <u>such</u> tedious work, and I do get <u>so</u> tired. Delia how I <u>do</u> <u>wish</u> you lived near me so could run in & see me every day, but I have already said more than intended & will change the subject. I am very glad Delia that my letters do you so much good but I am afraid you prize them altogether too highly, do you not? I am very sorry indeed that "Will" should have proved himself false both to himself and the girl he <u>so</u> <u>basely</u> <u>deceived</u>. I know just what <u>I</u> should do if I were placed in y<u>our</u> circumstances. <u>I</u> <u>should</u> <u>not</u> <u>have</u> <u>anything</u> <u>to</u> <u>do</u> <u>with</u> <u>or</u> <u>say</u> <u>to</u> <u>Will</u> <u>Williams</u>, for I think a young gentleman who will treat a girl so meanly is not worthy to associate with such "<u>pure</u> <u>minded</u> <u>mortals</u>" as "<u>we</u> <u>girls</u>" are generally supposed to be, dont <u>you</u> <u>think</u> <u>so</u>?

Friend

Well I only hope that Hammie will be true to himself & to you, and if he should cease to love you, will have respect enough for himself (as well as you) to come out boldly and confess it & receive an "honorable discharge", instead of "deserting the ranks" as Will did with out one word in explanation, and just as another young man did that I know of perhaps you know who I mean. Well it was Geo P. Delia although I have ceased to love Geo yet I can not entirely forget him. Many times I find myself, though unconsciously, thinking of him and it is at such times that I ask myself the question, Why will such thoughts of him rise unbidden to my mind? but I can give no satisfactory answer myself, and there the thing drops, though he has been false to me, yes & to many others, yet it is impossible for me to forget so easily one that I once loved, & you know when one loves truly & deeply we are apt to look over all the dark spots on the character of the one we love, & to dwell upon the virtues alone, so has it been with me, though I have heard many things in detraction of his character & principles yet I have been loth to believe them, for you know the eyes of love look only at the bright side of the picture, but Delia I have forgotten myself. I did not think of mentioning the name Geo. Prout, when I commenced writing this letter, but Delia now that I have said this, suppose I cant help it can I? and will you do me the favor not to mention one word of what I have said to anybody, not for the world. I did not intend to say another word to anybody about him, but I see I have committed myself. I shall "take care" in future. Now Delia when you "get married" to your old school teacher the Doctor I want you to send me a wedding card, also an "invite" to the wedding. Now do not forget! I commenced this letter about 10 oclock & here it is nearly 4 P.M. and it is not finished yet, but I have been interrupted several times & have had two calls. I think I have done pretty well after all, but I must close now so Good Bye ever your friend Mate. Please excuse this miserable ink. I hope I shall have some better next time. Please write very soon to Mate.

Columbus O.
Aug. 16th 1863

Dear Delia:

Your letter of the 9th inst. is received. I am glad to find that Nelia is getting well again and hope she will get up now and come to Columbus as soon as she can get ready.

I have found a good place for her now, and think there is nothing in the way of her enjoying herself here this Fall. The best I could do was to take a room on the third floor of a house with the prospect of getting one on the second floor in a few weeks if preferred, but the room above is the largest and most comfortable one. The gentleman who keeps the house, Mr. McCarter, is a Presbyterian Minister who is not now engaged in any pulpit. He lives in a fine brick house on Town street, about a square from Mr. Miller's. He has a fine piano, a much better one than I could rent, which Nelia is to have the use of.

I have not yet engaged a teacher for Nelia, but can readily get one, there is no trouble about that.

He will rent the room on the third floor to the two young ladies with light and fuel for seven dollars a week, which is a very fair price, considering the location of the house and the probable high price of provisions this winter.

I am much predisposed to like the place and surroundings and think Nelia will.

You must have had a good time down to the Lake Shore. It strikes me that I would like to see Dr. Cornell swim with a dress on.

I am glad to find that you have a prospect for preaching in our own church again.

I am getting along about as well as usual here. I am kept very busy, but do not injure myself any yet I believe.

Mrs Botsford was in the office to see me yesterday. She and her husband are staying at Camp Chase. He is Hospital Steward I believe, and she is Matron of the hospital.

She wished to be remembered to Mother when I wrote home. She is well acquainted with Arthur's wife and says she is an excellent young lady.

As I have no more news to tell, I will close with love to all.
Yours truly
Sheldon Colton

H. Colton

Saturday Aug. 22nd 1863

Dear Carlos,

The barrel of flour arrived day before yesterday and your advice of shipment yesterday. I do not know the present price of flour in Town but presume there is a saving of a few shillings aside from as I hope a gain in quality from any that we have had lately. I have been somewhat exercised about the "Third clause section second of the Enrollment act" and applied at Head quarters for an interpretation thereof. It would seem that others have been similarly puzzled from there having been a circular prepared on the subject — which they sent me in reply. I have also seen a farther decision of Judge Advocate General Holt, that it is not necessary the parents should be entirely dependent upon that "only son" — so that the other "only son" being three fourths disabled will readily exempt you, which we can honorably and consistently ask for since you have both "done the State some service".

Application under this plea need not be made till after the draft, the only one to be made previous is where parents elect which son shall be exempt. There will doubtless be directions & blanks published when the draft is ordered in this State ——

In case it should so happen the "aged & infirm parents" release you from conscription, they will not have altogether "outlived their usefulness".

All well as usual, & the women very busy preparing Nelia for her departure which is now near at hand
            Yours affectionately
            H. Colton

Nelia,

Columbus, Tuesday Sept. 8th/63

My Dear Father and Mother

Well, here I am at last in the city of Columbus; and having unpacked my trunk and become settled generally, I seat myself at the window to tell you of my safe arrival, and pleasant, though tedious, journey. We found when we reached Monroeville that Sheldon was right about the trains, and that we would have to remain in Shelby until five in the afternoon, but nothing daunted we went on, arrived at Shelby a little before nine oclock, and found that a freight train with accommodations for a few passengers would leave there at half-past twelve. The depot at Shelby is about a mile from the town, and though very comfortable and having a hotel attached is lonesome and affords no amusements in the way of books or music, not even a newspaper could we find, and we determined to take the freight train and jog along at any pace rather than remain there. I think I stood it rather better than the other girls for they are not very easily suited. David and I walked up into the town for pastime and so we managed to survive until the freight train came along. Mary & Maria were provided with a large basket of eatables and I lunched with them.

After we had arrived at Crestline there were so many passengers who were left from another train that the conducter attached a passenger car and it was speedily filled, so we came very comfortably, the only inconvenience being the detentions at small places. The girls wished many times that we had gone via Grafton but on the whole I enjoyed the day's ride. I made any quantity of <u>tatting</u> which the slowness of the motion of the train enabled me to do without any inconvenience, and helped to pass away the time. A very pleasant, elderly gentleman, who sat just before me remarked on my industry and opened a conversation with me. He proved very entertaining, and when we reached Columbus offered his assistance and conducted us to the depot. This train arrived about an hour sooner than the one Sheldon expected me to come in, and as there were no omnibusses there, we waited. I more particularly for my trunk, which could not be checked through on the freight train, just as the accomodation train from Cleveland arrived, Sheldon and Mary entered the depot, so we were soon in the carriage on our way home. Mary is much smaller than I had supposed and not so handsome as her picture represents, but she is pretty and lovable. She has a quick energetic way about her which is decidedly interesting, and I know we shall be very good friends. She has a sister Hattie about Delia's age, and Sheldon says they would make a "team". Mrs Smyth's family

Nelia,

consists of six children. The eldest, Emma who is about my age, leaves this evening for Oxford, (the place where Hattie Ashley is going) to attend school. The next is Myra, a year or two younger and then four boys whose names I have not heard the youngest of whom is about two years old. Mr Smyth (I beg his pardon for mentioning his children first) is quite an elderly gentleman, and has some very peculiar nervous movements, which are decidedly amusing. I have begun to love Mrs Smyth already. She is very pleasant. They are very plain substantial people, and I am perfectly at ease when among them. There is a melodeon, but no piano in the house yet. Sheldon expected to have one here before this. The teacher he has engaged is a Mr Shirner a German and organist in the Presbyterian church. They are coming around here this noon.

Broad Street is finely shaded and Mary says is the finest in the city. When we came last night Mr Brough was speaking on the State House steps. Sheldon pointed out to me the room where he writes and said that he would show me all over the Capitol and take me up into the dome whenever I felt like coming, to see him. I do not feel homesick today. I did yesterday, but I met with a much more cordial reception than I anticipated, and although it is raining this morning it is not gloomy. One thing I suppose that makes it more like home is that I am not at fault about the points of the compass here as I am usually on leaving home any distance. Our room fronts the north (as does the house) the street running east & west. I have been asking Mrs Smyth about having my washing done. She says that her girl will do it for her own benefit for 37 cents a dozen and only asks that I will iron my collars and undersleeves. I thought that very reasonable and accepted the proposition. Mary has the same privilege. Well I have filled my sheet and yet I do not know as I have said all I wished to. The church that they attend is Mr Trammer's. I must stop writing now, for want of room. My clothes all came in good order. My bonnet was not harmed in the least. I have not given Sheldon his collars & papers yet but will do so this noon. The boquet was withered very much but the rosebuds are still fresh and I am going to rearrange it this morning, the tuberose was entirely spoiled except the fragrance. Give much love to all and write to me soon. They wish me to have my letters directed to Marys Box which is No. 795. tell Lina & Delia to write to me soon and "When this cruel war is over" I'll <u>come</u> <u>home</u> <u>again</u>. Accept much love from your
Daughter
Nelia

Melia,

Dear Sisters Lina and Delia,

As I have nothing to say which will be for either of you exclusively, I take the liberty of addressing you in company, hoping to hear from each of you soon. I have been here <u>two whole days</u>, and indeed it seems like as many weeks! not that I am lonesome or homesick; I would not have you think so by any means; But every thing is so new and strange that it makes the time seem longer. I have not been out to see any of the <u>lions</u>, yet but I imagine they are under good control, so I apprehend no danger. Tuesday, after Miss Whiting had closed her school we went to the druggists to procure some Alcohol, quite a good beginning for two young ladies wasn't it? Sheldon has teazed us considerable about it. The State house is a grand structure as seen from the exterior, (I have not been inside yet,) and I was duly impressed with a sense of my own littleness when passing it. The building itself covers a space of ground I should judge somewhat larger than our Public square in Milan, and is enclosed by a much larger one. It fronts on four streets, that is, each of the four sides of the building are so exactly alike, that I question whether there is any front to it. But I can tell you more about that when I have seen the interior.

Last evening Mary and I walked down the street about half a mile to see the residences. This is called the finest street in the city and it certainly is beautiful. The most aristocratic & wealthy people live on it and some of the grounds are very extensive, and most beautifully planned with their evergreens nicely trimmed, and waterfalls & fountains & statuary. We walked as far as the Lunatic asylum which presents a fine appearance and as Mary is acquainted with the Superintendent's wife we are going there Saturday. This street leads straight to Camp Chase at the West & direct to Granville at the East so you can imagine the extended view as the one is four miles and the other thirty from the city. The hospital is nearly opposite Mr Smythe's and we see the convalescent soldiers around the grounds which are very pleasant. They have preaching there every Wednesday and Sunday evenings for the soldiers and any who choose to come in. Myra Smythe, Mary & myself, intended to go there last evening. But instead we went to the 1st Presbyterian church to hear a lecture by the Rev. Mr Masson from London. He comes as a committee from the clergy of England to inform the Americans of the feelings of the mass of the English people and the Queen towards the United States, and read an address from the clergy. It was really interesting. He says we must not believe what the London Times says for it is not the organ of the people and will make a statement one day & deny it the next without even apologizing. They appointed a committee to answer the address as coming from the loyal people of the state, Mary's acquaintances tell her. Mr Smythe is a copperhead and we have been trying to ascertain by conversation with him whether it is true or not. But so far he has been rather

Nelia,

guarded in his talks. But I believe the serpent usually bites in the dark, and does not dare to come out boldly with its sentiments. He told us last evening of an affair which happened next door to his office. It seems they had hung out their banner with the names of Vallandingham and Pugh upon it. Some soldiers riding by saw it, and their leader bade them take it down. They rode up and one of them was just about to attempt it when his horse slipped on the pavement and threw him, he regained his seat and the rest rode up, presented arms & threatened to shoot the first man who attempted to prevent him, he raised in his stirrups and succeeded in reaching one corner of it, and jerked it off the pole, and waving it behind him they rode off. But when they had reached High Street, the flag was gone, someone had snatched it from them and they were obliged to go without it. I do not know whether the affair has terminated yet or not.

I saw Mr Zenas King pass here yesterday. I strained my eyes to catch the "last glimpse of the top of his hat," for his is the only familiar face I have seen yet. I have not yet commenced taking music lessons, but shall probably take my first tomorrow. Sheldon and Proff. Shirner have not yet succeeded in getting a piano but I can practise at the next door until they do.

The only old friend I have met was a piece of music of Mary's a very sweet little song entitled "Weeping sad and lonely" or "When this cruel war is over". If you have never heard it I would advise you to get it as soon as possible. I suppose your R.S.S. will meet tomorrow evening please knock a few of the members on the head and charge it to my account. There will be no school for Mary tomorrow on account of the County Fair, and so we shall probably go to the State house & some other places, and then I will write to you of what I see.

I dont suppose there is anything in this letter that will interest you. But I have written because I felt like it, and just as I would have talked with you had I been where you are. I love Mary very much and we agree on a great many points where most of others disagree with me for instance we both dislike Dicken's writings, and I think as she does that they lack a high moral tone. We have a very pleasant room and are suited in every way with our boarding place. We pay only three dollars a week here, and at Mr McCarter's they have already raised the price of board, and the room there was an attic room designed for four persons. Well it is most time for my partner to come home and I must close. Tell Mother Mary has a fine Heliotrope here which she says, I pet more than she does. I wish we could have some more flowers in our room I miss them so much. Give much love to all inquiring friends and write soon, to

Sister   Nelia

You know I never could write a decent hand so you must excuse the scribbling. Remember the box, no. 795.

Nelia,

Dear Father and Mother

      I have practised four hours today and as tea is not quite ready will sit down to acknowledge the receipt of your kind letters. I do not feel any the worse for my exercise at the piano only a little fatigue, and it is something of a task for me to confine my mind for as long a time to scales and exercises when I have been used to playing whatever I pleased, besides I find I have a great deal to <u>unlearn</u>. But I guess patience & perseverence will carry me safely through. By Sheldons request I use the piano only during school hours that Mary & Mira may have the use of it at other times, so it is <u>going</u> all day. But even Pa could not object to the sound of it. It is an entirely new one and the sweetest toned instrument I ever heard. I have not been lonesome or homesick yet much. But I could not wait today for Sheldon to bring our mail at noon, (when he brings a daily paper for us,) but went to the Post Office with Mary just before school time after the letter <u>which</u> I <u>knew</u> <u>would</u> <u>be</u> <u>there</u>, and was not disappointed for I received a letter from Lina & some papers from Father. I guess the mail comes in during the night, and it closes about ten in the morning so you cannot get our letters until the day after they are mailed. I wrote a letter of this size to Carlos the other day and one to Carter Sunday evening. I shall write to Myra in a day or two. I feel perfectly at home here. Mrs Smythe is so pleasant and motherly to us.

      The other day she told us that whenever we wished to do up any collars to let her know, and so Friday she sent some hot water up to our room and we washed and starched collars & undersleeves and dried them on a little clotheshorse here and when we went down to dinner there was an ironing board all ready and iron heated so we ironed them and had it all done in short order. I tell you this that you may see how ready she always is to help us and to save our going up and down stairs more than is necessary. My knee does not pain me as much as it did before I left home and I have felt perfectly well all the time. Lina wishes to know how it was about our missing the train. George landed us in Monroeville at the time he expected to, and we took the train we expected to. But they told us at Monroeville that the train from Cleveland was passing through Shelby just about that time, so we could not of course overtake it. Mary was mistaken about our not reaching there in time for we waited fully ten minutes for the train. I have received calls from four young ladies. Two Misses Crosby, <u>rather</u> older than I and verging on to <u>thirty</u>. They are the stepdaughters and house keepers of Mr. Miller where Sheldon boards and he respects them very much. Their conversation was considerably in favor of "your <u>brother</u>" and "Oh! indeed, you must not persuade him to take his guitar away

Nelia,

from our house we should miss it <u>so</u> much." Another was a Miss Treat a friend & fellow laborer of Mary's another a Miss Ridgeway living in this same block. All of them rather old but better so for me.

Wednesday morning.

I was interrupted by another call from Miss Mary Leamon another teacher and an intimate friend of Mary & Sheldon. We persuaded her to stay and spend the evening, as Sheldon was intending to come. He came and brought with him Mr Ferson, who boarded at Mrs Ralstons where he & Mary did, and is a favorite of Sheldons. And also Mr Phillips a nephew of Gen. Hill's. He writes in the office with Sheldon, and he says he is the only person from the office he would bring here. We were much pleased with him. He reminded me very much of Edward Ashley in size in looks only he has dark hair & eyes. We had some grand singing. I can assure you. On Friday evening we are all going to the place where Miss Leamon boards.

Mrs Smythe requested me to ask you how you make watermelon preserves, and would like to know as soon as convenient.

Mary says she wore her hat all last winter & intends to this, so I guess I shall. The weather so far has been quite warm, and we have feasted on peaches & grapes which are most gone now. Sheldon bought us a watch to use in our room and while we are practising. It is a secondhand one and cost him only six dollars, but it keeps good time.

No one in the family drinks either tea or coffee except Mrs Smythe. She thinks it is quite convenient to have boarders who are so easy to please.

I know this letter is hardly readable but Mrs Smythe was anxious to know about those preserves and I had no news in particular to tell so I have written fast and not written much after all. But I will make no apologies for I shall be very likely to do the same thing again. I bought me a pair of thick shoes, but if I do not go out any more than I have this far — I shall wear my slippers out first. And, Pa will you believe it? I have actually <u>cleaned</u> <u>my</u> <u>teeth</u> every morning since I came. Tell Delia to write to me. I dont care about any great news. I want to know how she likes school, what persons she meets, who asks about me and every little thing she would tell me if I was there.

So you want me to <u>escape</u> <u>any</u> <u>home</u> <u>affection</u> <u>do</u> <u>you</u>? In the words of the immortal Shakespear I would say "<u>You</u> <u>cant</u> <u>come</u> <u>it</u>." I hope to hear from you all soon, <u>for</u> <u>I</u> <u>look</u> <u>for</u> <u>the</u> <u>letters</u> <u>every</u> day.

Accept much love from your
daughter
Nelia.

Music

When the soul with grief is bowed
　　In a sadness deep and lone
And the heart is all too proud,
　　For the tongue to tell its moan;
Turn to music's magic spell,
　　Lightly touch the quivering string,
Let the full deep cadence swell
　　Till the lips, responsive, sing.

When the heart with joy is thrilled
　　Till it scarce can be controlled,
And the soul with rapture filled,
　　Let it be by music told.
Music ringing wild and free,
　　Free from sorrow's saddening strain,
Till each listener's heart shall be
　　Throbbing to the glad refrain.

Sheldon Colton

Nelia,

Toledo Sept 17th 63

Dear Mother

In exchange for Nelia's letter to you I enclose one sent to me, also return hers — she writes a good letter. Aunt told me a few days since that when Mrs Shepard comes here she will go with her to Milan, dont know when she will be here. I met Banks on the street this morning in Lieutenants uniform, he goes into camp here with a Volunteer Company — Will see him again—

          I enclose $5.00   Carlos

Columbus Sept 12th 1863

Dear Brother Carl

I beleive I was owing you a letter when I left home. But I neglected many of my correspondents while I was preparing to leave, and now that I have more leisure will write to them all. I left home last Monday morning and had a very pleasant journey here though we were detained on account of missing a train and did not arrive until about nine oclock in the evening. I came in company with Mary Abbott and Maria Mowry who went on to College Hill to attend school. Sheldon and Miss Mary Whiting met me at the depot and we were soon at our destination.

We board at H.P. Smythe's 171 Broad Street, and we find it a very pleasant place. The family are Episcopalians and Mrs Smythe is particularly pleasant and accommodating. We pay three dollars a week for board with everything furnished except lights, and we get our washing done in the house for 37 cents per dozen. Our room is in the 3rd story, but very pleasant and fronts on Broad Street which is the finest street in the city. There are many beautiful residences on it many very extensive grounds containing fountains, waterfalls, statuary etc. The Lunatic Asylum is on this road about half a mile from where we are and as Mary is acquainted with the superintendents wife we are going there some Saturday.

Mr Smythe is called a copperhead by some of the people here and I have been trying to find out whether it is true or not. He makes a great many loyal

Nelia,

expressions, and occasionally some suspicious sounding ones. He prays for the President and the people who are suffering in bondage. But — he takes the Ohio Statesman. But I beleive these copperheads prefer to bite in the dark. Yesterday Sheldon took us up into the dome of the State House, and really I never saw a more imposing sight we were at an elevation of about 120 feet, and as the surrounding country is nearly level we had a very extensive view. I think the beauty of the city consists in its straight & parallel streets, and the great number of beautiful shade trees mostly maples. The state house is a very imposing edifice, with its marble floors & staircases, and I was impressed with a painful sense of my own littleness while looking at it, the winding stone steps which lead to the dome, remind me very much of the pictures of the tower of Babel.

I have not yet commenced to take music lessons, as Sheldon and Proff. Shirner had some difficulty in obtaining a piano. But they have engaged one now which will be here today, and I shall take a lesson Monday morning. I mean to improve myself a great deal during the next six months — after that it will not be my fault if I am any longer a burden to my brothers, and I am very grateful to them both for all they have done for me thus far. There is no one in Milan now who gives music lessons and I think that upon my return I could have a large class.

My roommate Mary Whiting is a very pretty interesting girl and I love her very much. She is very generous and warm hearted, and we seldom disagree in anything. As I have several more letters to write you will please excuse me from writing any more this time.

I shall hope to hear from you soon, and with much love remain as ever
Yours truly
Nelia

P.S. tell Annie that the hired girl who lived at Rev. Anson Smythe's is living here, and she was very anxious to know whether I was a sister of the one who visited Sarah Smyth.

Nelia,

Dear Lina

Your letter was received last Tuesday and I was truly delighted to hear from you. Mary and I went to the office and she received one from her sister at the same time. We could not wait to reach home before reading them but opened them on the way and both of us laughed several times at their contents. I received a letter from Mother last night, which was welcome and Mrs Smythe thanks her very much for that recipe. I do not expect you at home to write to me as often as I do to you for I know you have not the time and I write whenever I feel like it which is not seldom, and what I address to one is intended for all, and what I receive from one I consider as coming from all. But I am glad to receive as many letters as you have a mind to send. Last Thursday Mary went home with a friend to tea and in the twilight I sat here alone, humming "I <u>am</u> <u>haunted,</u>" and I felt the "home affection" coming and was on the point of giving up to it when Mary opened the gate and I hastily lit the lamp and her lively presence soon dispelled all homesickness and I have not given way to it since nor do I intend to for it is a miserable feeling. The next afternoon we both felt in pretty good spirits and laughed so much & heartily before and after tea that we had not become sobered when Sheldon and "George Phillips" called for us to go to Miss Leamon's and spend the evening. We carried our good nature with us and all enjoyed ourselves very much.

Saturday morning we went to the State house again at Sheldon's request and he conducted us to several different departments. First to the Paymaster's Office, where there are on exhibition relics ancient and modern of the wars. There were quite a number of rebel flags one elegantly made of silk & gold fringe bearing the motto, "Death before Submission," and also many flags that bore the marks of having seen hard service, some of them saturated with the blood of some poor soldiers. It was painful to look at them. There were many Revolutionary relics and ancient books. Swords, belts, sashes & epaulets worn by different men of note in the wars. He then took us into the Senate Chamber which is not much larger than "Andrew's Hall" but beautifully finished with carvings in the marble, & the speakers desk was of the purest marble. We did not visit the Legislative hall, we are going when the Legislature assembles. We then went to the Quarter master General's office, and were introduced to Gen. Wright. There we saw all the improvements in fire arms which was a pretty sight though I was hardly the wiser for having seen them. Then we went into the lower regions where the engines were working which supplied the rooms with water — the furnaces which heated the rooms. Lastly we went to the Library which is a very large room supplied with books of every description, and anyone has the privelege of selecting from them and reading them <u>in</u> <u>the</u> <u>room,</u> which is prepared with tables & chairs for the accommodation of visitors, persons connected with the State House and a few others are permitted to draw

Nelia,

books and retain them two weeks. Sheldon drew a couple for Mary and me. She took Litcomb's "Lessons in Life" and I took a work called "Mosaics" by the author of "Salad for the Solitary".

Please tell Mary Wilbor that her aunt Lottie has lived here where I am boarding and has visited here with Philo, that Mrs Smythe's oldest boy is named Arthur Wilcox. She made a great many inquiries about them, and I told her all I was able to for I was not personally acquainted with Mrs John Wilbor.

And tell Mrs Carter that if she has not used up all her cucumbers I would advise her to peel and grate them fine then strain them and add as much vinegar as there is juice strained off. Then season with horseradish pepper & salt, & seal it up for winter use, or it will keep a very long time without sealing, and it certainly makes the best catsup I ever tasted.

Sheldon came here this noon with a letter from Mother and Father, and I have been looking for the express wagon this afternoon but it did not come I suppose it will be along in good time.

I have asked Mary for her photograph and she says that in about three weeks when she is paid again she will have some more copied, and when Niles returns I would like two or three of mine to exchange here.

I have concluded not to take anything but my music for they do not teach French in the High School, and so Sheldon went to see a French lady here, but would not tell me what her terms were. I mistrusted they were pretty high, and so I called on her myself and found she charged $20. for 36 lessons and recite every day. I thought I would not incur that expense for him, for the little knowledge I could get of it in six months would not enable me to teach it. So I told Sheldon I thought I would not take it, he doesn't know why, though.

I must close now, but I will first tell you a couple of little anecdotes about our Perry, which pleased me considerable. He came home in fine spirits telling his Mother how he & another boy had been throwing potatoes at his Cousin Brainerd. "Why Perry" said his mother "didn't you know that was a very naughty thing to do?" "No" said he "I didn't know it was wrong, well, I wasn't so bad as the other boy for he stole the potatoes."

Every morning at family prayers the little boys repeat a verse from the Bible, this morning Perry's was: Set a watch Oh Lord before my mouth and keep thou the door of my lips. But he caused us to smile by saying, keep thou the door of my lips — shut. We enjoy ourselves here very much and I do not think I shall be homesick a great deal the days fly faster now. Mary returns love to you. I will write home again when I receive the letters from Father & Delia which I suppose will come in the basket.

Does your R.S.S. (Rattle-Snake Swamp as Will Osborne called it,) still prosper? and have you any new members?

But good afternoon, with much love I am as ever

Your sister   Nelia

Nelia,

My Dear Mother

I received a very welcome letter from you last Monday, and will attempt a reply this afternoon. Your flowers and plants were very acceptable. I fear however we cannot succeed in making the plants grow. Mary's Heliotrope is looking very pale. I suppose because the sun does not touch our windows at all during the day. The boquet was handled and admired by nearly every one of the family.

When Sheldon came in the evening to take Mary & me to Mr White's I went up to him, holding a dish of grapes in one hand, and the vase of flowers in the other: He very cooly commenced eating the grapes when Mary exclaimed: "Why Lieutenant how <u>can</u> you <u>look</u> at the grapes before you have admired the flowers?" All the young folks here call him Lieutenant. It sounds odd to me. I proposed that we should call him Lieut<u>ie</u>. We could not think of enjoying our "goodies" alone, and as Mrs Smythe told us that her nephew Brainerd Howe and a Miss McKinney, Myra's music teacher, were coming to spend the evening with us, Sheldon concluded to ask his friends, Miss Leamon, Mr Ferson, and Mr Phillips, to accompany him here too. So we expect a very pleasant little musical soiree, and think we will entertain them with "a little more grape." Our acquaintences here will see that we have a <u>home</u> at least, and how could the grapes and flowers come unless <u>some</u> <u>friends</u> <u>packed</u> <u>and</u> <u>sent</u> <u>them</u>.

Mary has made a couple of mistakes regarding my identity as follows: She introduced me to some ladies as, "<u>My</u> <u>Sister</u> <u>Miss</u> <u>Colton</u>," her embarassment can be better imagined than described, and last evening Mr White asked her who was her roommate. She very innocently replied Miss Colton's <u>brother</u>. She has not heard the last of that yet.

The Rev. Mr Nash, who used to preach in Milan, was here today. I did not see him to speak with him. Mrs Smythe says he is out of work and intends to sit down and wait for a call. He picked up my album and looked it through I do not know whether he recognized your faces or not.

This house is built for three families, and in the family of Mrs Drury who lives <u>right</u> to <u>our</u> <u>right</u> <u>hand</u>, there was a death last Thursday, her father, Mr Taylor. Although I was a stranger to her, had never seen her, yet I refused to open the piano on Friday and Saturday morning. Mrs Smythe thought it would not make any difference to them, but I feared it would, & afterwards, Mrs Drury asked Mrs Smythe to "thank Miss Colton for her consideration in keeping the piano closed." I took that day for sewing & accomplished considerable. I took a lesson of Proff. <u>Shirner</u> this morning. There is a thunder storm coming up and as it is getting dark I will close, with much love to all, to Myra & Nellie when they come from

Nelia

Delia will hear from me soon

Nelia,

My Dear Father,

       I mailed a letter to Lina yesterday morning, and was then in pleasant anticipation concerning the basket from home which your letter to Sheldon informed us was on the way. It arrived yesterday after-noon about four oclock, and I hurried up to my room with it anxious to get a peep at the contents <u>all</u> by <u>myself</u>. My hands shook so I had difficulty in cutting the strings, and besides <u>my</u> <u>eyesight</u> <u>was</u> <u>not</u> <u>very</u> <u>clear</u>: but finally the last cord was broken, and my eyes feasted on "<u>Flowers</u> and <u>grapes</u>." I had no idea they could come in such good order. The flowers were a little crushed, but Mary rearranged them when she came home, and placed them on the mantle down in the parlor, for Sheldon to see when he came in the evening. I think there was not a single grape crushed; and they are far superior to any we have had here. There is a small vine in Mr Smythe's back yard, (which yard, by the way, is just about large enough to swing a cat round in, but as we have no need to swing cats round, we make no complaints.) This vine bore a few grapes this Fall, but the most we have had came from market or the neighbors, and Mary's scholars keep her supplied with fruits of all descriptions. But every one acknowledges that Milan grapes are ahead of any here. I filled a glass dish with some for the family, but they refused to partake very freely of them, telling me that I could preserve them for our own use for a long time, and they would not deprive me of the pleasure of them. Mary says she is going to give her folks a hint of what nice things are sent to me. Sheldon came in the evening to go with us to call at Mr White's who is the editor of the Educational Monthly. Mrs White's sister is one of the teachers here and a friend of Mary's. They are a very pleasant highly intellectual family, and we spent a very pleasant evening. While there I met a Miss Risteyo, I beleive the name was, and we were conversing alone, the others having gone to see Mr White who is confined to his room with lameness of some kind. She is from New Hampshire, and our conversation turned upon lameness when she said that about seven years ago, <u>she</u> <u>fell</u> <u>and</u> <u>hurt</u> <u>her</u> <u>knee</u> <u>and</u> it was thought she <u>displaced</u> <u>the</u> <u>kneepan</u>. The Physician tried blistering leeching & etc until she was not able to walk, and her parents carried her to Boston where a Homeopathic doctor prescribed, <u>showering</u> it <u>in</u> <u>cold</u> <u>water</u> <u>and</u>

Nelia,

bathing <u>it</u> <u>in</u> <u>alcohol</u>, and <u>besides</u>, <u>to</u> <u>wear</u> <u>an</u> <u>India</u> <u>Rubber</u> <u>supporter</u> <u>on</u> <u>it</u>, she followed the advice for three years constantly, <u>and</u> <u>was</u> <u>cured</u>, and for the last two years it has caused her no pain nor weakness except occasionally a slight aching, on a sudden change from dry to damp weather. I thought it quite a coincidence to find a case as nearly corresponding with mine. She advised me to continue wearing my supporter for she <u>knew it would cure me</u>.

I thank you very much for the reproof and criticism in your letter. It was just what I needed. But I was grieved to think I had done that which merited reproof from you, <u>in</u> <u>your</u> <u>first</u> <u>letter</u> <u>to</u> <u>me</u>. I shall certainly be more careful in the future.

As soon as I had written both those words, and some others which you did not mention, I noticed how inappropriate they were but — I thought — "The letters are going <u>home</u> and they will make allowances, for they <u>know</u> <u>that</u> <u>I</u> <u>know</u> <u>better</u>," and as regards my handwriting, I will make no excuses only that when I sit down to write home, my thoughts travel so fast, my pen involuntarily, attempts to overtake them. Mary says "I wish our folks would criticise my letters." I hope you will do it often, for though it makes me feel badly for a while, it is better for me in the end.

General Rosecrans was an old friend and schoolmate of Mrs Smythe's, and indeed I know from some things Mr Smythe has said that she refused an offer of marriage from him. She says she never thought he would amount to much, and that he is entirely a self made man, his father was a hotel keeper! Can't Delight Jarvis take heart & hope from that? Who knows what might happen.

I received a letter from Carlos this noon. He says that they expect ten or twelve thousand soldiers there today to be reviewed by the Governor. That J.J. Banks is Lieutenant of a company & stayed with him the night before. He also says Aunt Sophia expects Mrs Shepard from Massachusetts to make them a visit and he thinks they intend going to Milan. I wish to write to Mother this afternoon and by your leave will close my letter, with much love to all   I remain
Your Daughter
Nelia.

Nelia,

Columbus, Sept 30th 1863

Dear Father and Mother

As you two were made <u>one</u>, longer ago than I can remember, perhaps it will be no harm to address this to you in <u>unity</u>, and I must ask you to accept a <u>small</u> letter this time for I have not the "<u>wherewith</u>" to fill a larger sheet. I have not been out to see any new sights yet unless I except last Saturday when Mary and I were out paying some calls.

We went to Mr Miller's where Sheldon boards, and found it a very fine oldfashioned house well-shaded and very homelike. The Misses Hattie & Lida Crosby were very sociable and wanted me to come there often on Sheldon's account. When we were coming home we went down by the Penitentiary and had the pleasure of seeing a massive stone structure with iron windows, the grounds finely laid out which surround it, and saw a few men in the "striped costume" but I think the "redoubtable John" kept himself in the background.

Sunday evening, Brainerd Howe, Sheldon, Mary & I went to the Presbyterian Church to hear a discourse on the death of an aged minister one of the first settlers in Columbus, and it was interesting even to a stranger.

Since then I have not been out of the gate except last evening when Sheldon & Mary, Myra & I went to Miss McKinney's to spend the evening. We returned early and had a little music all to ourselves.

Mary and I have come to the conclusion that Mrs Smythe is about as nearly perfect as any person <u>away</u> <u>from</u> <u>home</u> can be. She is just like a Mother to us, and Mary said this morning, "I do wish I had had such a friend & home last year as I have now". She is just as careful who

Nelia,

we are introduced to as if we were her own daughters. She was speaking this morning of a lady here who she said took boarders <u>for</u> <u>the</u> <u>money</u> and did not make it a <u>home</u> for them. She seems to make it an object to have us feel that we are under the same influences we would be at our own homes. During the time we have been here we have not heard one impatient or unpleasant word from her lips. She never scolds or punishes her children though they are pretty trying sometimes, and they are taught instant obedience. I dont know what I should have done to have gone into a city without a brother to advise me. The young people that he has introduced me to are <u>all</u> church members, and appear to have unexceptionable characters. <u>I</u> introduced <u>him</u> to Brainerd Howe and he has expressed himself <u>satisfied</u> with <u>him</u>. He is a member of the Presbyterian Church and his father is a minister. So while I have such friends as Sheldon Mary & Mrs Smythe there is no danger of my getting into bad company.

Mary says she agrees to the compromise it suits her exactly.

Yesterday morning I avowed my intention of "<u>washing the dishes</u>" as Mrs Smythe and the girl were very busy canning peaches. They "didn't beleive I knew how!" But I received many thanks when I had finished, and she said "tell your Mother you have not forgotten that it is the healthiest work imaginable to wash dishes." I hope you will all keep will, and Pa must not work so hard as to bring on his headaches.

I find it is almost impossible for me to write a decent hand but "hope on."

Much love to all from
Nelia

Nelia,

Dear Brother Carl

I received a letter from you about a week ago, and should have replied to it before this but I thought by waiting I might have something interesting to write, and here it is Friday morning and I am no better off than I would have been several days ago. But I wish to acknowledge the receipt of your letter and say that I shall hope soon & often to hear from you, and if this does not contain any valuable information you will please excuse it and hope to receive a better one when I have been out more and seen the sights.

I take lessons twice a week and practise four hours every day which about fills up my time for it tires me so that I have to rest after it. Mr Shirner was obliged to be absent from the town last Thursday and consequently I did not take a lesson and feeling rather lonesome in the afternoon with no practising to do, I went around to Esq. Miller's where Sheldon boards, and spent the afternoon with the Misses Crosby. They were very sociable and would not hear of such a thing as my leaving before tea, so I stayed until evening and Sheldon accompanied me home I was very much pleased with the whole family, which consists only of the two young ladies and their Step Mother, and this place of residence and manner of living are very fine indeed. This afternoon Sheldon is going to bring me some "garments" to make for him and some socks to run the heels of, and I have already hemmed him some handkerchiefs. So I have no idle time to get into mischief you see.

The troops have been pouring through here in large numbers for a few days. I believe the whole of Hooker's division have gone to reinforce Rosecrans. What an awful battle that was at Chattanooga. Nearly every one we meet here is anxious about a brother or son who was in the fight. Our next door neighbor heard that her son was killed, then he was reported to have had both feet shot off, now she has heard from reliable authority that he has only lost one foot. I see the 101st was in the battle but have not yet found any familiar names among the lists.

This neighborhood is very pleasant indeed and the neighbors have been very friendly about calling on us and showing us every attention, and if everything continues as pleasant as it has been thus far, I think I shall spend a very pleasant winter. I wish you was in business here, it would be so pleasant for us all, and it seems as if living was cheaper & wages better than elsewhere. There is the breakfast bell and I must close accept much love and write soon to
Nelia.

Nelia.

Dear Mother

I received a letter from you and one from Lina yesterday, and should have written to you then, but Mrs Smythe had promised to accompany me out to the Blind Asylum, this afternoon, and I thought I would wait until I could send word to Mrs Abbott that I had seen David. But a cold rainstorm set in this morning and prevented our going, so I will not wait but write again when I have seen him, which I intend shall be sometime this week. The weather has been so cold for two or three days that I put on the green Merions, but as it is a little warmer today I have on my brown dress & brown spencer and they look nicely together, and feel very comfortable. I like the idea of the cloth bonnet very much, and so does Mary & Mrs Smythe. Send all the pieces you can, for the style of making bonnets this winter requires a very large piece of cloth, not that they are any larger. But the bonnet is made of one whole piece, with the exception of the crown and cape. You ask about my sewing. I have not yet made my new drawers, but the rest of my plain sewing is done. My dress waist is not done. I have not looked at it since I came. If I find I cannot make it fit there is a dressmaker three doors from here who can do it for me.

Last Sunday Sheldon spent the afternoon in our room reading to us, and we enjoyed it very much. When he had finished he handed me a letter he had received from Father, and I was glad I did not see it before, for it made me cry. Can I _ever_ do _anything_ _that_ _will_ _not_ _merit_ _reproof_? I am sure I _try_ hard enough, but the _more_ I _try_, the _worse_ _it_ _gets_. I had a letter ready to send to Delia, but I will retain it for I see he thinks I write home too often. As to the Soldiers' letters I have nothing to say. I did not consider it any harm to give Alice a chance to correct mis-spelling, for I know it always did the scholars good where I taught, and I suppressed the name. I _have_ _no_ _idle_ _time_, as he thinks I do. I will deny my self the pleasure I had anticipated in giving you a little surprise when I return, and say now, that I give Mary music lessons and she gives me drawing lessons, that occupies about six hours a day, then I do Sheldon's sewing, have already made him two pair of flannel drawers, run the heels to two pair of socks and hemmed a couple of pocket handkerchiefs, besides my own sewing, and he is here — a part at least — of nearly every evening. I am sorry about the extra postage. I will enclose some in return. I thought I was only doing as Father had always taught me in writing letters to "spin it out" as he called it. But I suppose many of them have been very much out of a little, and after this will try to write home only once a week. But

Nelia,

I thought as I had only two correspondents out of the family I might indulge myself in writing home every little thing I did or saw.

Last Sunday was Communion day. There was a preparatory lecture on the evening previous, & as Mrs Smythe was not well enough to go I had given it up, but she came to my room about church time & said if I wished to go, she could furnish me with the very best of company. I went down to the parlor and was introduced to Mary Hurd, an intimate friend of Emma Smythe's, a very pleasant girl about my age. The church is near here on the opposite side of the street, and with a young brother of hers to guard us we went, and I enjoyed it very much. I like Mr Grammer better if possible every time I hear him preach. When I returned found Sheldon and Gen. Hill here. I dont like the General, he makes Sheldon work too hard. Putting my hand to my head just now reminded me to tell you that my hair has grown so long that I wear the roll under instead of over it, and it looks very much better.

Mary says "Tell your father, 'I want to know if Nelia may bite her nails off, they are so long she <u>scratches</u> me." She also sends much love to all the family. We enjoy ourselves very much together, evenings when we have not too much work to do and are alone. We take turns reading aloud to each other. I will put this by now till morning for Mary Hurd is coming for me to go to Prayer Meeting.

Thursday Morning

Myra has not come yet has she? I was in hopes she would be in Cleveland when I return home for Mary King still insists upon my making her a short visit as I pass through there. When I gave Sheldon that Ohio Statesman to send to Father I did not know that the few words written on it would require letter postage or I should certainly not have sent it. My letters <u>do</u> <u>not</u> "lie around loose." If there is anything in them that I think Mary would like to hear I read it to her otherwise they are put away. There is the bell for us to go down to "Prayers," and I must close, with much love to all from

Nelia

A black or brown Alapaca would make Delia a very pretty Sacque for this winter, and if I were you I would get her a felt hat The young girls here wear them very much and they are pretty. The new shape is a tall crown with the sides turned up and the back & front drooping. I must close now hoping to hear from you soon again.

Nelia

Nelia,

Columbus Oct 11th 1863

Well, I have attended Sunday School and Church this morning, and now will write a few lines to my <u>Dear</u> <u>Father</u>, if it will be acceptable to him. This is a bright, beautiful day, and we had a heavy frost last night, which has stripped many of the maple trees of their beautiful foliage. I enjoy this weather very much, and indeed I have not felt in such good health in <u>a</u> <u>year</u> as I do now. My face is fuller, and fresher looking, and Sheldon says, "I do not think you have grown very poor since you came." I think it arises from my regularity in dieting. I do not "<u>run</u> <u>to</u> <u>the</u> <u>cupboard</u>" at any hour in the day, and constantly eat whatever I fancy, and it keeps me in a healthier condition, I know. Last Thursday, was the day appointed for the Union Convention here, and although it was rainy & the streets very muddy, yet a large number of the citizens formed in the procession which passed here. Myra, Mary and I sat at our windows watching them, and were quite interested. I cannot remember the order in which they passed and very many of the mottoes we could not interpret, but a few were the following: First came the largest wagon I ever saw, mounted on six wheels and drawn by sixteen horses, and occupied by girls to represent the States, dressed in Red, White & Blue, with their Goddess of Liberty bearing the <u>flag</u>, and the Goddess of war waving her <u>Sword</u>. They called themselves the "<u>Soldiers' Friends</u>." Another large wagon drawn by eight horses, was filled with Soldiers dressed in the Invalid Uniform, and arranged in <u>tiers</u> so that those in the centre were plainly seen, and on the wagon in large letters was painted: "The Invalid Corps Of Honor." You may be sure we waved our Flag & handkerchiefs at them and they touched their caps to us and hurrahed for "Brough." But the best of all was a <u>miniature "Monitor"</u> on wheels, and a <u>large</u> "<u>miniature</u>" it was too. I had no idea there was any "machinery" connected with it, and you can imagine my surprise when it "presented" its guns and fired right before our window. Altogether there was a much better display than at the Vallandingham meeting, a few weeks ago. In the afternoon I had been practising and was feeling a little "blue" when there was a ring at the doorbell and <u>Mrs Botsford</u> was shown in. She was as glad to see me as I was to meet her, and she said I deserved a <u>scolding for not letting her know I was here.</u> Sheldon had told her to bring me to the State House if I wished to come and so we started. On the way we stopped at the hospital which I have told you is nearly opposite here. We went through several wards and found everything looking even better than I expected. The building was formerly a female Seminary, and has all the conveniences of <u>furnaces gas</u> and a <u>reservoir</u> from

Nelia,

which water is conducted to the rooms by pipes. Mrs Smythe has often tried to persuade me to do as her daughters have done: carry books and papers over to the soldiers. But I disliked to go there, and now have found how I can do it very conveniently. There are always a number of the patients out by the gate and I noticed as I passed there coming from church this noon, that several of the ladies handed them their Parish Visitors, and they took them eagerly & thankfully, so I guess after this I will carry my Harper's Weekly and Registers over to the gate and hand them to some of them. Dont you think it would be a good plan? as they told us they depended entirely on the Ladies of the City for Reading Matter. But to return to my story, when we reached the State House we went into the General's Room to call on Sheldon, and he took us into the Governor's room and we were introduced to Gov. Tod, who said as he shook hands with me, "How <u>are</u> you <u>my</u> dear." I thought he was remarkably <u>free</u> on <u>short</u> acquaintance. Sheldon thinks a great deal of him. Mrs Botsford's object in calling on him was to offer her services as a nurse <u>in the front of the ranks</u>. Mr Botsford is about leaving Camp Chase and she does not wish to stay, without him. The Gov. gladly accepted her services and I think she will soon go. Her daughter Emma is teaching school. Hattie, Lily, & Ulysses are keeping house with Etta Bradshaw, a twin sister of Arthur's wife. I spent a very pleasant afternoon with her and she says that the first of the week she will send a private conveyance for me to spend the day with her; nearly all the soldiers have gone home to vote and it will be a good chance to see the grounds.

Mrs Smythe went with me out to the Blind Asylum Friday and we saw a great many things that were new to me and I will write more about it another time. I saw David Abbott, and indeed I think he is looking much better than when he left home, and yesterday he came to see me and I played & sung for him and read to him, then went with him to the corner of Town and 7th streets, and then he went on alone.

I expect to see him oftener now that I have found the way. Sheldon wishes to enclose a few lines and so I will be obliged to close this time. I have tried the experiment of writing <u>more</u> on <u>less</u> paper & if it can be read perhaps I will try it again. You will please excuse the mistakes. I was anxious to have this ready to mail in the morning & attempted to write with Sheldon & Mary talking in the room so I find I have made several errors.

Hoping to hear from you soon I remain your <u>well</u> <u>meaning</u>
Daughter
Nelia.

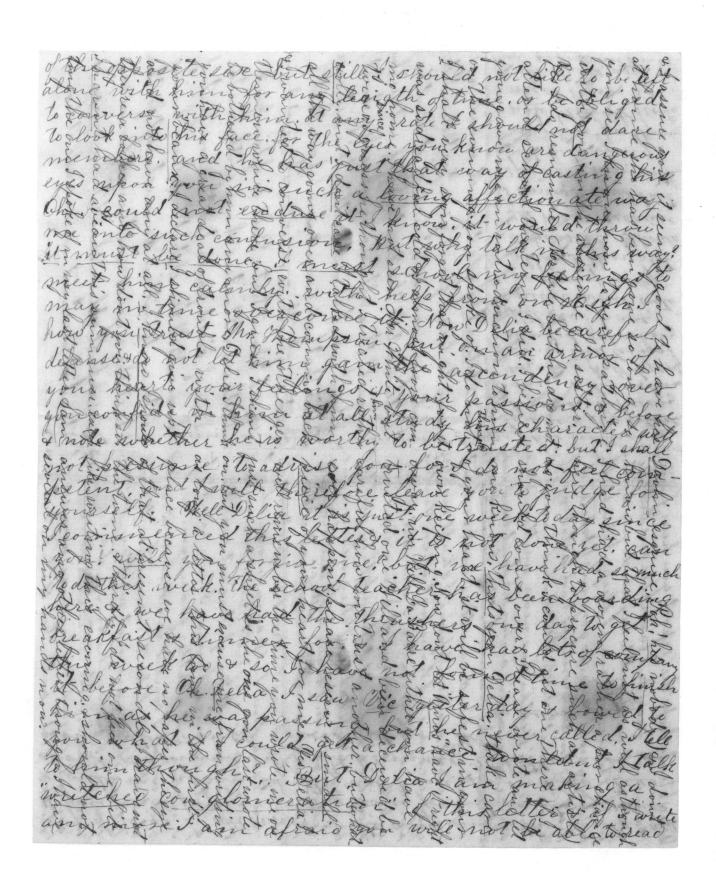

Friend

My Dear Friend Delia

I received your letter the 15th of last month and was <u>tolerably</u> glad (just as I always am to hear from you. Yes! Delia I do pity you ever so much if it is'nt too late, & to tell the truth I feel rather "<u>blue</u> myself this afternoon, & I really dont know why I should either. It is <u>so</u> <u>strange</u> Delia that you never knew before that I had any brothers or sisters & I used to speak about Sister Bell so often. Yes 2 brothers & 2 Sisters share with me the love of kind parents & the comforts of home. Bell the eldest has been living with an Aunt in Connecticut, for the last three years, & returned home very unexpectedly a short time since, so that at present we are all at home & I assure you it seems good to have her at home she has been gone so long, so you see I know how to sympathize with <u>you</u> in the abscence of a sister. Yes I do remember Mr Kyle but he did not attend school that term I did. I believe you gave me an introduction to him on the evening you spoke of. I do not think <u>I</u> shall very soon forget that night, for it was so <u>dreadful</u> cold & I almost froze coming home. I have not seen Mr White but twice since I guess he thought I treated him rather <u>coolly</u>, but <u>I</u> <u>don't</u> <u>care</u>. I talked with him all the way going over and coming back & I wanted to converse with the other gentlemen while there, but I guess I shant be bothered by him any more, Delia. I think you have a great deal of trouble with your <u>beaux</u>. I declare I should give up and not have any at all. <u>I</u> <u>know</u> <u>I</u> <u>should</u>. They're a bother any how dont you think so. I have'nt had a beau this summer, excepting the one I spoke of in my last letter. <u>Sam Davlin</u> Esquire. <u>Poh</u>! <u>he's</u> <u>nobody</u> & I don't know but that I feel just as well as though I had had a dozen (rather a poor chance here though to procure such an article) do you think I could get one there if I should come over? Please write and let me know. <u>That's</u> <u>you</u> <u>Delia</u>. Take care of your heart, it will be safest in your own keeping. Now dont let "<u>Amos</u>" have it right away, nor Will LaBarre either you have trusted one Will and been deceived, be careful how you trust another, but what ever happens, please reserve a <u>small</u> <u>piece</u> of your heart for me. Yes Delia I well remember the time you wrote me on just such a sheet as the one you last wrote on, but you must excuse <u>me</u> in the first place because we have no paper the size of that at present, secondly I have not the time, & thirdly I do not feel one bit like writing this evening, & should not answer any other letters though I have several on my hands now. Delia I truly hope the report you hear from Hammie" may be a favorable one, but like you I shall be obliged to lay aside my writing for this time, for I am so sleepy I can hardly hold my eyes open, so goodnight & heres a kiss

Monday morning. I have seated myself to write just a little bit while I have the time. No! Weltha has never written to me since she went away, & I dont know why either for she promised too, her sister is expecting her down this week or

Friend

next on a visit, so I suppose I shall see her, if she comes. I have not seen Beattie since last winter. I should really like to attend some of your reading Societies. I should think they would be very profitable if they were conducted right. No! I have not the honor of an acquaintance with Miss Wilbor, though I have heard her spoken of. Now Delia dont talk anymore about your writing, just write as much as you want too, if it is'nt written quite so nice, I guess I can read it. I never got a letter from you yet but what I could read every word of it. I always like to receive good full letters if they are not written so well, & when I have the time I always write them in return. Now I'm not going to be jealous because you went and took a ride with Geo. Prout. but then I dont like it much, but <u>why</u> <u>should</u> <u>I</u> <u>care</u>? he's nothing to me anymore. I have not seen <u>him</u> a dozen times no! nor a half dozen since the term I attended school in Milan. I have never went into any company where I thought it possible I should see him, because I knew I could not speak to him with out betraying my love for <u>him</u> <u>now</u> I think I could meet him as calmly as any other acquaintance of the opposite sex but still should not like to be left alone with him for any length of time, or be obliged to converse with him, at any rate I should not dare to look into his face, for the eyes you know are dangerous members, and he has just that way of casting his eyes upon you in such a <u>loving</u> <u>affectionate</u> way. Oh! I could not <u>endure</u> it. I know, it would throw me into such confusion. But why talk in this way? <u>it</u> <u>must</u> <u>be</u> <u>done</u>. <u>I</u> <u>must</u> school my feelings to meet him calmly, with help from on High may in time overcome it. Now Delia be careful how you trust Mr Thompson, put on an armor of defense & do not let him gain the ascendency over your heart your feelings & your passions, & before you confide in him at all study his character well & note whether he is worthy to be trusted, but I shall not presume to advise you for I do not feel competent, and I will therefore leave you to judge for yourself. Well Delia it is just one week today since I commenced this letter & it is not done yet, can you? <u>will</u> you forgive me? but we have had <u>so</u> much to do this week. The school teacher has been boarding here & we have had the thrashers one day to get breakfast & dinner for. I have had lots of company this week too & so I have not found time to finish it before. Oh, Delia I saw <u>Vic</u> yesterday & bowed to him as he was passing but he never called. I <u>tell</u> you what if I could get a chance wouldnt I talk to him though? But, Delia I am making a "<u>wretched</u> <u>conglomeration</u>" of this letter & if I write any more I am afraid you will not be able to read any of it so I will not write any more, this time but if you will forgive me this time for not writing sooner, & write me again shortly & let me know how it is about Hammie, <u>I</u> will promise to do better also so now with much love — I bid you adieu.   As ever
                                                                                    <u>Mate</u>.

[letter written in normal fashion, then crosswise over each page]

Cleveland Oct 15th 1863

Dear "Pa".

   I should have replied to your questions concerning "Mr. Jacksons opinion of the best mode of keeping grapes" — ere this — had I not thought I might visit Milan ere this. He does nothing but cut them carefully — and put them in a dry place and they keep until after Christmas. There was an old English Gardener, here this morning — and he says — dip the ends of the stem in Sealing Wax and hang them in a warm dry place.

   I think now I will visit Milan with Mrs. Shepherd — but am not fully decided. I have such discouraging letters from Henry — I sometimes think I ought not spend my money in visiting. Henry is doing but very little — and cannot collect anything that is due him in Nashville — still he wishes for some reason to keep by himself. Sometimes I cannot help feeling pretty <u>blue</u>.

   Aunt wrote me Mrs. Shepherd was to here next Tuesday on her way to Milan — and wanted me to meet her at the Depot. I supposed she intended stopping here and have written Aunt — if Uncle thought best he might write for her to do so — as she has never been West. I supposed she would like to see something of Cleveland. I am glad to hear through Aunts letter — that Carlos has gone back there to board — as I think it will be better for him on many accounts — than boarding with strangers.

   We were rejoiced yesterday in the good news of Broughs victory over Valandingham — and to day feel sad that the news from the Potomac Army is so discouraging. I cannot but think all will yet end well. I am sorry you still suffer so much with Sickhead — it is so wearing.

      Give my love to all
        Myra

Mr Jenkins was here a few days ago — he looks completely broken down. I saw Mrs. Carnahan (Jackson) yesterday in town — and also met John Blinn — he came in town in the morning & was going away last night. We would like very much to have had him stay here over night.

Nelia,

Columbus Oct 16th 1863. Sunday Evening

Dear Sisters Lina and Delia.

As I am owing you both letters, and moreover am a little tired tonight, I hope you will not object to my addressing you both together again. I have quite a number of little items to tell you which may not be interesting, to y<u>ou</u>, but as it will be pleasant for <u>me</u> <u>to recall</u> <u>them</u> by writing, I will do so: asking your kind attention for a few moments. By the way, this is the evening for your R.S.S. isn't it? I imagine you enjoying yourselves, as I know I should were I at home. Before I forget it, I wish to say to Delia that her accidental mention of Miss Cornelia Keller, was quite a coincidence, as connected with something I had heard only the day before. When you see the young lady again, please tell her that Will Alling spent six weeks in Milan this fall. If you do not gain any information further from her I will tell you a little incident, next time I write, which I have not the space to do now. In my letter to Father, Sunday, I mentioned visiting the Blind Asylum. You can tell Jennie Norton that I saw Miss Lipton, and became somewhat acquainted with her. She teaches music at the Asylum, and is a member of the Episcopal Church. She sang and played a great many pieces for me, some of them original; one she called the "Ohio Volunteer's March" and I think I have seldom heard a piece I liked as well. She sent much love to Jennie and invited me to come out often to see her.

I have never witnessed so sad a sight as those poor blind people of nearly every age, under thirty, pursuing occupations which we would deem it impossible to do <u>without</u> <u>light</u>, and yet they seem perfectly happy. There are two young Soldiers there, this year, whose eyes were shot out in battle and it was said to be very difficult to reconcile them to their fate. But they are all very comfortably situated; the grounds around the building are tastefully arranged, and the scholars seem to have no difficulty in finding their way about them. I shall go there again soon and have a better opportunity of seeing the different departments. Mary and I expect tomorrow to visit the Lunatic Asylum, and I wish

soon to go to the Idiotic, also. Well, what have I done <u>this week</u>? let me see. Oh! Monday evening, Sheldon brought his <u>guitar</u>, <u>and</u> Mr Phillips, & Charley Stevens of Toledo, to spend the evening with us. The <u>guitar</u> is <u>here</u> <u>yet</u>, the <u>rest of the company are not</u>. We spent a very pleasant evening, as we usually do when we have so much good music.

Tuesday morning, Mrs Botsford drove up in the Chaplin's carriage and signified her intention of taking me out to Camp Chase to spend the day with her. I had practised my music very thoroughly the day before and consequently thought I could afford to lose a day in recreation, and seeing something of the manner in which "Our Brave Boys" in the field live. We crossed the Sciota River at the foot of Broad Street, and proceeded directly West, on the same track, for about four miles. —(indeed the road is so straight that as far as the eye can reach it is a white extended line)—and arrived at the Camp which is situated on the left hand, and as the little "white houses" of which the "town" is composed burst upon the sight, it was really imposing. The camp is about a mile & a quarter in length, and the "houses" are arranged in straight lines with regular streets between them, and they have their Barber Shops — Bakeries, Apothecary Shops and Sutter's Stores, and indeed it is said that a countryman, in passing one day remarked, "<u>Well this is a right</u> smart <u>little town</u>, what do <u>they call it</u>?" We went directly to the hospital buildings where Mrs Botsford's room is, and indeed she is not so comfortably situated, as a woman of her age ought to be. She is the Matron, and receives & delivers the clothing & keeps it mended, which is a great task for her, and does everything just as she would for her own family. The three Surgeons and Chaplain have neat carpeted rooms in a separate house, and Mrs Dr Barr has a piano there, which was diversion for me. We went through all the wards, and found very few sick, and <u>none</u> who were then considered dangerous, nearly all who were able had gone home to vote, and among those who remained there were 175 votes raised, and <u>not one</u> for Vallandingham. As Mr Botsford was away she urged me to remain with her over night and I did so. We

Nelia,

slept under one of the wards on <u>little</u> <u>iron</u> <u>bed</u> <u>steads</u>, and the constant walking & talking over the unplastered ceiling, disturbed me very much, though she had become so used to it, it did not trouble her. I was struck with the devotion of the nurses, (who are all convalescent soldiers) to the sick men. They take great pride in keeping every thing as neat as wax almost, and are constant in their endeavors to relieve & amuse the patients. I should not have remained over night had I known what grand proceedings were going on in the city. There was speaking at the State House steps, and a torchlight procession, & a large bonfire, built upon a wagon, to which was attached another wagon filled with men, and drawn by horses. Thus they went all over the city until the fire had consumed the <u>wagon</u>. I missed seeing all this, but from the camp, I plainly saw the fireworks which were sent from the dome of the Capitol. Last evening Secretary Chase spoke and they had another grand Rally. Sheldon took Mary and me to hear him and it was very interesting. The men hurrahed for "Old Greenback" & etc. Mr Smythe did not vote for either of the candidates for governor, they say only because he was <u>afraid</u> <u>to</u> <u>do</u> <u>it</u>. I am very careful not to mention either of the names, "Brough" — Vallandigham" for he is so nervous & excitable, and moreover quite an old gentleman, that I wish to <u>keep</u> <u>him</u> <u>as</u> <u>cool</u> <u>as</u> <u>possible</u>.

You will perceive I write just as things come into my brain and now comes the recollection of another addition to one of Perry's verses, which was too supremely ridiculous to keep. He spoke up in a loud voice the other morning when his turn came & said, "I love them that love me and those that seek me early shall find me <u>up</u> <u>early</u>."

When you send my shawl & etc please enclose all those drawings that cousin Alphens sent you. I will bring them safely home to you again. Mrs Botsford sent much love to all. I must close now with love from Sheldon & myself to all the family and inquiring friends, write soon and often wont you? to your Sister

Nelia

There was speaking at the State House steps... & a large bonfire, built upon a wagon, to which was attached another wagon filled with men, and drawn by horses. Thus they went all over the city until the fire had consumed the <u>wagon</u>.

Nelia,

Columbus Monday Oct 19

My Dear Mother

As Mary is writing a few lines to Father this morning I will employ the same time in writing to you I can hardly express my gratification at the acceptable present which Mary received Saturday evening from my home and friends. She was very much pleased and will not soon forget the attention thus shown her. Sheldon was here yesterday afternoon and after sitting with us about an hour went out to the Blind Asylum to see a Mr Lindsay and David Abbott. We sent them each some of the grapes and they were very thankful for them. Last evening we attended the 1st Presbyterian Church where Sheldon and Mary sing, to hear a Mr Chidlaw who has been a Chaplain, and is now an energetic, hardworking, delegate of the Christian Commission. I was very much interested indeed, in his reports of the moral and temporal condition of the army, and he brought tears to many eyes by the affecting anecdotes he related. After the service he had a collection taken up for the aid of the Christian & Sanitary Commissions, and the way the ten & five dollar bills went into the box was a comfort to see. We concluded last night that the contribution must have amounted to at least $500. Thinking of his remarks reminds me of some things Mrs Botsford told me with regard to the Hospital clothing, which perhaps you would like to know. She says that the bosoms to the shirts ought to be at least eighteen inches long, that she has had to alter a great many on account of not being able to get them on to a sick man, and it is also a very good plan to make a great number of the drawers, and the sleeves to the shirts, open on the outer edge with tapes to fasten them up, that is I mean, to tie them together, as it is very inconvenient to dress wounds on the legs or arms with the close drawers and sleeves.

Mother, every one declares here that I am better looking than when I first came, because I have fattened up considerable, for me, and indeed we made a mistake in fitting my clothing to my form as it was when I left home. I have enlarged my corsets about an inch and shall have to do it again in a few days, for you know I can not bear anything too tight around me, & I find I must let out all my winter dresses, it is

utterly impossible to get the lining of my blue dressing gown anywhere near together. Now I think that is really encouraging don't you? and Mother I will tell you one little thing that I had not intended to, before I came home. That is, Mrs Smythe found out my <u>industrious habits</u> and proposed that I should assist her, in my leisure hours about her sewing etc. (I have already trimmed hers & Myra's bonnets to their entire satisfaction) and she pays me liberally for what I do, so I am kept in spending money, and have several times refused it from Sheldon, though he doesn't know why, and I think I can save enough to fix my hat & perhaps my bonnet without asking him for any. So with all this, I do <u>not spend an idle moment</u>, nor do I neglect my music and drawing, & no one can complain <u>here</u> that I am <u>on the street too much</u>. Mrs. Smythe when she proposed it said she knew I would feel much more independent to do so and she should enjoy having me do it for her as she would be obliged to hire it done away from the house if I did not. So I am perfectly contented and really happy here, much more so than I ever imagined I could be so far away from home. Well I must close though I wish to say to Father that his dear good letter was very acceptable, and I <u>should think he knew better</u> than to make fun of Will, for what he cannot help, perhaps the young man has never had an opportunity of <u>shortening his understandings,</u> and I should like to know, really, which is the <u>worse,</u> to laugh at men because they have <u>neglected</u> the <u>priveleges of education which are offered</u> to all in a free country, or to make fun of a young man because he is made somewhat taller than others. I wonder where I inherited the "funny" propensity? I could tell you a capital joke on Sheldon & perhaps will next time I write. Tell Delia to go up stairs immediately to that large box in the little back Chamber and find a piece of music which Sheldon composed, called the "Marie Serenade" & send it forthwith to him by mail as he is anxious for it.

Mother I dont know as you can read this but it is most time to take a music lesson and we over slept ourselves this morning so you will please take it as it comes & be thankful. I find I have not told you all I wished to, but must close now, until some othertime. Accept much love from Nelia I <u>have</u> answered Emma Brace's letter.

Nelia,

Columbus Oct 27th 1863

My Dear Father

I had been intending to write home tonight and was trying to make up my mind to whom to address a letter, when a welcome one from you was received, and of course that decided the question. I will warn you beforehand, that I have nothing new or interesting to write, and moreover (I may as well acknowledge it) I <u>am</u> <u>homesick</u> <u>tonight</u>, and have felt that "<u>home affection</u>" considerable during the past two or three days, after a crying spell this evening I feel a little better and doubtless it will all wear off in a short time. Whenever I sit down to my sewing or have time to think I <u>imagine</u> what you are all doing and it seems as if <u>I</u> was <u>there</u> and some <u>one else</u> was <u>Nelia</u> <u>Colton</u> <u>at</u> present.

Mary and Sheldon have gone out to spend the evening at Lizzie Wheaton's. I should have accompanied them, but that I accidentally <u>thumped</u> <u>my</u> <u>knee</u> <u>against</u> <u>Mary's</u> the other night and I have been so lame ever since that I have not tried to walk much and although I am stronger tonight, yet, I thought it prudent to remain in my room. Sheldon now has Tuesday, Thursday and Saturday evenings to himself and is then at <u>our</u> disposal. Saturday Mary went out in the country to spend Sunday with a Schoolmate of hers, and I was left a widow. Sheldon came as usual right after dinner and we had a pleasant visit together. Mary returned about five oclock and Sheldon stayed to tea & spent the evening with her while I went to church with the family. I love Mary very much. Her greatest fault, and I might almost say her only one, is similar to <u>one</u> of mine, and that is: "<u>Put it away</u>" but we are both improving in that respect and indeed if you would look into our room, closet & trunks, you would, I think generally find them in pretty good order.

I was quite amused Saturday evening at Arthurs. He had been with his father to see Mr Grammer who is sick and as he returned I was about leaving the room, "Oh Miss Colton" said he "Wait a minute I want

Nelia,

to tell you what Mr Grammer said about you." There was company in the room and I did not care to hear him then for I knew from his actions it was something flattering So I said "no, no, I dont care to hear" and in his eagerness to tell me before I got away he expressed himself thus. "Well he says you are the best <u>boy</u> he has got in his Bible Class." I thought that might be very true when there were no <u>other boys</u> in it.

"That poor Mr Smythe" is only in the house at meal times, and after nine oclock in the evening, so he seldom hears the "fiddling". I should think though it would make any one, not concerned, rather nervous, to hear a piano going so constantly as is this one. It seems to me you are suffering with your headaches more than usual are you not? I fear you try to work too much. <u>Do you have to get breakfast in the morning</u>?

I did not mean that I only wanted the pictures Alphy drew himself. I want those he sent for patterns, though the case is not an urgent one.

There was a gathering at the Gov.'s house Friday evening, of all the men connected with the State House. Sheldon's note of invitation read "to drink a cup of coffee" but from what he said of the proceeding they used a drink considerable stronger than coffee. I think it is such a shame for the Governor to set such an example to the young men, and from what I can hear of Brough I imagine will not be much better when he takes Tod's place. I am tired and sleepy and you will please excuse more this time. My pens <u>were poor</u> & I have stolen Mary's gold one this time which by the way was a present from Sheldon. I thank Mother for the Fuschia blossom. It seems Lina's & my letters pass each other usually. I shall write to her soon again. With much love and many wishes that your health may improve I remain as ever

Your daughter,
Nelia.

Detroit Nov 1st 1863

Dear Niece

I arose this morning feeling much better than I had for some time past, but did not feel well enough to attend Church, so I thought to myself, I will write a few lines to Lina as I was getting writing utensils together. Clarinda came in from Church, with your letter which Hatty handed her, you may believe we are none of us in a very amiable frame of mind. Hatty said she was so angry and so grieved after reading your letter that she did not know what to do with herself she had no idea that she could go to Milan as she left home in a very great hurry, did not receive Johns letter until about time for her to be at the Cars: you may be sure if she had known of the arrangement, John had made with you she never would have returned without making a visit, and bringing you back with her if you could come. I have no idea but John intended to do as he told you he would, and will probably make provision for Hattie to fulfil his promise as regards your travelling expenses. Lina I think you can spend your time very pleasantly here, the coming winter your Aunts and Cousins are all living so near each other, that you can see them all every day if you choose and still be Hattie's <u>boon</u> <u>companion</u>. I suppose you are not aware that we have street-cars on the <u>Avenue</u> which run from the corner of Jefferson Avenue, up Woodward, about half a mile above here, they run from six in the morning to ten at night, every twenty minutes and for the small sum of five cents you can have quite a long ride. Mrs Boylen will be quite a near neighbor of your Aunt Lucindas that is for the winter, you probably recollect the house they now occupy in going from Mt Calm Str to the Avenue, you turn the corner at the grocery where Phin got the most of his supplies the next building to that is a two story brick house painted white, that is the house your Uncle George will occupy until spring when one of his new houses up here will be vacant. Your Aunt Fannie is very nicely settled in one of those brick houses on the opposite side of the Park from where they used to live. Hattie has a very nice house, and is very pleasantly situated. Clarinda is very pleasantly situated and living, <u>On</u> <u>the</u> <u>Avenue</u> on the whole Lina we are a very <u>pleasant</u> <u>people</u> come and see for yourself. Is Mrs Boylen coming soon, if not do not wait for her, it would be pleasanter to have company but there would be no difficulty in coming alone as I know Phin would meet you at the Cars if you would let us know when to expect you. My health has been very poor all summer, and so far this fall, I think however two or three of the last attacks have been less severe so I hope they are going to have me for a few months at least. I am weak and miserable the most of the time not able to do anything of consequence except walk from one house to the other I visited at your Aunt Lucindas a week ago last Saturday with Mrs Brigham wife of your Mothers Uncle Bela she had been to Chicago to visit her oldest son Charles Brigham

I would like to see your father and mother, also Lottie and her family not forgetting Delia. By the way I hear that you wrote to your Aunt Lucinda, that I had not acknowledged the receipt of your photograph. I certainly thought I had both of yours and Mr Carters, if not accept my very best thanks for both, and attribute the cause of the neglect to ill health.

Love to all from all Do come and come soon, you will get a letter from Hatty probably by the same Mail with this. If I mistake not your father is owing me a letter

Your Affectionate Aunt

C Bill

Nelia,

Columbus Nov 4th 1863

My Dear Mother

      Sheldon received letters from home yesterday by which we were informed that Lina had accepted a <u>good</u> <u>offer</u> (as all young ladies should I <u>suppose</u>) and intends going to Detroit to live. You did not say how soon she expects to leave, and so I will write immediately and enclose the letter in the little package I wish to send to her. I made this bead collar purposely for her some time ago, and will also send another collar and a velvet bow for her hair. Mary threw in the red bow. If she wants either of my undersleeves, she is welcome to them as neither of my winter dresses have open sleeves. I am glad she has the opportunity of spending the winter in Detroit. But fear you will need one of us at home wont you? I mean no distrust of Delia's abilities to fill our places but you will be lonely, only three of you. Well, you can tell how it will be when I am all alone with the old folks there is nothing like "getting used to it."

      Yesterday afternoon there was a meeting of the Ladies Benevolent Society at Mrs Medbury's and a Sociable in the evening. We Episcolians attended and though it was rather dull, still I enjoyed it very well considering I was a stranger to nearly every one there. Oh! I believe I have never told you of that capital joke on Sheldon which we teaze him about, yet. I will tell it for Pa's benefit as I beleive he enjoys anything of that kind, at any rate I have a slight recollection of his fun over a similar mishap of Mr Bower's. Mrs Drury lives in this same house and the front doors are so near together that the same flight of steps lead to both. One evening Mary Sheldon & I went in there to call, after returning they sat up until about eleven oclock when on going home he could not find his cap. He <u>had</u> <u>left</u> <u>it in Mrs Drury's</u> <u>on</u> <u>the</u> <u>parlor table</u>. Mary gave him Arthur's to wear home and he returned it early in the morning when I went and got his. What made it worse was that the two other young men who board where he does were at Mrs Drury's that same evening. When they left at ten oclock there lay his hat yet. We supposed that the family here knew nothing of it until yesterday Mr Smythe was looking for his hat and Mrs S. looked up slyly & said "<u>You</u> <u>can</u> <u>borrow</u> <u>Arthur's</u>." It was all out then, they had known of it all the while but were too polite to speak of it first. I think this was rather "badder" than Mr Bower's. Please dont let Sheldon know that I have told it to you he might not like it. But Pa made so much fun of Mr Bower. I could not resist telling him this. Of course you have seen accounts of the arrests made here of rebel spies. There has been a great deal of excitement in the city, and just think what might have happened had they succeeded in letting out the prisoners at Camp Chase. It is time to mail this and I must close, with much love to all from Mrs Smythe, Mary &

      Nelia.

Columbus Nov. 9th 1863. Monday.

Dear Sister Delia,

I had been intending to write to you this afternoon, but thought I would wait until after mail time as there might be letters from home. Sheldon brought me a good long one from you so I have further inducement for writing, and I guess I have enough to tell you this time to fill this sheet. Well, to begin, I must tell you what I have been doing for a few days past. Mary wished very much to go home Friday night & spend Sunday, as her oldest sister Lillie Denman was there with her children. Her father wrote there was "room in their buggy, <u>room in their house and room in their hearts</u> for Sheldon & Nelia too." So we made arrangements to accompany her. I was to go with her Friday & Sheldon would come on Saturday night. But on Friday noon Mr Mitchell, who is a brother of Mrs Smythe's came from Granville, and told us that Lillie's baby, which was about the age of Carrie Belle had died, and they had taken the body home to Coshocton to bury it. Mr Mitchell said, Mr Whiting told him not to let that make any difference in our plans, and said particularly that I must be sure and come. Sheldon concluded he had better not go, as it would hinder his work, and he had been anxious to see Lillie who was not not there. So Mary & I started off about three oclock, for Granville. Myra went with us as far as Pataskala, where Brainerd Howe's parents live, at the depot there, we met Brainerd who had gone home the day before, and his cousin Miss Dell Harris. They went on with us to Granville. Mr Whiting met us at the depot at Union, which is about three miles from their home. I met with a very warm reception from the family which consists now of only Mr & Mrs Whiting and his sister, "Aunt Gray." Hattie who is about my age is teaching away from home, and George who is only a few years older is in the army, then comes Mary & then Lillie Denman, so the old folks are left all alone. In the evening Mr Whiting took Mary and me over to the village to a festival which was given for the Aid Society. I was introduced to a great many of Mary's friends and all of Mrs Smythe's relations. The latter welcomed me cordially saying they had heard of me so often they felt almost acquainted. I enjoyed the Festival exceedingly, though nearly all there were strangers to me and the house was so crowded it was almost impossible to move around. We had a great deal of "fun", indeed every one was on the <u>broad grin</u>. <u>We</u> laughed particularly, when I, (or <u>some one else I do not know which</u>) tipped a plateful of oyster soup <u>into my lap</u>, all over my red merino dress, and Brainerd accused me of trying to <u>pocket that dish of soup</u>. The next morning there was not a trace of it on my dress. I was glad twas not my cloth one. They sold a great number of fancy articles besides the supper. Brainerd bought a very handsome lamp mat for Mary & I'm partnership & a freind of Mary's bought her a card basket, altogether it was a

Nelia,

grand success, and they <u>cleared</u> over $300.00 which was considerable in a town somewhat smaller than Milan Saturday morning we spent at home, quietly with the exception of a couple of calls, one from Brainerd, the other from Dr Harry Tassett who came to see if we would be at home in the evening as he wished to bring his sister to see us. In the afternoon we went to the village to take tea at Mr Mitchell's. Frank Mitchell is a young lady somewhat older than I, and a very intelligent & interesting person, by-the-way, I discovered that she is a cousin of Mary Mitchell's though they have not seen Mary since she was seven years old. We had a very pleasant visit there with Frank & Dell Harris, and Mr Whiting came for us at evening, & we spent the evening at home in company with Dr. Tassett and his sister. Sunday morning I went to church with them and at noon Mary & I went to her Aunt's, Mrs Partridge's, to stay until the time for Episcopal service which was three oclock. The church is a very neat one, not very large but handsomely finished. When it was time for service to commence who should enter the pulpit but <u>Mr Bower</u>. Newark is only six miles from Granville and he supplies both pulpits. After service as we came out I stepped up to speak with him, and if you ever saw a man astonished as at an apparition, he was the man. He talked with me some time, and said if I would go back with him to Newark I could take the cars from there in the morning. But that was out of the question of course, and he made me promise that when I came home with Mary again in the holidays, I should come and see him. I made Mr Whiting laugh considerable by telling him as we came home that I <u>always</u> <u>liked</u> <u>that sermon of Mr. Bower's</u>. It was one of those excellent ones he preached Sunday evenings last winter. Well we arrived home safely about noon today and I have enjoyed myself every moment. They all regretted very much that Sheldon did not go with us. But Mary said she thought there was attraction enough here for him, which means that Frank McMillen has come here to teach in one of the schools, and called on me Friday, leaving word for Sheldon to be sure & come to see her. Well, here I am at the end of my paper & have not begun to answer your letter. But I must stop now until evening as Mr Shirner kindly consented to give me a lesson at five oclock, so that I need not lose anything by being away. The snow is about an inch deep on the roads this afternoon and this first snow storm has nearly set the boys wild.

I went over to the Hospital Thursday and took from there five pair of socks to darn, and such an amount of darning as they needed I cannot describe. I spent Thursday evening at Mary Herd's. My last visit with her as she is going to teach this winter away from home. I shall miss her for I had become strongly attached to her. Well Supper is ready & I will finish this this evening on another piece of paper.

[remainder of letter not found]

Adj. General's Office.
Columbus O. Nov. 16th 1863

Dear Father:

I have no special news to communicate, but as I have finished my work and am in possession of a little leisure time, I concluded to inform you that I am still alive and well, both of which items I am quite sure will be interesting to you.

I am not quite so much pressed with work just now as I have been, and hope to have it a little easier for a while.

Nelia is getting along finely. Keeps well all of the time and is getting pretty well used to things so that I hope she will not be homesick any more. By the way, who and what is the "Will Osborn" that she and Delia mention once in a while? I have a slight recollection of meeting such an individual at our house some time, but can hardly place him. I think he was there one evening and took part in our singing.

I presume you have had something of a scare up on the Lake shore. I imagined "Pater Familias" cleaning up the old musket and making various preparations to meet the bold intruder in case he should venture up the sacred waters of the Milan Canal.

The principal reason of my writing to you this evening was for the purpose of sending to you a photograph of Mary. I got this one from her yesterday to send to you, as she had just been having some taken. You need not flatter yourself that the receipt of this is any token that wisdom and old age can compete with youth and honorable scars in the race when beauty is the prize, even though said youth travels with a cane.

I do not know as I have any further remarks to make on these or any other subjects, and will therefore close with love to all.

Yours truly
Sheldon Colton.

I would like to have you send me the piano cover that I gave to Nelia, if you can fold it so as not to wrinkle it too much. Send by Express or otherwise as most convenient.

S.C.

An Old Love Song

I envy not the sceptered King,
    Who proudly sits on a shining throne,
Though wide domains with his praises ring,
    And countless subjects his ruling own;
I boast of a diadem far more bright,
    Than on his head is glittering,
And know of a realm more pure and light,
    Where I am subject at once and King.

I know of a maid, whose lustrous eye
    Beams kind on me with love's warm light,
Whose rosy lips will in sweetness vie
    With the honey concealed in flowers bright;
Her heart is pure as the calm moonbeam
    That falls at eve on the fountain cool,
And thence returns with a milder gleam,
    That heart is the realm where I bow and rule.

Sheldon Colton

Carlos

Toledo Nov 17th 63

Dear Father

I was surprised yesterday upon receiving your note to learn that Lina was not coming at present owing to a "Prevalence of Company". We are aware that Myra and her mother are there but as they were there when you wrote that Lina would come today, we dont know but what you have had some new arrivals. Am sorry Lina did not come today, as Annie has word from Miss Turner of Salina (or some other place) that she is to come here "Wednesday or Thursday" — this week — Annie thinks she will stay perhaps two weeks. So that when Lina does come we will probably have to send her along to Detroit the same day — though we will give her a chance to have dinner at the house and wait an hour or two.

Nelias letters are still as interesting as at first. I hear from different sources here that Sheldon is soon to marry, and I have had quite hard work to convince Aunt Sophia that I dont know anything about it particularly as Mrs Shepard told her "Confidentially" that <u>she</u> was "Confidentially" told that Sheldon and Miss Whiting were engaged — but then you know it was a secret, Oh yes! and <u>they</u> wouldnt speak of it to <u>any</u> one Oh No! bless their hearts — and tongues — I received a lengthy poetical letter from Ino Johnston yesterday — two or three extracts will I think appear in tomorrows "Blade" (18th). Had a short letter from Kent Hamilton a day or two since, written at Chattanooga he was acting as Adjutant of the Brigade as well as regiment

I enclose a duplicate of 1 Owe "Wayne Street Mills" Flour — price $7.00 all well as usual
            Carlos

Freight on Flour paid to Norwalk

Nelia.

Columbus Nov 24th 1863.

My Dear Mother

I was very much disappointed at not receiving letters from home today. Sheldon and I were comparing notes this noon, and came to the conclusion that the folks at home had forgotten us. I received a letter from Lina last week but have not heard from Father or you for a long time. I intended to have written to you last Sunday but was prevented by my numerous duties. Well, to tell you the whole story, last Thursday, Mrs Smythe was surprised at the unexpected appearance of Mrs George Smythe, and her daughter Julia, a girl about my age, both of them rich, fashionable, & dashy. They had a little boy of about six years of age with them. It never rains but it pours you know, and so of course the next train brought two nieces of Mrs Smythe's, Dell Harris, a young lady about twentyone and her half-sister, a little girl of about eleven years of age. The house was as full as it could be comfortably before, but by a little managing the five were accommodated with sleeping room.

I must proceed with my story in a systematic style, so I will go on to state that on Thursday evening we had a little party of young folks who had been previously invited, among them were Frank McMillen Mary Leamon and Mr Phillips. We enjoyed the evening very much. As Miss Julia & her Mother intended leaving on Saturday, Dell invited her cousins Brainerd and Archer to spend the evening here. They came bringing some of the other young folks with them so we had another party, Sheldon and I entertaining them a part of the time with music. On Saturday the Hack that was engaged did not come for the passengers & they were obliged to remain over Sunday. Now comes the "fun" Annie, the hired girl, was taken very sick, and unable to do anything. Myra, dont know how to do anything and is lazy besides. Dell, knows how but had no energy to take hold and assist her aunt, so what did Nelia do but get up early Sunday morning and get breakfast all alone while Mrs Smythe washed and dressed the children, and I have helped her all the time since, making bread today getting the meals and washing the dishes. I tell you, Mother I am not ashamed that I am as much at home in the kitchen as at the piano. Mrs Smythe said today "I

Nelia,

don't know what I should have done without you, you make the best kind of a step daughter." Her baby is sick now too. We think it will prove to be the Scarlet fever as he and all of us have been exposed to it. I think it is real nice to be in the kitchen once again. It seems like home. So you see my time has been fully occupied and is likely to be for a few days to come. I suppose we will spend a very quiet Thanksgiving. Mary will have no school after Wednesday this week and we will have a nice time together. I intend to make my bonnet this week and think I can do it with very little expense. I have altered my cloth dress only three times & now there is a wrinkle on one shoulder which however I think I can remedy by <u>another trial</u>. I am getting along very well with my music I think, though sometimes I get a little discouraged and then I am homesick. Though I cannot yet make much of a show of what I have learned I can see that I have acquired a great deal more practical knowledge than I ever had before of music. Shirner is very particular indeed and it is hard for me to learn that I must play a piece as it is written, not as it sounds the best.

Wednesday Morning.

I am glad to say that Eddy is quite smart today and I hope he will not be any worse, than he is now. Annie is no better and I got breakfast again and washed the dishes. Bishop McShane preached here last Sunday confirming fourteen at St Paul's in the morning & six at Trinity Church in the afternoon. Etta Page was one of the latter.

Mrs Botsford called here last Thursday to tell me that she expects Hattie to come from home today to make her a visit and stay until Monday, & they are coming for me to spend one night with them, and she will stay with me next Sunday so as to take the cars early in the morning. I am anticipating a very pleasant visit from her. David Abbott spent Saturday afternoon with us bringing with him another blind boy, Eugene Bigelow. Mary and I entertained them as well as we could with music & reading and went with them to Town Street, which leads directly to the Asylum, or at least so nearly that they have no difficulty in finding it. I must close my letter now, with much love to all from

Your daughter
Nelia.

Nelia.

My Dear Father.

I had intended to write to you earlier in the week, in reply to the kind letter received in the package; but several things have happened to prevent, and now at last, on Friday evening, I have determined to cancel that debt. I wish I was owing a few letters to that Brotherinlaw of mine wouldn't I pay him with interest? Well, I'll see if I can tell you all that I have been doing this week. You know I spoke of anticipating pleasure from Hattie Botsford's visit. Her Mother intended to have Mary, Myra & me spend last Friday with them at the camp. But the ambulance failed to call for us, and we were all disappointed, I saw nothing of them until Monday, when Hattie came for me to go out to the Asylums with them. We rode out to the Blind Asylum & at an urgent invitation from Miss Brown, the Matron, who is a lovely woman, Hattie & I remained to dinner while Mrs Botsford went back home. I saw a great many things there that I had not before! and we had the opportunity of hearing several classes recite and the choirs sing, and after dinner Miss Brown sent for David Abbott & Mr Lindsay and we enjoyed a very pleasant chat with them. David is very well and seems quite contented & happy. After leaving there we went to the Lunatic Asylum for the purpose of <u>showing</u> <u>Hattie</u> the place rather than a wish to see the inmates again <u>myself</u>. And though I did not witness any of them "dancing on their heads," yet a new inmate pleased me considerable. The worst cases are kept in small rooms, that open into a large hall, and are allowed free access to the whole hall, the grated door of which is kept locked, as we went to the door a great number of the women came forward wanting to shake hands with us. I shook hands with them all through the bars, and could hardly keep my face straight at the medley of sounds, from Dutch & Irish and the preaching of the new inmate who was evidently crazy on religion, and the horrid laughter & grimaces of others. We then went to the State House and Sheldon went up into the Dome with us, after that you may imagine we were a little tired, but in the morning we accepted Brainerd Howe's offer of going over to the Penitentiary with us. As he has been there often on account of Mr Hayden's employing three hundred of the prisoners to work for him. We were satisfied that he would show us all that was to be seen, and we were very much pleased with what we saw. There were about 700 prisoners, and it was a queer sight to see them all in their striped clothes march to dinner in companies. We went into the

Nelia,

dining hall and there they all sat in rows, eating from tin plates, and drinking from tin cups, and "mum" was the word. The guide showed us the knives which he said were all that Morgan and his men had to dig their way out with. You know they sometimes "lock the barn door after the horse is stolen" and consequently we were not even allowed to see where Morgan and his men had been confined. We passed through all the workshops and I saw a great many things which were new and instructive that I cannot write for want of time & room. We then went to the depot with Hattie & saw her safely started for home. I took great satisfaction in being able to make Hattie's visit a pleasant one as I think I did, and was also pleased and amused myself. Tomorrow night we are all going to hear "Gottschalk," & I think that will end this weeks dissipation. I have felt very well all this week, but last week I <u>was</u> just <u>as homesick as I could be</u>. It made me miserable & disagreeable I know & I have concluded not to feel so anymore until <u>next</u> <u>time</u>. Do you remember joking me about using "molasses" just before I left home? I have all I want here, and they say it is so like Emma, to want molasses that it seems natural to them. I beg your pardon I should have said "syrup."

I inquired the other day at a drug store for some of "Weaver's Salt Rheum syrup" and they had it in bottles holding about three pints for a dollar, and in no smaller quantities, so I did not take it. My fingers are pretty rough and sore now but I am hoping they will sometime be better. The drawings you sent in the Blades were received, though I did not discover one of them for several days. We had a great deal of fun here over them. I received a letter from Mother Tuesday, which I will answer in due course of time. The family are all well and there seem to be no symptoms of Scarlet Fever now. We hope there will be none of it too. Well I will lay this by for tonight & see if there is anything more in the morning which I wish to say. I hope you will all keep in good health. Tell Delia to "hold the reins" carefully until I come home and then I will relieve her. Good night, I hope you will rest well and not wake up with a headache in the morning.

Saturday morning

I hope you are well. I am and in good spirits. There is nothing of importance to say and I will close so as to send this letter by Mr Smythe. I dreamed last night that I was at home. Write soon and accept much love from your daughter

Nelia

Nelia,

Columbus Dec 8th 1863

My Dear Mother
      I received a letter from you last week, in which you said you almost looked for us home Thanksgiving day. When I read it, it almost made me want to go home, but I knew that was impossible for the day was already passed. I expect to be quite lonely Christmas, for Mary is going home in the afternoon, and Mrs Smythe is going to Oxford to visit Emma, and has told me that if I will stay here with Myra until she returns, and take the charge of things, that she will not consider me a boarder that week. As it will be an accommodation to her and no very great detriment to me, I have agreed to do so, though when she returns from Oxford perhaps we will both go together to Granville. I "whistled before I was out of the woods," for now Annie's Aunt is very sick and she has left for a time to take care of her, so the work devolves again upon Mrs Smythe. I help her occasionally about getting meals and washing dishes, and as she is tired tonight, I think I will arise early and mix the bread for her in the morning. I received a letter from Luther this morning also some papers. I was much obliged to him for remembering to send me the "Sermon" but I had read it only yesterday. I forgot to mention before that I am supplied with the "Independent" every week to read, but no matter "Howe." I will send this one to Aunt Clarinda in the morning as Sheldon has not time to read it.

      Last Saturday all the Photographers in town took pictures for the benefit of the Aid Society and I was strongly tempted to go and have mine taken, but thought I would not this time. Myra went and I will enclose one of her pictures to you, to be returned to me sometime when convenient. We think it a perfect likeness. She is considerable younger than Delia. I like her very much. She says I have talked so much about my sister that she has a great curiosity to see her. You know when I heard that Mr S. was a bookkeeper I thought of course he was a young man. But it is not so. From several things that I have heard this is about the amount of their story. Mrs S had considerable property in her

Nelia,

own right before her marriage, and her husband was doing a good business. As soon as they were married he used all her money & his own in some speculation and in ten days they were not worth a cent, and now for fifteen years he has kept books for Mr Hayden. His present salary is $1500. and he has bought this house which of course had to be done in her name as he cannot hold any property himself, and he has his life insured for $3000. so they are living very comfortably, though not one woman in a thousand could do all that Mrs Smythe has done. Mr George Smythe of Newark is very different from his brother, being a good looking jolly gentleman, but perfectly irreligious. Why when he is here he will stand in one corner of the room and read the "Ohio Statesman" <u>during</u> <u>prayer time</u>. Does Delia find out yet who the young folks come to see at our house? I hope she has enough friends to keep her from longing for the two who have left her. Just let her come down here & spend Christmas with me, wouldn't we talk <u>all</u> <u>day</u> though? We expected Mrs Lindsay & David Abbott to spend last Thursday evening with us. But we received a "blind" letter saying that they would come next Thursday instead so we are looking for them and anticipating a very pleasant time.

I received a letter from Delia Saturday which was very welcome. I do not care for the Beaver, as my white hat looks very well trimmed as I have it now, am just as much obliged however. I am sorry Lottie was disappointed about that house it would have been so pleasant for us all. Sheldon said he was going to write home for the timing key to the piano, if he does, will it be very much trouble for you to send the book "January & June?" I must close as I will have no eyes left to see daylight tomorrow morning so good night. Write soon and often and do not forget to direct some of your letters to Sheldon he thinks the folks have forgotten him since I came.

Much love to all from
Nelia

Nelia,

Columbus Dec. 13th 1863

My Dear, beloved, adorable Sister,

I received a letter from you about a week ago which deserved a more prompt reply, but as I was owing Mother one, concluded to answer that first. I have made this discovery with regard to the mails, although they do not leave until ten o'clock in the morning yet they are closed the evening before. I presume because there is only one man in this office at present to attend to everything. If I get my letters in, at evening, they go in the morning, but if they are left until morning they lie over one day. So although Mary is reading aloud to Sheldon who is reclining nearly asleep on our bed, I must try to finish this to send by him when he leaves. We have had quite a "spell of weather" during the past week, every day has been clear & warm, until Friday night when a warm rain set in which has continued until now with no prospect of clearing off.

Well Delia, what do you think I have done? went to the Opera last Thursday evening. I had some doubt about its being right for me to do so, and asked Mrs Smythe's advice. She said that if her daughter was away from home and wished to attend once to satisfy her curiosity she should make no objections in the world. But she would not consent to her making a practise of going. Sheldon gave his consent readily and invited Mary to go, but she did not care to. I was quite interested with the performances & indeed fascinated, and am convinced that 'twould never do for me to cultivate a desire for attending such a place, & I think that if I do as Mrs Smythe would have her daughters do I shall not commit many errors in such things. Miss Caroline Richings was the chief performer, a very fine singer and good actress.

This week there is to be a grand Bazaar for the Soldiers' Aid which I think will be a success from the extensive preparations that are being

Nelia,

made, it will last from Tuesday until Saturday. I can tell you more about it after it is over with.

Sheldon received a letter from Lina last week. I shall write to her tonight or tomorrow.

I do not sing in the choir all the time They invited me to go up there once to take the place of the Alto Singer who was absent. I have not of course intruded myself since. I attended Sunday School & church this morning. The teacher of our class was absent and I was the only member there. So Mr Fisher the Superintendent asked me to take a class of little girls whose teacher was also absent, remarking at the time that I seemed to be the most useful member of the school as he always comes to me if any of the teachers are absent. I enjoy the Sunday School very much but often wish I was back in our own once more. I am occasionally homesick now but not so often as I have been heretofore. If there is any probability of my having a class in music upon my return I would like to know it, for I mean that my brothers shall not spend another dollar of money on me after March unless some unforeseen event deprives me of the power of supporting myself. I <u>will</u> <u>do</u> <u>something</u> if it is only to teach a district school. If there are music teachers enough in Milan perhaps I can do better to go away from home again. I think I will have no difficulty now in teaching music for I have become pretty well initiated into the system and principles of teaching it and am really anxious to get to work. Well, I must close now with much love to all from your sister

Nelia

Sheldon stayed to tea & then went to Church from here so my letter must <u>lie over</u> until tomorrow. The enclosed is a specimen which amused me exceedingly

Carlos

Toledo O Dec 18th 1863

Dear Sister Delia

I received a letter from you a day or two since and was glad to hear from you. Hope you have not got the Scarlet fever yet nor Small pox, nor any thing that you dont want, but trust you have everything that you do want and more too. My first vaccination wouldnt "take" so we tried it again and am inclined to think I will not take it at all, doctor claims that the old vaccination is still good, hope it is. Before we were vaccinated I told Aunt that if I was attacked with the Small Pox I should go immediately to the "Pest House" and didnt want any of my acquaintances to come and see me. "Well" Aunt said I "Might be assured of one thing <u>My Mother</u> would come and see me whether I wanted her to or not." I do hope to escape it, for I dont want to <u>have a muss</u> with Mother — I think there are only a few cases in the city but whenever a person is taken sick it is called the Small Pox.

We have had <u>awful</u> weather lately — all kinds — today we have had a cold hard snow storm — if the weather continues cold as today we will soon have skating.

It is getting towards time for closing of the mail consequently time for closing of this letter. I have been talking some of going to Detroit for two or three days about the Holidays — perhaps with Aunt, have been urged to do so. Would like to go to Milan to see you <u>folks at home</u> but can of course do that sometime before Spring — dont know yet whether I shall go to Detroit or not — I enclose $5—

Your Brother
Carlos

Relative

Big Valley [Canada] December 20th 1863

Dear Melinda

We received a letter from you some time ago containing pictures of yourself and other friends and were much pleased to get them as well as the papers you are so kind as to send us. The children are delighted with their little papers. You wished to know about churches and schools in this part of the world. I have had but one opportunity to attend Episcopal services since I left home, that was five years ago when Bishop Kiss visited Jackson. We had the children christened. As for Sunday schools the poor children hardly know what they are, although Fanny used to go regularly (when we lived in Jackson,) to the Methodist Sunday school. We are now living three miles from the nearest school house and as our children cannot go far, we teach them at home and Fanny who is nine years of age is quite forward she is studying Geography Arithmetic, reading spelling and writing. Maria who will be seven the 26th of this month can read and spell very well, and Molly, aged two years and a half studys mischief. You see by this how many boys and girls we have. We are living in a beautiful country and what is better very healthy. I wish you could look in upon us in the spring, then the hills around are covered with wild flowers. It would do Myra good to see them, she would have a grand time botanising. I hope she wouldnt break her back again though. I often think of your beautiful garden and wish I had a few seeds from it. I wish you would send me a few in a letter and I will try and save some wild flower seeds for you.
We have quite a nice little orchard and vineyard, if you will visit us next fall we will give you some grapes, peaches and apples, to eat, how I wish you could come and see us. It makes me feel old when I think of your daughters, (who we knew as little girls) now young ladies and one a married woman with two children. Sheldon and Carlos two old bachelers. Oh dear how time flies. We received a letter from ma lately she sent pictures of Hatty John and their children. John has not changed much but I would not have recognised Hatty. I feel very anxious about Ma as she wrote that her health was very poor. Tell Cornelia that Fanny has a letter which she, C. sent her five years ago, she says she is going to write to her soon. The last time I wrote to Ma, Fanny wrote a little letter also, which her Grandma answered. I soon after wrote to your Mother and Myra, and Fanny enclosed a letter to her Grandma Allen, perhaps they were not received as we have heard nothing from them. Maria and her family were well when we last heard from them two weeks ago, we have not seen them since we moved here, but hope to next season. Maria has four children three boys and one girl. When I commenced writing I thought I would make out a long if not a very interesting letter, but I will be obliged to close now with love to all my friends. Jane Norton among the number.
Yours affectionately
Mary Allen

*The Indian Booth pleased Sheldon the most and he bought for
Mary a very handsome box of Indian work, and for her sister
Hattie... a little canoe.*

Nelia,

Columbus Dec 21st /63

My Dear, Dear, Father,

I awoke this morning hugging & kissing you, and almost cried when I found 'twas all a dream. I was intending to write to you yesterday. But Sheldon was here reading to us all the afternoon and after Church in the evening I was so sleepy and tired that I was only too glad to rest, for you must know that we have all been dissipating at the "gay Bazaar" this last week. It opened Tuesday and the lunch hours were from ten till four. Then they had a few tableaux every evening. Wednesday evening Sheldon, Brainerd, & Ed Herd, (who is a younger brother of Mary's) and Mary Whiting, Myra & myself, all went together. I could not begin to give an adequate description of what I saw. There were booths fitted up to represent the different nations. The Indian Booth pleased Sheldon the most and he bought for Mary a very handsome box of Indian work, and for her sister Hattie (to be sent to her) a little canoe. I knew two of the young ladies who were dressed in costume, Miss Broderick & Ella White, and they certainly looked beautiful. Another was the Yankee Booth, with two signs hung out, one: "Miss Slimmens Milliner," and of all the old fashioned bonnets, I never saw the beat: the other sign was: "Boarders, gentlemen <u>taken</u> <u>in</u> and <u>done</u> <u>for</u>." The booth was festooned with <u>dried</u> <u>apples</u>, and there was for sale from nutmegs & mousetraps, to the finest embroideries, and laces. I cannot begin to tell what the others contained. But there was a post office & an Adams Express, & a fishing pond, similar to a grab-bag. And what pleased me the most was a stand of most beautiful boquets one of which I brought away with me. One objection that a great many raised to the proceedings was, that everything of any value was <u>Raffled</u> for. A $500 piano was sold in shares of $5. each and fell to a gentleman in the city. An elegant moire antique dress pattern valued at $100 was drawn by an old bachelor. The "Journal" wonders <u>what</u> <u>he</u> <u>will</u> <u>do</u> <u>with</u> <u>it</u>. Thursday night Mr. Smythe took his family including Mary & myself, and Saturday night I was invited again to go with Mary,

Nelia,

Ed Rob & Alice Herd & their cousin Will Kidd. So I have not failed help patronize the institution. But the best part of all happened Saturday morning when, each township in Franklin County contributed wood for the soldier's families. The township that furnished the greatest number of loads received a premium. It would have done you good, (it made <u>Me</u> cry) to see the streets literally blockaded with teams hauling wood. The street cars were obliged to stop running. I believe it was estimated that there was in all about four hundred cords of wood, and as it is worth four dollars a cord here now, it was quite an acceptable present. Those who brought the wood received their dinner free at the Bazaar.

Oh! Dear I shall think of you often on Christmas day and no doubt shall wish many times that I was there with you. Mrs. Smythe and her sister Mrs. Howe are going to Oxford on Friday noon. But I shall have one consolation Mary will stay here until New Years but I am afraid she will not come back next term. I do not think her health is sufficiently good nor is she naturally strong enough for a school teacher. I do love her with all my heart, and next to her I love Mary Herd, they are two of the best girls that ever lived I am sure, and I wish a great many times a day that I was only half as good, but the more I try the worse I find I am. I wonder if it isn't natural for some folks to be good. Mary Herd has seen enough trouble to <u>refine</u> her. She is now supporting herself though her father is immensely rich but very "close" & peculiar. Still I like him, and her stepmother is a very good woman. Mary has an invalid sister Lottie, older than herself who is now at the watercure about three miles from here.

Well, I suppose this is not interesting to you but I like to have you know all about all my friends, here. I was talking with Mary (Herd) yesterday & she almost made up her mind to go to Milan with me and attend the Normal one term. I must close now with much love to all from

Nelia

Delia's letter was received

Carlos

Toledo Dec 23rd 63

Dear Father

Your letter with the "fascinating" remarks was recd and laughed at. We tried the vaccination again but our arms wont "work" as Mothers does — guess the Small Pox will not be able to beat the vaccine matter in that respect — Aunts servant girl is sick with Neuralgia but after considerable urging I have concluded to go without her and will probably go tomorrow evening ("Christmas Eve") to remain till the forepart of next week. It is very dull and quiet on the docks now. I send by this mail a Harpers Magazine and "Weekly" to Delia and the January No of the "Atlantic Monthly" as a Christmas present to Mother. I intend to send it to her monthly, during the coming year. I enclose $7— the "2" is for Delia to buy candy or something else for Christmas with. Hoping you all may have as merry a Christmas as I expect to have I will proceed to finish up my evening work ——

Carlos

Lina

Sunday Evening
Detroit Dec. 27th 1863

Dear Father & Mother

We have no services at St. John's to night. It is too cold and dark to go to St. Paul's. Carlos is about entering the land of dreams here on the sofa, so I seat myself to write. We were delighted at seeing Carlos last Thursday night. All are trying to persuade him to remain over New Years, but thinks he must return to Toledo Wednesday morning. He received Fathers note with the letter from Nelia enclosed yesterday.

Well, I suppose you want to know how we all spent Christmas. The children were up, of course, before daylight, and down stairs to find their presents, and had a merry time over them. While we older ones looked on with long faces, thinking of the times when Santa Claus never forgot us, and regretting that we were now too old to "hang up our stockings."

Seating ourselves at the breakfast table Carlos raised his plate and was astonished at the appearance of a "dancing Jack" beneath. It was a comical little effect and caused a good deal of fun. I did not expect him here until New Years or should have had something ready for him: Next was my turn to be surprised, for under my plate was a Season ticket to the Skating park. Also had a present of a nice handkerchief. Hattie was watching us eagerly, and for some time did not see that she had a very pretty needle cushion. Cousin Phin's family including Alfy were here to dinner. Hattie and Clarinda made their Mother a present of a few Victorines to match her muff. I had a needle book commenced for her, but had to present it without finishing, not having time. Uncle Hyde's family were at Uncle George's to dinner. So Aunt Fanny had her <u>turkey</u> yesterday, and invited Carlos and I there. I arose up to go to Sunday School in the afternoon. Carlos staid there until this evening. Uncle Hyde has shown him a great deal of attention.Tomorrow Clarinda is to have her Christmas dinner. We are all going there. The church celebration has not yet taken place. The infant school are to receive their presents tomorrow afternoon. The older ones on Tuesday evening. They never have their trees on Christmas eve, as it interferes with family celebrations. It will be a beautiful sight Tuesday. I wish you could all witness it. I received Delia's letter and will try to answer soon. Don't know whether I shall reply <u>this</u> <u>year</u> or <u>next</u>. John has not been at home for some time. He may possibly be here to spend New Years. Hattie expects Tom Ballard tomorrow, to stay a week or so. We are not alone all the time. Still we do not feel at all timid when there is no man in the house. For this part of the city is very quiet, this street in particular. Expect to see some Milan faces — soon — Will Stevens — and Ralph Lockwood. It will be <u>q</u>uite a <u>treat</u>. I am tired of meeting strange faces — still am making some very pleasant acquaintances. Let me correct a mistake about Cousin Phin's salary. Instead of $1500. he receives but $800 a year. Perhaps Mother will think better of him when she knows he has not <u>very</u> much to do with. Would like to read Nelia's <u>Soldier</u> <u>letter</u> if she returns it. The enclosed picture is for Lottie. Mrs Boylan will send her husbands when they <u>can</u> <u>find</u> <u>it</u>. Have not found my way to an Aid society yet. Shall go some day this week with Aunt Fanny. She takes sewing home to do. All unite in sending love to both familys Too late to wish a "Merry Christmas" I close by wishing all a "Happy New Year."

Your daughter
Lina

Nelia,

Columbus Dec. 28th 1863

Dear Mother.

      I am rather tired this morning but will write you a few lines in reply to the letter that Delia wrote for you. Mrs Smythe, you know, has gone to Oxford leaving Myra & myself here to take charge of things in general. Though Annie does all the kitchen work on her own responsibility. This morning being wash-day we had the kitchen work to do and the chamber work beside, and Myra was taken sick right after breakfast, so I have had it all to do. But it has not hurt me any. I feel better for it. I received a long letter from Father yesterday morning enclosing one from Fort Leavenworth. No one could have been more surprised than I was, for I had actually forgotten all about that pair of socks. 'Twas a good letter wasn't it? and I think deserves an answer. I will do as Father told me to about answering it. But I wish to know if it will not be as well, if I send him an exact copy of my letter for his "perusal & edification" & mail one from here. For if in the course of my writing I want to speak of the soldiers I see here it would be rather out of character to have the letter mailed from Milan. However, he knows best and I shall wait for permission. I will send this letter home but would like to have it returned again immediately for I wish to keep it. Sheldon thinks it is "one of the romantic incidents of the war" & says he can find out something about the <u>young</u> or <u>old</u> <u>man</u> who wrote that. <u>I</u> think he showed good judgment in saying <u>we</u>, and did not seem to be of the class of young men who wish to "exchange photographs." I am glad you succeeded so admirably with your Christmas tree. I wish you could have seen ours. It was trimmed entirely by <u>myself</u>. I would not admit any one else into the room, and after trimming it very beautifully with all the presents that had been purchased I was perfectly satisfied with the result. I did not want anything on it for myself & was perfectly satisfied to find that only one article bore my name and that was a neat little shawl pin from Arthur. Well, we went to church in the evening leaving Sheldon & Mame to guard the tree. When we returned the family were all assembled except the two youngest, and Mr Smythe cut off the presents. To my surprise the first one was handed to me & on opening a box I found a very handsome money bag, then in due time I received a little steel breastpin. A collar & cravat, and a handsome scarf in all amounting to over six dollars these had been hung on after I had gone to Church. They were all from Mrs Smythes family. Mary & I agreed not to give each other anything, and I made Sheldon promise not to give me any extra present. He gave Mame a handsome portfolio and she gave him a silver fruit knife. Altogether we had a happy time that evening. Mary is going home tomorrow. Mrs Smythe and I will probably go the next day & Sheldon will come out the day after to spend New Years with us and all return together on Saturday.

Monday evening.
I have concluded for several reasons not to go to Granville this week. I must now bring my letter to a close and go about something else. Much love to all
Write soon to   Nelia

Bishop Bedell preached in Trinity Church Christmas morning, in St. Paul's Sunday morning & Trinity in the evening.

1864

On March 9, Grant is appointed general-in-chief to command in the field. He fails in his objective to destroy Lee's army.

In July, General Jubal A. Early controls the Shenandoah; the valley's agricultural resources are of great value to Lee's army in northern Virginia.

Sherman, with roughly 100,000 troops, captures Atlanta on September 2, but allows the Confederate army to escape.

From September 19 to October 19, in the Third Battle of Winchester, General Philip H. Sheridan drives Early out of the Shenandoah, completely devastating the valley and the grain supply for Richmond.

President Lincoln is re-elected over his opponent, General McClellan.

On November 15, Sherman begins his celebrated "March to the Sea" from Atlanta to Savannah, with some 60,000 troops. Savannah is evacuated on December 21.

Detroit experiences unprecedented freezing conditions.

Lina remains in Detroit, teaching Sunday School and visiting among the numerous relatives. Later, she moves to Columbus, assisting Sheldon as a copyist of muster-out rolls and cavalry information, and attends many of the city's military and patriotic events.

Sheldon and Mary Whiting are wed in October.

Carlos is employed in the shipping business, by a Mr. Strong.

Delia is invited to Columbus to work as a copyist in the Adjutant General's office.

Nelia has a brief stay in Winchester, Ohio, where she gives music lessons. A sudden onslaught of illness causes her return to Milan where she instructs a small group of piano students.

Lottie's husband, Mr. Carter, attempts to find work in Toledo.

Carlos

Toledo New Year 1864

Dear Father

I dont know that I ever dreaded "out door air" so much as today. Suppose you are getting the same kind of weather. Yesterday and until late last night it was raining almost constantly, but today everything is frozen stiff as a poker and Ugh! Whew! how the keen wind cuts through all wearing apparel. I recvd your letter enclosing one of Nelia's whilst in Detroit. I had a very pleasant visit there and returned Wednesday — found Lina looking in excellent health. Will not attempt a description of the visit now, have been in the office most of the day today catching up lost time — it is tea time and I will stop

Wishing all of you a "Happy New Year" —

Carlos

The Coltons do not keep "open house" today ——— I presented Annie a photograph album — Enclosed find $5.

Relative

My Dear Sister.

"A Happy New Year" to each of you in the dear old Home. The year opens cold and blustering, may its close be more pleasant. And Oh if the will of God could be wrought out and this War brought to a close, during this year, how many hearts would be filled with thankfulness.

Alice and Lucy have great causes for thankfulness that their Husbands have been restored to them in safety, this year that has just closed. Do you know any thing of Addie, whether she went to Vicksburg. I have heard nothing of her since I was in Elmore. I have deferred acknowledging the reception of Nellie's stockings, for which I am very much obliged, that I might write you something about our new brother, but they have not yet returned. The Father is very sick and they have remained there on his account and now think they will visit Maggie as she is quite urgent they should — When Father left he expected to be Home Christmas. Alice had her Friends here to dinner. We trimmed the Parlor & Alice's room with Evergreens, and she made some wreaths of Autumn leaves, which she varnished. I regretted that I did not think to bring the leaves you had pressed for me. William went to Franklin with Steve, and engaged in a Flour Mill and Produce business, and returned here Christmas Eve to spend the Holidays. He will stay with us until Monday, he is so cheerful it is quite pleasant to have him here. Alice feels that it is a great trial to be separated from him again so soon, but as he did not go into the Army to make money, it is necessary to do something for that purpose now, and he cannot take his family there at present.

Kate, the girl Alice has had nearly four years, leaves to day to be married. She has brought an old maid here in her place. Alice feels very badly to change girls now, just as our new Mother is coming. I went to Mrs Kings Wednesday and staid until the next morning — had a very good visit. She is quite feeble, is better than it was last week. Mary had just written to Nelia. Mary seems much pleased that Nelia has such a fine opportunity for improvement. I have not heard from Detroit except through yours & Aunts letters. Nellie is well and often asks for Delia, Carrie Bell & Libbie. Tell the children Nellie had a Boy doll dressed in Soldiers clothes Christmas, from her cousin Jennie, and a blue dress from her Aunt Julia. I have no news from Henry to write. I cannot but hope this new year may dawn brighter for me than the last, but I try very hard to say with truthfulness, "Thy will be done" —

I wrote urging Henry to spend Christmas with us, and was sorely disappointed that he did not come. Perhaps if I had not the trial of living as I have done since my marriage, I should have a greater one in some form. Give my love to the Boys and Girls when you write them, and accept a large share for "our Pa" Delia, Lottie and yourself — from

Myra

Lina

Detroit Jan. 5th 1864

Dear Delia.

Are you all <u>frozen up</u> in Ohio? or why dont I hear from any of you. I will not begin to scold for there may be letters for me in the Office tonight. Shall go tomorrow and get them, that is, if I remember to carry an order. I cannot get my letters from John's box without presenting a ticket with his name signed.

Believe I have written how we spent Christmas. Oh, if you could have seen how we spent New Years. Never have I known such a bitter cold day although sitting by a roaring fire — [the remainder of this sentence illegible due to fading] There was a gentleman that came up here that day of an errand and froze both his ears on the way. Strange reports have reached us about people being frozen to death in the city. Can hardly credit them. Still they may be true. One report came direct to us from Dr Kermott. He said the stage driver from Lansing to Detroit was frozen while coming here last Friday. The horses came direct to the hotel that they were in the habit of stopping at, with a dead driver — men had to cut the reins from his hands. Did you receive calls? That reminds me of something, Aunt Fanny was anxious for me to come there and help her keep open house. I promised to do so and intended to go there Thursday but wind and weather did not permit, neither could I go next morning on account of the cold. After much hesitation concluded to remain at home. Next I heard of Mrs Hyde, she had gone to Trenton to avoid receiving calls. Now, just imagine how agreeable it would have been for me, had I got down there and been obliged to help Uncle Hyde entertain his democratic friends.

Should style any man a goose that would venture to make calls on such a day as that was. <u>Del.</u> has been here since and left his card for me. I was not at home. Should like to show it to you. It is new style entirely, never anything of the kind having been seen, this side of the <u>city</u> of <u>New York</u>. Enough about New Years and weather.

... the stage driver from Lansing to Detroit was frozen while coming here last Friday. The horses came direct to the hotel that they were in the habit of stopping at, with a dead driver...

Lina

I have a class in Sunday School of eight little girls about the age of those in Mothers class. I think I shall like them very much. There will be another social gathering Friday night, that we all expect to attend. Tell Mother that I have sold my nubia, and am going tomorrow to get me a merino scarf. The nubia's are not worn at all here. Hattie got me some cherry velvet, for my bonnet. I had a wide band of it put across the outside with black lace on each edge, a <u>triangle</u> trimmed the same on the cape. Had also two plumes donated, one cherry and one black. Wear them on my hat through the week and on the <u>bonnet</u> to go to church. It is no disgrace to be poor, but some times it is <u>very</u> inconvenient. Have taken the wide velvet off from my merino dress. Shall bind it with some narrower and put on large white bone buttons. My cloak is the right material and made just right. Aunt Lucinda has a new one of broad cloth cut the same pattern. Ben has resigned. He reached home last Friday. Do not know what he intends to do now. I have received papers from Father. Suppose the Independent is intended for Aunt. John is at home. He is fast asleep on the sofa, as you might have known, for he could not stop talking long enough for me to get a letter written if he was awake. Thinks he will stay at home until some time next week.

How is Henry. I received his regard and send mine in return. Such teeth I have not seen nor eyes to match his own, in the whole city of Detroit.

Ruckers Shoe store

Have just been to the office and got a letter from Mother. Was glad to hear from home.

Saw Betsy in Toledo. She seemed quite delighted to meet me. Has a very pretty little girl. Will try and do something for the fair. Mrs Shepherd is coming tomorrow night, folks are all well.

Am in great haste for I want to mail this now.

Will write again soon.

Lina

Nelia,

Columbus Jan 9th/.64

Dear Father.

I commenced to give Sheldon the usual number of "lovetaps" in commemoration of his birthday, this noon. But he laughingly prevented me, saying, it would take too long a time, as he is twenty nine years old. He showed me your letter which he received today and I wish to explain to you a little about some things! First, I do not like Frank McMillen any better than you do and am not thrown in her company but very little, except at meal times. I have not been to her room to visit with her at all, indeed Mary and I have spent every evening together since she came here. Sheldon is of course at liberty to choose his own associates, but if I was left to my own discretion, I should not choose her company. I am glad you spoke of it however for I shall be more careful to avoid being thrown in contact with her, in the future. Do you understand that Mary has come back to teach this term? I should judge you did not by what Mary Abbott told me. When Miss Whiting talked of going away Frank was very anxious to come here & take her place. But Mrs Smythe told Mary that "she should not consent to it, for she wished Myra & Nelia to be thrown in company with some one who had a little more refinement than she should judge Miss McMillen had." and she only took Frank in for a few days till she could find another boarding place, & she leaves Monday. Mrs S. was very glad, and so were we all, when Mary concluded to return, to take an easier school this term.

And another thing is, that my knee does not trouble me this winter only in sudden changes of weather and I do not now wear my India rubber cap, on it. I do not think I need it but should probably continue wearing it, but that the large one is worn out & the small one is so tight as to be painful. Do not be troubled

251

Nelia,

my dear Father on my account for I think I am doing very well without troubling Mother to watch over me. I have not taken any cold hardly this winter, and you know how I suffered last year from imprudence. I am very much obliged to Mother for the stockings but would have been better pleased had they been dark ones. ("Ain't my pride coming down a little?") I bought me a pair of dark fleecy lined ones in the Fall and so have saved my white ones some, but this coal dust is beyond description for intruding itself where it is not wanted. Mrs Smythe says, if I wish to, she will buy one pair of these and I can get some dark ones, what do you think? what did you pay for them? (this is to Mother of course) We awoke this morning to find it very cold indeed. I wish we had a thermometer here. I think the cold must be more intense in Milan than it is here I went out to the Blind Asylum Thursday to see Mary & Maria. They were just getting ready to come & call on me, so we came back here and went to the State House, then they returned to the Asylum, intending to leave for College Hill next morning.

I must close now and go to practising so you will please excuse me from writing more. I hope dear Father I shall not give you cause to be anxious about me. I try very hard to do what I think would please you, but I fail sometimes of course as I always did, for I think it is hard to tell always what will please you most, you are so quiet.

But I think when I find I have offended you, you seldom find the offence repeated at least intentionally.

Give my love to Mother & Delia with many thanks for their kind remembrances of Christmas.

Write soon to your
Affectionate daughter
Nelia.

Nelia,

Columbus Jan 13th 1864

My Dear Mother.

Now that I have practised and <u>darned</u> <u>Sheldon's socks</u>, I feel somewhat like writing a letter this afternoon, and hope you will have no objections if it is addressed to you as I am owing you one. I imagine Father will not see much improvement in the hastily written note I sent to him last Saturday. But 'twas the best I could do in the short time allowed — and I was anxious he should receive a correct impression of some things which I fancy he misunderstood. Christmas when I did go skating, I only stayed a short time, had not been before nor did I intend to go again; <u>only</u> <u>wanted</u> <u>to</u> <u>experience</u> <u>once</u> <u>more</u> <u>the</u> <u>pleasure</u> <u>of</u> <u>having</u> <u>on</u> skates.

In Delia's letter which I was very happy to receive yesterday, she says: "Kitty Harry just asked Pa to let him come in." Now any little thing like that brings you all to my mind very vividly, and I can almost hear Harry's "<u>p-r-r-m-e-o-w</u>" — as he jumps from the window-sill to the seat & then to the door, where Pa stands rattling the latch to fool him. Then Pa goes to the stove and holding his hands over it yawns out — "<u>hi-ho-hum</u>" — or brings his boots to get them warm preparatory to splitting the kindlings & bringing in the wood. — Mother looks over her glasses and smiles, or laying down her papers folds her hands and wonders what Lina & Nelia are doing now, and Delia keeps on busily with her writing occasionally glancing at the clock to see if it is time to get supper. I have thought of Pa many times during these two weeks of cold weather, and almost wished I was there to build his fires for him. Mother can imagine me Sunday afternoons sitting in my room with Mary and Sheldon, the latter reading to us or telling war stories, though for the past two Sundays since Frank McMillen has been here he stayed away, and Mary and I went last Sunday afternoon to an anniversary at their Sunday School, which was very interesting. A missionary from India addressed the scholars — & that reminds me that the Rev. Dudley Smith is a brotherinlaw of Mr Grammar's, and has preached here. I liked him very well indeed, he preaches here again Sunday, and I shall take more pleasure in listening to him <u>because</u> <u>you</u> <u>heard him this week.</u>

Monday afternoon, Sheldon called for Frank Mitchell and me to go to the State House steps and hear the Inaugural address. We went and secured a good position for <u>seeing</u> everything. But could not <u>hear</u> a word, and after looking a while at the "maneuvers" of the Regiment that conducted the governors from Gov. Tod's house, and taking a good view of Brough in all his "massive<u>ness</u>", Frank and I came home preferring to read the papers next morning rather than stand there and <u>hear</u> <u>nothing.</u>

... I can almost hear Harry's "p-r-r-m-e-o-w" — as he jumps from the window-sill... Then Pa goes to the stove... — Mother looks over her glasses and smiles... and Delia keeps on busily with her writing...

Nelia,

Now Mother I want you & Father's advice about something and only hope you will agree with Mary & Myself. When I left home, Father said perhaps I could secure a school here — and as I have found it will be impossible to have a class in music here on account of the great number of music teachers now employed, I concluded to attend an examination which was held here a short time ago, and Mr Grammar (who was one of the examiners) told me yesterday that "I did great credit to myself." At any rate my name appeared in the Journal which signified that I could have one of the public school upon application. Indeed Mr Kingsley, the Superintendent told Sheldon that I could have had a situation this term if I had said the word. Now Mary & I have been talking it over & thought it would be very pleasant, to have me teach here, next term, which commences in March, and we will still board here & room together & probably teach in the same building. I am determined at least to do for myself after the first of March and think this would be a good beginning, better than attempting to do anything at home at present, for you know "a prophet is not without honor save in his own country." The wages would be probably $7.00 per week, and I could keep the piano (Mrs S. paying half the rent as she offers to do) and keep up my practising.

Then Mary & I will come home to spend the summer vacation. I have talked with Sheldon about it and after due consideration I think he has come to our opinion. — I dont propose this because I do not wish to see you all, for you know I should like nothing better. But I have another plan still, which is to have Mother come & visit us if I stay. I hope you will think favorably of this & write soon to let me know. I have not made many acquaintances here but all that I have become acquainted with, seem for some reason _not_ to <u>dislike</u> me. So I think for a time I would get along here at least until folks found out how ugly I am.
As I wish to give this to Mr Smythe to mail, at tea time, I shall be obliged to bring my letter to a close.
I will enclose a photograph of Sheldon's for Delia's album, and perhaps another time will send one of mine, back. I do not know that I shall have any more taken but Mary & Myra are not satisfied with these in exchange for theirs.

We are all well and Myra & Mary who are sitting here talking while I write wish to unite with me in sending much love to all my relatives in Milan. Write soon to your

Affectionate daughter
Nelia —

Sheldon Colton

Dear Brother:

Yours of the 3rd inst. is received, and I am glad to find that Lina is having such a good time in Detroit and hope she may spend a pleasant Winter there. Nelia is doing well, her health is good and she enjoys herself generally. She complained of having to let out all of her dresses a while ago, so I think she is not pining away at all.

You see that I still date my letters at the Adjutant General's office; and for some time to come. I expect to do the same thing; as the new Adj. Gen. tells me that he wants me to stay here with him. I like his appearance very much. It is useless to go on and tell about the inauguration, as you have already seen accounts of it in the papers. Nelia myself were among the spectators, and got a pretty good position for seeing, though not so favorable for hearing. The weather was rather pleasanter that day than it had been for a few days previous, and altogether, the show was a pretty good one.

Gen. Cowen, our new chief, was formerly Secretary of State, and now holds a place as Paymaster in the army, from which he has a furlough to take his place here. He is very pleasant and agreeable and I think I shall get along well with him. He has an idea that our work can be done in a less number of hours, and I think he will soon stop our night work. So you see I will not have to "change my base" at present. I like to stay here very well and the work is not very hard, but I do not learn anything about business, and when I leave here I shall have to commence at the beginning again, I expect. That is all the objection I have to staying here.

I suppose you know your own business best, but if I was offered a place in a bank, the same as you was, and had as much experience in that line of business, I think I should take it.

On my way up town last night, I stopped in at a Museum to see the original "What is it?" He is curious looking specimen, and if he goes your way it would pay to take a look at him. In the same show with him was a man, who is seven feet and eight inches high. I thought I had seen large men before, but I had not. He was a fine looking, well proportioned man as could be found among those of ordinary size.

Nelia has received the music which you sent her, and I presume she is correspondingly obliged and will return thanks for the same in due season.

Remember me to all friends of mine in Toledo, who care enough about me to inquire after me; and let me hear from you again soon.

Yours truly,

Sheldon Colton

H Calton

Milan Jany. 22nd 1864

Dee Pet Daughter,

The month of February is near at hand and will not be long in peeping away, — O' then 'twill be joyful if Dee comes marching home, as you mention in your letter of 15 is now probable, though we are glad to learn that you are not particularly anxious on the time and will stay longer should it be necessary We wish the chance for employment might continue and that Lina could return there when you leave. She is in the poorest kind of business now, visiting around for a living. At last advice from her she had just returned from Trenton to Detroit and seems to have lost the chance at Mitzdens, if there could have been any pleasure in retaining it, as Arthur and wife were there and she thinks "they will remain as long as they are invited."

Mr Hyde is worse again and as Lina says quite discouraged. I suppose there can be small chance of his recovery. Mrs Turner left for Toledo on Wednesday where she intends to make a short visit and then proceed from Detroit to Chicago. She is about Sheldons age and a good sensible old girl. She is the oldest of ———— mothers family and has devoted her early years to their support, has been teaching almost constantly for fourteen years, with only the usual vacations.

Her mother was my most intimate cousin whom I have not seen for about the space of thirty five years.

With regard to the weather, we had an unusually heavy fall of snow about two weeks ago, which has remained on the ground with very cold weather, making good sleighing but no skating, young people seemed pleased with the style of weather while older ones were not. I reminded Nelia sometimes of the anxiety expressed in some of her letters last winter to be at home so as to get up and make fires for me cold mornings.

H. Culton

She thinks "tis distance lends enchantment" in such cases.

Am glad to say we are having a thaw now and the snow is wasting away. Hope we have had the hardest of this present winter. Old people are more sensitive to cold and especially snowy weather than the young, but your Mother and I are making ourselves as comfortable as may be, looking forward to "the time of the singing of birds with hope.

We have been pleased to hear of the usually proper and profitable manner in which you employ the Sundays and church going privileges that you enjoy there, and of the seemingly favorable impression they have made upon your mind, we trust that any good seeds that might have been sown may remain and bear fruit in after life one hundred fold.

We hope that so long as it may seem proper for you to remain away from home, you may continue well and contented, and that when the time does finally come for you to return to us that you may be as glad to come as we shall be to have you.

Alice Blinn is still here. She has been with Mrs Carter mostly the past week as an option to Bruin — this evening Lottie is spending alone with the children for the first since Mr C. left. She seems anxious to try the experiment of living alone and declines offers of company, though perhaps she wouldnt object to having you or Lina with her if you were at home. On account of the "inclemency of the roads" it is at times difficult to reach the P.O. in time to mail letters in the morning so that you may not calculate with much certainty hereafter of getting news from home. Tuesday morning. We have no branch office since Esq. Carter left & without any mail Boy, have to do the best we can in that regard

Nelia,

Columbus Jan 26th 1864

My Dear Mother,

I have a few moments to spare before the mail closes tonight and must write a few lines to tell you what has happened to me today. I awoke this morning feeling as if I should like to hear from home, and sent Arthur to the office to get the mail at eight o'clock. But no letter was there — Then I consoled myself with thinking that Sheldon had probably received one, and waited patiently till noon — But when he came and said there were no letters "Why, Sheldon" said I "now I am going to cry" — But I mastered myself by an effort yet I tell you, the practising went on mechanically enough until about four oclock, an imperative summons to the front door disclosed to me the welcome fact that by placing my name upon a book which was handed me I should come into possession of a tempting looking basket which sat there — I hurried to my room and was soon among the fruits & letters. Everything was very acceptable, and you don't know how glad I am that one of the cans was marked for Myra. She is one of those sensitive dispositions that every little attention does her good, and she says that when I write to Father again she wishes to send a line of thanks. Mary has gone up town but will probably be in before I have finished my letter — I have not seen her since the basket came — There she has just come in and sends her thanks, love, and kind wishes. I assure you I do not need many inducements to tempt me to come home — I value the place too much to think of staying away from it unless I can do better pecuniarily — I have talked with Mr Kingsley, about a situation in the schools here next term and he can of course give me no encouragement for he knows nothing of what vacancies may occur. But assures me that tis a bad time of the year for any opening, that the Fall term is the time for young teachers to apply ———— now Mother it is just

Nelia,

what I want — the plans you have laid — and I want to ask another favor of you which I hope you will not refuse this is — that if Mary Herd comes home with me she may board at our house — She is about twenty two years of age and such a quiet lady-like unassuming girl I do not think you would regret having her become a member of our family — and I know she would be glad to come and live just <u>as</u> <u>we</u> <u>do</u>, for they are very plain people — If you think you can take <u>us</u> <u>both</u> please let me know soon & also state the price of board.

I have time only to write these few lines tonight — will write again in a short time —

I have not been as well for a few days as I was before but am feeling better tonight and hope I shall continue to do so — I have received the soldier's letter and will reply to it and send you a copy this week —

Write soon and accept much love from
Nelia ———

Thursday Morning

Dear Carlos

Your letter of 26 arrived last evening — Your Mother wrote Nelia advising her to come home, take a few young music scholars that she can have, & continue some studies at the Normal for the Spring, & in the Fall make such other arrangements as may seem desirable — She expects to bring a particular friend, Mary Herd to attend school here — Your letter will be sent to her so that she can form her own opinion & reply for herself, we think she will prefer being at home for the Spring Term at least — This unseasonable weather is not favorable to health of "the old folks at home," though we are <u>moving</u> ———

Yours affectionately
H. Colton

Lina

Detroit Feb. 7th 1864

My Dear Brother
        It is too stormy to attend services this evening, so I sit down to write. Mother wanted me to send you this letter of Aunt Marys for the folks to read, then wishes it returned to her, so that she can send it to Aunt Myra.

I cannot realize that Winter is so near gone, and that I have been here nearly three months. Am enjoying myself well as ever, and, like Alfy, have become so much attached to the city that I do not want to leave it. It certainly has done Alfy a great deal of good coming here. He is pleasant, polite, and talkative. Will come in here of an evening and entertain me as well as "<u>any</u> <u>other</u> <u>man</u>." When Phin is absent from his meals — he takes the head of the table and <u>does</u> <u>the</u> <u>agreeable</u>, calling it one of his <u>Detroit</u> <u>accomplishments</u>. The ice suddenly disappeared about two weeks ago — and there <u>has</u> not been much skating since.

Last Friday evening we went to the park to see the celebrated Haines skate. He belongs in New York. The managers of this park engaged him to <u>perform</u> here on the ice. It certainly was a sight to behold. No one attempts to skate while he is on the ice — they are so intent on watching him.

Aunt Lucy has been here nearly three weeks. Leonard has been sick most of the time, so she could not have enjoyed her visit very much. Think they intend starting for home tomorrow. I have not been down there since the forepart of last week. How is the sickness in Toledo? Does the small pox still rage? I was vaccinated — but it did not work, so the Dr. would take no pay. He wants to try it again. It does not seem hardly necessary, although he probably knows best. Mrs. Shepherd started for home, <u>at</u> <u>last</u> on Friday evening. Tommy has been sick here some time.

John was at home all last week. I mean week before last. He started for Cleveland on Monday and expected to be in Milan by Tuesday of this week.

His brother Tom was with us most of the time last week. He is in Kalamazoo now. Expects to return in a few days and stay a couple of weeks before going to the Regiment. You see we are not unprotected females — <u>all</u> the time. This is fast becoming a <u>sinful</u> city. Scarcely a night passes but some man is knocked down in the street and robbed. In almost every instance last week, it was done early in the evening. I expect to attend a social gathering tomorrow evening at Mr. Rose. You noticed the house particularly when here. It is a large brick one, on Woodward Avenue.

Want to write to Nelia tonight so must close. Give much love to all.
                Your sister
                Lina

Nelia.

My Dear Mother,

It seems to be your turn to receive the news of the arrival of any welcome packages from home. I watched yesterday for a letter, and was sadly disappointed at not receiving one, for both Father and Delia were owing me letters, the former, I have written to twice since hearing a word from him. I very much fear I have again unwittingly committed some breach of propriety, and I feel very sorry if such is the case. But I shall still look for one of his ever welcome letters hoping it will all come out right "sometime." Well! I comenced to tell you that when I found this morning there was no news from home, I was ready to cry. I did receive a letter from Lottie this morning which was very welcome But still I wondered that neither Sheldon nor I, had received our usual weekly mail. I practised after dinner, until about halfpast three oclock, and then I said to Mrs Smythe — "I cannot stand this — I must go to the office and see if there isn't a letter from Lina at least, I haven't any heart in my practising." In the P.O. I met Sheldon — There was nothing for either of us, and I came away quite low spirited. He asked me to go to his office with him — and I think it is a perfect little "snuggery" — He says he is contented and happy now and I know he is much better suited under the new administration. Well after sitting and talking with him awhile I came home slowly and wearily as if I was walking to my own funeral. The express wagon was opposite me in the street all the way home, and when it turned up to the gate, a faint hope sprang up in my heart which I immediately thrust down, for I did not suppose you had anything to send us — But when the man delivered the box my spirits rose ten degrees, and I hurried back to the State House to tell my brother the good news. He could not come around until supper time, so I had the extreme felicity of sitting an hour and a half catching glimpses of <u>something</u> <u>through</u> <u>the bars</u>. Well! at last I

Nelia,

have found what it is, and must say I <u>am</u> <u>delighted</u>. You have showed excellent taste and skill in your arrangement of the leaves and manufacture of the frame — I would make one suggestion in case you make more of this sort for the fair, that is that you leave a little more of a margin to the white paper on which the leaves are placed — I think it will show them off to better effect —

I thank Delia for her kind letter and will probably reply to it tonight — I like the appearance of the sweet modest face that looks out of the little frame of shells and "stone wall". Mary fell to admiring the workmanship of the frame — & Sheldon asked her how she liked the looks of the centre — "not a bit" said she "I wish it had been your picture instead, for me."

Well! I have made quite a long story out of a seemingly small matter. But any thing that comes from home is not a <u>small</u> or <u>insignificant</u> <u>thing</u> <u>for me</u> and as the time approaches when I expect to return to that home I grow so eager and count the days, and weeks that I am more homesick than I was two months ago — I do not know but I shall stay until the middle of March — Mrs S. has been very, <u>very</u> kind to me all the time that I have been here and she seems so anxious that I should remain and become acquainted with her daughter that I feel inclined to do so, though if you think best I will come sooner or even meet you in Cleveland, at the time of the Fair, though I think if I wait, Sheldon may go home with me. I tell him I shall need his trunk to help carry home my things for I have the piano cover and the fruit cans, besides I could never pack my clothes as you did, and what good would it do to take his trunk if he didn't go too. I think he will not withstand my pleading — well I must close now.

Kiss Pa for me (I should like to see you when you do it) and imagine yourself kissed by your

Affectionate
Daughter
Nelia

Carlos

Toledo Feb 11th 1864

Dear Mother

The pictures and letters brought by Bang's I got today. I shall prize your "Winter Boquet" exceedingly. Aunt says the arrangement of the bouqet and the making of the frame exhibit a talent that she has not got, they praised it at the house very much. I think it very beautiful. I am afraid you will overwork yourself in your efforts to help the Soldiers, the crayon sketch of a pear by Nelia is very pretty and neatly done (she is a splendid girl, and I hope the Lord will give her good health to keep pace with the growth of her mind, then I am sure she will give us still further reason to be proud of her), her reply to the Soldiers letter was neat and good —— It is just one year today since I commenced work for Mr Strong. I have had two or three talks with him about raising my salary but am convinced now that he does not intend to do it, he says he does not want to make any change in the office, that he wants me to stay at my present salary, which he thinks is liberal for the amount of work to be done in his office, that when his business is heavier than it has been he will be glad to pay better wages & etc., it is true the work in his office is for the most part of the year comparatively small. I like the place much better than any situation I have filled heretofore, but I must do better if possible soon as regards salary. I know that you at home need more money, much more in these times than you receive to live comfortably and respectably, and it is the great wish of my heart that I might be enabled to send home many more of the "almighty dollars" than I do. I could of course to a certain extent do so if I denied myself many little extravagancies that I do not, but I am only human and as "all flesh is weak", I am — "all flesh" — Well, we can't tell what is best for us in this big Strange World, and I can only hope that it is all for the best <u>as it is</u> now, and that some time it may all be for the best if we should happen to be blessed with any greater amount of this worlds goods than we at present posess. I have made no engagement to stay but have told Mr Strong that when I do get a chance to do better I will give him time to "break in" a new man. Lucy Blinn was here a few days since with her child. Went along the same day to Fremont. Mrs Shepard has also gone home — via Canada much to the relief I am told, of her Detroit victims —— Abram went over to Detroit yesterday will probably return tomorrow. I think of nothing further to write. Lina sent me Mary Allens letter a day or two since requesting me to return it to you. I enclose it herewith. I also return Nelia's letters, and enclose $5— all well as usual here — Much love to all, from

Your affectionate Son
Carlos

Cleveland Feb. 23rd 1864 —

My Dear Sister.

I received your letter enclosing this one from Mary, both of which were quite welcome I intend writing to Hiram & Mary soon as I can find the suitable time for so doing. Shall I direct to Lakeport Lake Co. if this is the right direction you need not be troubled mention it in your next. I received a letter from Lina tonight telling me, of the severe turn Ma had a week ago & alas of Mr Hydes illness. I feel very anxious about Ma, thinking she will be taken away quite suddenly soon. I wish it was as I could be with her more. I suppose I shall go to Louisville — (but cannot yet tell if I should. I would try to go to Detroit first though it is very late, am <u>scribbling</u> a few lines to you. Lina writes that Lucy is to move here in the Spring, if she does, how pleasant it would be for me if Henry would return here, but, I do not anticipate such happiness. I have always hoped since my marriage, I could have a home here of my <u>own</u> when I could feel at liberty to send for my friends, and welcome them to <u>my</u> <u>home</u>, and not be dependent so long as I have been I now fear when I do have a home it be so far away, our dear Mother can never the journey of coming to me. Henry said in his last letter he hoped he should have a home for us soon —

I attended the "Inauguration" yesterday, with Father & Mother, & went with them to the Bazzar this afternoon. There is so much to be seen we did not attempt to visit any of the other Halls to day, we got very tired "standing around", although there was much to interest us. I was glad to see Miss Gordon, her Booth looked very nicely.

I saw a Lady with a pair of y<u>our</u> little socks, which she had purchased. I think your Cone Work and the Boquet very pretty indeed I would like much to have purchased one, but felt that I could not afford to buy any of the fancy articles, but what I do purchase must be of the <u>useful</u> I saw some of Delias work too, but am afraid it is marked too high, Miss Gordon thinks whatever she finds is marked too high she must offer far less. In the sets I sold for a dollar, were a Table, Sofa, four or five chairs & two ottomans — the Beads added very much to them. When there is such a great variety & quantity of fancy articles they have to be marked rather low to find sale — for there are so many ways of spending money at the Fair. I am sorry you cannot attend the Fair, for I know you would enjoy it, if you was well enough to go through the crowds & see all that is to be seen. This is certainly a grand affair — you were wise in not coming as the delegate — you never could have endured the fatigue. We live so far out it is quite a journey to go back & forth, so I do not suppose I can go as often as I wish. I met Mrs Ely, she seemed very cordial, said she should come soon to call on me. I was very glad to see her, she seemed so friendly. I also met Mrs Sprague whom I had not seen for years — Those "Chemise" Mrs J.C. Lockwood made sold & were laid aside before I saw them. She marked them very low I thought. I suppose Floral Hall is exquisite I know you would enjoy that. That is a treat. I hope soon to enjoy
Libbie Sands wrote me she expected to come to the Fair this week. I shall try to call on her. Good night dear Sister. Give my love to all dear ones. Nellie is very well, & was much pleased with Aunti Coltons kiss.
  Myra

Nelia,

Columbus Feb 25th 1864

My Dear Mother,

Itakes a comparatively small matter to <u>please</u> <u>children</u>, doesn't it? When I received the package from home yesterday afternoon, and opened the note from Father, the loving words, "<u>Me darling child</u>," made me the merriest hearted girl in Columbus. His warning to look out for the express when the bell rang was heeded for early in the afternoon I told Mrs Smythe, I would answer the door bell for I knew twas the express-man. I found twas <u>two</u> <u>ladies</u> instead, and a short time after, I went to the door again and found twas another lady caller, the third time when the bell rang I sat still, telling Mrs S. I wasn't going to be fooled any more. So she smoothed her hair, cast a parting glance in the glass to be assured all was right and hastened to the door. She returned in a few minutes laughing heartily. She had got the package after all.

The Valentine is a very nice one but I agree with Father that twas "Love's labor lost," especially if it came from the quarter he thinks it did. Was there no post mark? and did you have to pay 18 cts to get it out of the office? I <u>wouldn't</u> have <u>done</u> it. Thank Father for the papers and stationary, and Delia for her good long interesting letter. I hope to be in Milan to enjoy some of your frolics etc before long. Mary and Sheldon were quite pleased with their share of the contents of the package.

Mrs Botsford was one of the ladies who called here yesterday. She has been confined so closely at the hospital, that she has not been in town since Christmas, there have been about ninety five cases of small pox at the camp, only five proving fatal however. She is still undecided as to where she will go and what she will do but says she finds so much to keep her busy there that she cannot bear to leave. I have promised to go out & spend a day with her before I go home.

I was sorry to hear that Father is still troubled so much with his sick headache but suppose he has quieter times now than when Lina and I were both home.

Nelia,

The enclosed little piece fell down on my paper just now. I have had it pinned up here on the wall nearly five months, and as "them's my sentiments," I will send it along —

Wouldn't you like to have us bring home that picture of Sheldons? the maple leaves. I would like to alter the back of the frame or rather the sides. It might be stained or have acorns glued around the edge to hide the bare frame it would present a better appearance at a side view. Sheldon suggested it and I will bring it if you say so. If there is any shopping you or Lottie or any of our friends want from here, let me know and I will gladly do it for you. If Mrs Abbott wishes anything from David, I shall be glad to take it for her. There comes my music teacher. I must stop now for a while.

There, I can now finish this I hope that I may give it to Sheldon to mail, this noon. Mary and I went to Squire Miller's to tea Tuesday, and had a very pleasant visit. They have two young gentleman boarders beside Sheldon and intend to move the First of April taking their boarders with them.

I have received another letter from our Soldier at Ft Leavenworth. I will bring it home with me, and also the reply that I intend to make — I did not send the other letter of mine home for any one to see, but because I thought Father wished to know all that passed between us which I thought all right. If I had known twas even going to Detroit I could not have written at all, for it is very embarassing to think that a third person is to read the letters one writes. I know I always find it so even in writing to my brothers, when I am home. Please dont send away any more of my correspondence it looks too much like trying to show one off, and I know I have enough of that disposition in myself, and it needs checking and conquering. I will copy a few sentences from Will Stone's last letter, for your and any one's else benefit, you please.

[the enclosure mentioned in this letter is a tiny newspaper clipping, attached to the second page with a straight pin]

NONE ON EARTH LIKE MOTHER

Sweet is the song of birds,
    In autumn's leafy wildwood;
But sweeter far the words
    That grace a loving childhood
But streamlet utters low
    The love no ill can smother —
The human heart alone can know
    There's none on earth like mother.
When far in distant lands,
    Though skies be bright above us,
We sigh for gentle hands
    And smiles of those who love us,
So down the weary years
    We follow one another,
Yet murmur through the blinding tears,
    "There's none on earth like mother."

[reverse side contains a portion of a testimonial]

weight, as it were rested upon my brain; also a feeling of sickness would occur at the stomach, and give pain in my eyes, accompanied with which was a continual fear of losing my reason. I also experienced great lassitude, debility and nervousness, which became avers to society, and disposed only to seclusion , and having tried the skill of a number of eminent physicians of various schools, finally came to the conclusion that for this disease, at my present ageing years, there was no cure in existence. But through the interference of Divine Providence, to whom I devoutly offer my thanks, I at last found a sovereign remedy in your Dyspepsia Pills and Tar Cordial, which seem to have effectually removed almost the last trace of my long list of ailments and bad feelings, and in their place health, pleasure and contentment are every day companions. JAMES M. SAUNDERS
  No. 453 North Second street, Philadelphia.

Dear Mother:

Yours of the 14th inst. is received and as I have a few moments spare time before I go to supper, I will write a short note to you.

Father's letter of the 20th and the box came along in due time and we were all much pleased with the pictures etc.

I have got leave of absence to take Nelia home, two weeks from today, and think you will then have the pleasure of beholding the faces of two of your <u>little</u> <u>ones</u> again. Hadn't I better bring along another one whom you have not yet seen, as <u>Mrs</u> <u>C</u>:?

I have been getting good lately I presume, as, by request of several of the teachers I have taken charge of the Library of the Presbyterian Sunday School. Who would have supposed that I would commence attending Sunday School again at my age? I have to be on hand at nine oclock Sunday Morning and have just time to get from the Sunday School to the choir, so that my time is pretty well occupied every Sunday morning.

I like my new employer better all of the while. He is a Free Mason, and also a member of the Methodist Church, and as pleasant a man as I ever had anything to do with. He never loses his temper at all.

I am as well situated here now as I could be anywhere I think, and feel quite contented. Nelia seems to be well and has certainly improved a good deal since she came here in every way. I do not know what Mary will do without her. They have become very much attached to each other.

I enclose five dollars in this, and will pay Father the rest that I owe him on this installment when I see you. I enclose this letter of Carlos' which Father sent. I received a letter from him today, in which he proposes to send for Lina and have a regular "<u>pow</u> <u>wow</u>" when Nelia and I go home.

I believe have said my say and will close with love to all.

Yours truly,
Sheldon Colton.

Youthful Frolics

The wearied mother is taking
    Her needed noonday rest,
Leaving the busy prattlers
    To work out their own behests.

Each room in the house is ringing
    With merry laughter and shouts,
Till at last an ominous silence
    Brings the mother some anxious doubts.

A crash of tin in the pantry,
    An indescribable sound —
In spite of her tired muscles
    The mother is there with a bound.

The elder boy is drinking
    His coffee direct from the pot;
The younger is prancing and howling
    For the share he never got.

A lake of maple syrup
    Is slowly spreading around,
From an up-set can, which the rascals
    On the lowest shelf had found.

The elder boy is drinking
  His coffee direct from the pot;
The younger is prancing and howling
  For the share he never got.

272

The horrified mother is saying
      To each little precious pet,
O, sweetest of sweetest of darlings,
      Don't come to my bosom yet.

For fingers and faces and jackets
      Were smeared with the sticky mess,
Until the original color
      'Twere a difficult thing to guess.

Their little tongues were seeking
      What was left on their white arms, bare,
While they longed for the "wasted sweetness"
      That was not on the desert air.

For water and soap and muscle
      Were called into play galore,
Ere the traces of their wild frolic
      Were gone from the pantry floor.

                              Sheldon Colton

Adj. Gen. Office.
Columbus, O. March 16 ~ 1864

Dear Mother:

I arrived here about nine o'clock last night, as I got to Grafton a few minutes too late for the Columbus train; the first time that I remember of having missed a train.

I then took a freight train to Crestline and spent the afternoon with John Burt and his family, and took the regular train at six oclock.

I found the people here all well. I have delivered Nelia's letter and the cough medicine.

I discovered upon opening my valise that it was partly filled with Raspberries, as the cover came off from one of the cans; it having been put in upside down. There was no great damage done however, as the paper held most of them in. The lining of the Valise was somewhat stained and also one of my shirts. I left the broken can at Mrs Smythe's and will give the other one to Miss Hattie.

I have no other news at present and only write to let you know I am here all safe.

Yours truly
Sheldon Colton.

Lina

Detroit Mich.
Sunday March 27th 1864

Dear Mother

For the first time since I left home a week has passed without my receiving letters from any of you. I had a few lines from Sheldon, with the name of my class very nicely finished. He told me nothing of Nelia's whereabouts. I am owing her a letter but do not know whether she is at home or in Columbus. You will judge from the size of this paper that I am visiting on Woodward Avenue again. Cousin Phin and Clarinda went to Trenton yesterday. Hattie and I wanted to go to choir meeting last night, so, of course, the children had to come over and stay with Grandma. Then we returned and lodged here too. I was up this morning and started for Services at half past five. There is something solemn and interesting unusually so in this early Easter Service. Aunt is getting ready for church now at ten, and I will keep house until she returns, improving my time by writing a letter.

This afternoon we have the Sunday School Easter Celebration. The children will meet in the church instead of the chapel, sing their Easter carlos (excuse me — I intended to write carols — instead of <u>carlos</u>) There will be baptism of infants and remarks made by two missionaries, one from Africa, the other from among the Indians, somewhere. The latter said this morning, that a <u>year</u> <u>ago</u> this morning he was addressing three hundred christian Indians. In our church, the pulpit-reading desk, and baptismal font, are decorated with flowers.

I send a paper to Delia in this mail. The account of the death of Mrs Witherell may interest Dr Cornell, as she was the only sister of his Aunt Mrs Backus. Judge Witherells first wife was a cousin of Uncle Hydes. So the two families have visited more or less for a number of years. Em Stevens, also, told me that her husband was in some way connected with the Witherell family — and that she intended to visit here this Spring. Perhaps Lucy has not heard of this mournful accident.

This is a <u>beautiful</u> Spring morning. I hear birds singing that sounds very much like our blue birds at home. Am afraid city life, in the Summer, will not be quite as delightful as at "Rose Hall" I can tell better though, after this Summer has passed.

I have urgent and repeated invitations to visit at Mr Hanchetts. They live three miles below Trenton at a place called Gibralter. Hattie and I have promised to go as soon as the weather becomes settled. We will take the boat to Gibralter — and after visiting them, Henry will take us out to Col. Saunders, make a short stay with them, come from there to Trenton, and visit a few days with Mrs Wm Davis, Mrs Slocum, Mrs J. Saunders <u>and so on</u>. If a week or two passes without your hearing from me, you may know that I am <u>rusticating</u>.

Aunt Lucinda wants me to spend the day with her tomorrow. I would like to spend the week, but Hattie is alone and I have to befriend her at night.

Monday morning

I went to Sunday School at two and did not get home till six, then attended evening service. So there was no time to finish my letter. Am still at Clarinda's. Shall go home soon and prepare to go down to Uncle's.

Grandma seems to be quite well. She walks occasionally up to St Johns. Uncle Hyde is quite miserable. He coughs hard and still raises blood. There will be confirmation at St. Johns next Sunday. Uncle George is among the candidates. Last Saturday there were twenty one adults baptized. Mr Armitage expects to have a large number to be confirmed.

Saturday evening I met Mr Shaw, from Milan, in the street, being closely veiled, suppose he did not recognize me. Do not know as he would have spoken, any way, as we are but little acquainted. But it <u>looked</u> <u>good</u> to see a Milan face.

I shall call at Mrs Boylans this afternoon with Aunt. Aunt and Hattie unite with me in sending love to all the family. I received three papers from Mr Carter last week. Also the usual number from Father. Am glad to get them.

Love to Lottie and family, and all inquiring friends.

Your Daughter
Lina

Sheldon Ogden

Columbus O. March 27~ 1864.

Dear Nelia:

I presume that you will be nearly ready to travel when this letter reaches you, and I shall expect to hear from some of you by Tuesday morning, telling what time you expect to be here. Mary has written to you to come by way of Newark and Granville, which you could do by going to Monroeville, without changing cars, but we thought you would be more likely to come here Wednesday for the sake of seeing Annie Smythe before she goes. There is an Anniho line from Newark to Granville.

I have had some trouble in trying to get a piano for you. Mr. Woods will not rent the one that is now at Mrs Smythe's any more, as it is a new one and he wishes to sell it. I can get it for $280, paying down as much as I please and giving interest in the balance. I can however get a piano from Mr. Minster, which he says is a good one, and he will let it be taken out to Winchester. I wish the piano at home could be sold for seventy five dollars, or even a little less. I should then feel more like getting a good one.

I am inclined to think that you will like to live in Winchester, as every one whom I hear mention it speaks of it as a pleasant place.

Mr. Minster talks as if he would like to have you try to sell pianos for him out there, of course he would allow you a commission on them if you did, and it would not cause you any extra labor.

I received Delia's letter a day or two ago. I am not ready to receive any assistants yet, as the books are not prepared for the writing, and I am not sure how many I can employ, but I have no objection to her coming here with you if she wishes to and if I cannot find anything for

her to do I can send her home again when she has seen enough of the city. I am quite sure I could employ her for a month or so, however.

If she has any clothing to fix up let her bring it along and fix it here, as it will be some days before I can find anything for her to do.

Mrs Smythe is willing to take her for a few weeks at least, probably as long as she would care to stay. If she does not conclude to come with you she had better wait till I get all ready for her.

Mary went home Saturday. Gen. Cowen came down to take the same train and I introduced them, and the last I saw of them they were sitting together very comfortably, apparently well satisfied. No matter — he is married.

I expect we will change our habitation this week, go down near the corner of Long and Fourth Streets.

The people here are generally well and I have no more news to tell, I believe.

I enclose five dollars, should Delia come, and if you want more to get yourself here, you can borrow it, and I will send it home as soon as I get my month's pay, next Thursday. I have only two dollars left.   Love to all,

Yours truly,

Sheldon Colton

If you take the early morning train, you will have but a few minutes to wait at Grafton, and will reach here about one oclock. When you get to Grafton, you must change checks on your trunks, you will see the baggage master on the platform with his truck, ready to change the baggage from one train to the other.

Nelia,

Columbus April 3rd 1864

My Dear Father,

I have seated myself this bright Sunday morning to tell you of my safe journey and some of the particulars thereof of my safe arrival and some incidents pertaining thereto. Well, to proceed to business, I enjoyed my short visit in Cleveland very much indeed. Myra suffered all the time I was there with a severe tooth-ache which prevented her going around with me at all, and probably I should have found it rather dull, had it not been for Willie Standart. He is about thirteen years of age and remarkably smart & intelligent, rather more boisterous than his older brother Harry, but both are little gentlemen, and they exerted themselves to entertain me with excellent success. They took me to the depot Friday morning and as we had some trouble in finding the baggage room I had just time to get my checks changed and jump on the cars. Was too late to buy my ticket — so when the conductor came round I opened my portmonnaie to pay my fare, which was four dollars, to my blank amazement, I had lost one dollar somewhere, probably in taking out my checks. I told the conductor so, and said my brother would meet me in the depot. He said it was all right, & so I came through on my face, rather an uncomfortable mode of traveling I think. After a while a gentlemanly looking young man came and took the seat beside me. He was very intelligent and lively and helped to make the time pass pleasantly, for we were from eight oclock until two reaching Columbus. Sheldon met me at the depot — and as it was April fool's day, and he reached the house before I did, he made Mrs. Smythe and Myra believe I had not come. Well I am settled in Columbus and only wish I was in Winchester. Sheldon has bought me a piano, a second-hand one which however is a very good one, & I like it better than the one we have here and there is a hundred dollars difference in the price, and he pays $170.00 cash for it after it is set up in Winchester for me. We concluded that was the cheapest way to do, and he will probably write to you what to do with the one at home. I suggest that you rent

Nelia,

it for about three dollars a month, and in a short time you will get the worth of the piano.

Mrs. Smythe says she would rather wait about a week before Delia comes though if she has a good opportunity to come as soon as she pleases and she would rather have her now than later in the season, for through the warm weather she don't want any one. When Delia does come, let her bring the piano cover and the bunch of piano wire that is I think in the passageway cupboard.

David called yesterday afternoon after his packages. I have nothing more to write that I know of and will wait until I am settled to write a longer letter. I dreamed all night of my troubles in getting to Winchester. Hiram McMillen took me over on a hand sled, and found Miss Haynie at Mr. Comstocks, she said she had got angry at her pupils and called them "little urchins" so they declared they would not take lessons of her, nor me either, and she advised me to go right back home.

Sheldon will be here this afternoon and if he has any word to send will finish this then.

Sheldon says to rent the old piano by all means if possible. You might get Buckley to put it in good tune first and then perhaps Mr. Draper or Mr. Mackey, or perhaps Mary Wilbor would take it. We are all well and in good spirits, only I dread going away tomorrow morning alone at eight oclock.

Well good night. Much love from Sheldon and Mary and Your affectionate daughter

Nelia

I had a poor pen when I wrote this.

Milan April 12 ~ 1864

Dee Pet Daughter

I wrote Sheldon this morning that your mother would make inquiries to day about juveniles with music proclivities for Nelia, which she has done & met with general & earnest expressions of satisfaction with Nelias disappointment at Winchester, & desire that she should return & open an office of instruction here, by the first of March, which we have given the neighbors & friends to understand is highly notable. We have promises more or less definite from the following. — Homer Page two, Tom Butman two, A L Moury two, Mrs Will Bates one, Taylor one, Collins one, Wilbor one, Williams one, Mackey one, Smythe one, Frith one — 13 We think she might calculate with some degree of certainty of opening with ten scholars. If that should prove inducement for her to return we shall be glad to see her at home once more to remain, at least till you can be with us again — I have almost forgotten when you left home it seems so long ago, though your Mother & I have got along very well keeping house alone ever since you left, hope it dont seem so long to you as it does to me.

We hope you can be spared to visit us the fourth of July even if you shouldnt be able to stay more than a week. The only event of importance that has occured since you left is that Mr Carter went to Toledo this morning. Mr Ballard was here last evening but having left home a week ago knew even less than we did about the folks at Detroit — Said he intends to bring Hattie & Lina & the children next time he comes this way.

Perhaps Lina will not wait for him though we have heard nothing from her since you left, I think.

I have waited for your Mother to return & report progress this PM. till it is now quite late & I must close as to take it to the office when I go after the mail and the milk, dear me, how many things I do have to attend to now.

Affectionately yours & all the childrens' in
Columbus belonging to us   from your
Father

Wednesday Morning

We recd a letter from Nelia last night she was not well & we are anxious to hear that she is at Columbus. If not when this gets there & you know nothing certain about this some one ought to go to her — Her letter was written Saturday, I have opened this at the office   H.C.

Carlos

Toledo O April 17th 1864

Dear Sister Delia

      Just before you left home for Columbus I received a letter from you, and have since heard by way of home of your safe arrival at Columbus, and how you were situated amongst your new friends, and was pleased to know that thus far you were <u>all</u> <u>right</u>, and trust you will have a pleasant and profitable time there. About a week or ten days ago a letter from Father said he had just got a letter from Sheldon in which he mentioned that he had been writing to me, please inform him that up to this time I have not got any letter from him since the one in which he enclosed my knife, and would like to know if he really did mail one to me which I have not received. A short note from home last night spoke of Nelia's safe arrival home. She had a severe cold but they were in hopes that a little rest and quiet would cure her, poor girl. She must have had a sorry time of it down there amongst strangers with her illness and disappointment and I am glad she has got safe home again. Rain, Rain Rain, oh what <u>awful</u> weather we do have these days, it seems as though we must have a change for the better soon.

Mr Carter was up here one day last week but Mr Raymond was in Washington, so he could not have a talk with him about the place in his office. Henry Raymond is now staying in the office with his brother, and I dont know whether Mr Raymond will want any body else or not yet. I think it will be decided in a few days. We expect Lina here about the middle of this week on her way home, at least so the folks at home think. I havent heard anything from Lina.

Alpha has been at home a week or more, he has made some very nice paintings and is now painting the portrait of a little curly headed Irish boy named "Jimmy" who stays around the docks a good deal and asks every body to give him "<u>a</u> <u>cent</u>" ——

The folks are well as usual at the house with the exception of some troublesome colds ——

I hope to hear from you soon giving an account of your experiences in city life — Would like to hear from Sheldon — good bye ——

           Your brother
           Carlos

Milan April 24th 1864

Dear Delia

I have not been at home long enough yet, to hear the Milan news but concluded to write a few lines to enclose in this letter that I received from Carlos last Winter while in Detroit. Of course there is nothing <u>laughable</u> in it but I thought you and Sheldon would like to read it. Everything seems quite strange to me, having been gone all Winter, and I have been accustomed to having the noise of children, that there is a <u>death</u> <u>like</u> stillness about this house. Another thing is y<u>ou</u> are absent and Nelia will not play with me. She is <u>more</u> <u>sedate</u> than usual since her stay in Columbus. Wonder if it will change you as much. It is to be hoped so. I am just learning the Milan news now. Why did you not write it to me this Winter? Betsey Stowe, Betsey Gwinne, Libbie Holling, Clara Prout, Lib. Edridge and Mrs Bates <u>all</u> <u>married</u>, and <u>I</u> knew nothing about it, what an oversight? Then, too, you was very careful not to let me know that the Dr. was sick at our house, was you afraid I would come home? Mr Carter is feeling better tonight, the rest of the family are well. Nelia was intending to write to Sheldon, but has been to church Sunday School, and to Mr Carter's twice. At last has gone to sleep on the lounge. So there is not much prospect of a letter. Do not destroy this letter from Carlos.

Shall expect a call from the "Shirt Chandler" this week. He has gone East for goods, and <u>proposed</u> stopping here on his return. If he comes will write soon after and let you hear all the <u>particulars</u>. Much love for Sheldon and yourself from all the family.

Lina

Detroit April 30 1864

Dear Brother

Yours of the 30th inst was duly received, and I hasten to inform you that an <u>apology</u> to me is unnecessary for addressing a few lines to me at any time that you feel disposed to do so, rest assured that you are not "<u>troubling</u>" me in the least. Lina has not made her visit in the country, she came in here a few minutes after I received your letter, I was reading it at the time and when I came to when you spoke of Delia going to Columbus, she said "I must go home it is too bad to have Pa and Ma alone, notwithstanding, we saw the justice of her remark, yet we all feel a reluctance to part with her. She has appeared to enjoy herself and it is a pleasure to her numerous relatives to have her in their midst, but no one will feel the loss of her society so much as Hatty, she says she dont know what she shall do if Lina leaves her. It has been a great comfort to me to have her make it her home with Hatty, as well as a relief, as I did not feel obliged to be there whether sick or well, do not think me selfish, however as I should have been unwilling, to have had her remained, as long as she has if she had not seemed perfectly contented she has seemed to appreciate her Church privileges, very highly. We would have been very much gratified if Sheldon could have extended his visit as far as Detroit glad to learn that he is doing so well, in his case you can truly say that Fortune favors the Brave" I hope Nelias lameness will not prove serious. How can you spare your right hand man Delia? it is a fine chance for her, but you and Melinda will feel very lonely without her as she has never been from you, any length of time. Should you and your better half chance to take a trip to the City of the Straits, you will find Cousin Phins local habitation, on Woodward Avenue, four doors above Charlotte St. you can take the street-car, and be landed right at the door. Cousin Johns is on Park St. 227 next street back of Woodward Avenue, and about three minutes walk from Phins, Mr Truax and Mr Hyde will probably change their places of residence on the 1st of May next when we will endeavor to inform you where they are located. It would be "quite an unexpected pleasure to us" to have you drop in upon us. I suppose Lina has told you that Affy has been spending the winter with us for the purpose of taking lessons in drawing and painting, he bids fair to rank high on the list of American Artists.
I am glad to still receive the Independent, I send them to Maria, and presume they will meet with a favorable reception. As Affy is waiting to take this to the Office I shall be obliged to close with love to all,
Yours Affectionately
C. Bill

P S. Please <u>trouble</u> me again, soon

Lina

Milan May 8th 1864

My Dear Sister,

This is a lovely May morning. But how strangely <u>still</u> it all seems. Nelia and I wander about as though there was some sick person in the house. I like it though, it is really pleasant. You will notice the change very much more — after having been in the city two or three months. Everything will look <u>very</u> <u>queer</u> to you when you return — the trees and shrubbery I mean. There is no place, in particular to <u>go</u> <u>to</u>, except Mr. Carters and the post office. We start for those two places every evening at six and get home again about seven. The mail will change this week so I do not know what time we will go for it.

Our Independent company intend to start for Columbus tomorrow morning. We did not know it in time to send you word so that you could <u>look</u> at them in the depot. But as they are ordered to Camp Chase you may have an opportunity of seeing, Mr. Draper, Penfield, Horace, Lucius, Phil, Azra, Danforth, Ed Story, and others too numerous to mention. In fact, there is hardly a man left. Pa says he tried to count the men on the public square the other morning and counted <u>Mr. Mann</u> <u>twice</u>, that was all he could see.

Hattie Lockwood is clerking for J.C. and Lilla Stuart for her father. Mr. Lockwood says he has had more female applicants for situations than he could get <u>inside</u> <u>of</u> <u>the</u> <u>store</u>. Casper feels that a great responsibility rests upon him — that of taking care of all the girls this Summer. He will be the only young man left here. James Banks goes as Lieut. in a Sandusky Company. Will Osborne called, a few evenings since. He is a member of the Norwalk guards. Friend after friend departs.

We have fitted up the front bedroom as a music room. It is much pleasanter than the Library ever was. Nelia has seven pupils now and the promise of more — when School closes. George Daniels is very anxious to take lessons — but Nelia declines receiving any young men over fifteen years of age. Mary Herd writes that you have had some photographs taken. Do not forget your friends at home — in distributing them. Julia Cornell did not come — we have heard nothing from her. The Dr. went to Youngstown last week. We heard by way of Mrs. Butman that you have taken a new boarding place. Do you intend remaining there the rest of your time?

How is Arthur Smythe? Hope he is better by this time.

Carrie Belle wants me to go where Aunt Delia is and tell her to come right home. Mr. Carter has been ailing about all the time since I came home. First with a gathering in his head and now with a bone in his back. The rest are all well.

I may possibly, return to Detroit this Summer. Hattie says she is coming for me and will not go back without me. Shall not go however, until after you return, for they want some one here to 'wash dishes'. Much love for Sheldon & yourself from all the family. Write whenever you have time to　　　　　　　　　　　　　　Your sister
　　　　　　　　　　　　　　　　　　　　Lina

　　　　　　　　　　　　　　　Monday
We send a paper in this mail with some flowers. Ma sends the blue eyed Mary to Sheldon. Lieut. Banks and Sergt. Jenny were here yesterday. James expects to see you in Columbus

Milan May 15~ 1864

Dee, Pet Daughter

I have been thinking for some time that I ought to acknowledge the receipt of two or three letters that I have written to you but somehow have put it off from day to day, till I am almost ashamed to say anything about it, as I can offer no reasonable excuse for the delay. You may think they were short & not worth mentioning so I will not tell that I have sometimes been sick & sometimes busy as usual at this season of the year whenever the weather will permit, indeed rather more so as I have no Stout Boy to help me now. Nelia is willing of course but does not amount to much for outdoor work. I have been obliged to hire Geo. Markey occasionally, in consequence of your absence but have told him several times that he wasnt half as good help as Delia especially about building fences. His father & mother gave consent that he should go as drummer in the Milan home guard, but repented them as soon as he had gone. Mr. Markey got a team & went to Sandusky after him. It so happened that he hadnt yet signed the roll & so he brought him home to the great relief & delight of his mother who was sorrowing as one without hope. I think one of the girls mentioned to you that Della Barton went with them. I fear that their stay was so short in Columbus that you had no chance to see the young men who made soldiers of themselves so unexpectedly, one of the best jokes of the war though they mostly failed to see it in that light. They didnt expect to leave home except in case of invasion, but the Governors invitation was so cordial that they could not well decline taking a ride at Government expense.

H. Culton

Some of the bereaved wives consoled themselves with the hope for a day or two that the Company would remain at Camp Chase, where they intended to visit & have a good time generally, & regretted to learn that it was not a very pleasant place for residences, perhaps they dont feel relieved now they know that they will not be obliged to go there.

You must not think that we wouldnt be glad to see you any time but thinking that a few months residence in Columbus would be of service to you in many ways, I should be sorry if a little homesickness should induce you to abandon your post & return before your term of enlistment expires, & cant believe it will. We have no fears that you will learn bad tricks from your playmates — besides a casual meeting with a fellow boarder is different from being obliged to room & mate exclusively with an objectionable person. Should think you must be rather pleasantly situated there & hope you will enjoy it to the best advantage besides improving yourself in various ways. Presume we shall be ashamed of our countryfied actions at table when you get home, & hope you will not forget while absent how much taller you are when you straighten up, than when you pop on like the "bended bow" we read of. I suppose one of the young ladies will write you all the news soon, they have no time for that purpose to day as Julia has been with them since Friday evening. Bellie was here yesterday & Castor Bean last evening — which is about all I know on such subjects   Yours affectionately

Father

Lina

Milan May 22nd 1864

Dear Delia

      I have nothing in particular to make out a letter with But suppose you would like to receive one whether there is much in it or not. Nelia wrote to you last Friday and suppose up to that time told all the news. Since then <u>nothing</u> has happened. Milan never was so quiet as it is now. There is a dearth of boys, and girls too. Julia Butman Jennie Norton, Nelia and I seem to be the only <u>unmarried</u> ones that attend the Aid Society. Jennie leaves here next Thursday to attend to a class in music — at Ft. Seneca, Ohio

      I have been to Sunday School today — They still have it at noon. Mr Rockwell superintends the School, and hears the bible class recite. He is a good teacher, but not quite equal to Dr Cornell. Casper comes now and then to attend to his duties. Nelia and I went to Lottie's after Sunday School and brought the children home with us. Then Mr Carter came for them about the middle of the afternoon. They expect to have the house that Mr Shaw has just left, across from Capt. Shipman's, and will probably commence moving tomorrow. It will be much pleasanter for them than where they are.

The regiment that "our boys" are in has gone to Arlington Heights. Mrs Penfield had a letter from her husband last night. They are all well. The 169th, to which Lieut. Banks belongs has gone to Washington.

The Spring term of the Normal closes this week. The School has <u>dwindled down</u> to about twenty scholars. <u>Henry</u> <u>Howe</u> and Delia Farnsworth spent Friday evening with us. <u>We</u> had a pleasant visit. Mr Howe said he was going home yesterday. His health is poor, has had an attack of bleeding at the lungs. He intends returning here to School this Fall. Miss Viles is teaching somewhere. If we have made no remarks about your Ferrotypes, it was all a mistake, for we consider them excellent. The best pictures, in fact, that you have ever had taken.

Nelia has gone to bed, and as I have not <u>slept</u> <u>much</u> <u>this</u> <u>afternoon</u>, must close my letter and go and do likewise.

Much love to all. Write soon to

                Your Sister
                Lina

Mother sends a sweet scented shrub for Sheldon, Mary, Myra, Hattie, Frank, Emma, and yourself. Put them in your — your — your — <u>bosoms,</u> you will be scented up to the highest pitch.

They will be found in the paper which will probably arrive in this same mail.   Nelia

Columbus July 31st 1864

Dear Delia,

I have handled the pen so much, of late, that today — well — I do not know what <u>is</u> the matter — but my fingers seem <u>kind</u> <u>of</u> <u>stiff</u>, and it is rather difficult to <u>write</u> just now. Sheldon brought Mary and I some muster-out rolls, last week that he wanted copied — soon as possible. Up to halfpast eleven last night, they were still unfinished — so we put them by for Monday morning — and must have them done by two oclock. Let me give you a slight idea of the <u>job</u>. It would take us a whole day, writing steadily, to copy one. Will probably amt. to $1.75 apiece. Aside from the names, dates, places etc. etc. there is, opposite each man's name, an account of what has become of him, whether died of disease — killed — wounded — or taken prisoner, name of place where it happened, date, and so on. I have not worked so hard since coming here — as last three days of last week. My regular business is a larger Cavalry Book. I like the occupation very much, indeed. The only trouble is, the days and weeks <u>fly</u> so fast I cannot <u>accomplish</u> enough. For, board is 14 dollars a month — washing $2. and coal oil $1.20 a gallon. We think of wearing clothes that will not need washing — and going to bed by the light of the street gas.   Am perfectly contented here. Mary said the other day she did not believe that Lina had been homesick a moment. Do not believe I have, although I should not object to seeing you all at any time.   There is enough <u>Military</u> to be seen in Columbus isn't there? Just after tea, every evening, Broad Street is <u>alive</u> with "Blue coats & brass buttons".

It disturbs my writing. Friday afternoon there were two poor soldiers passed here together both on crutches. It was a very warm day. They stopped to rest under the shade tree right by our gate. They looked <u>so</u> tired — we <u>almost</u> <u>cried</u>. Hattie said she felt inclined to run down stairs and throw them a handsome boquet that she had in the parlor. There are said to be a large number of patients in the Hospital now. Mr. Denman has been, and is still, very sick in the Hospital at Fortress Monroe. They feel very anxious about him.

Mr. Williams says he forwarded a letter to his wife that he thinks was from you. She and Emma are still in Granville, are expected home some time this week. Mother need not return the letter of Addie's. Sheldon sent money home by express yesterday. Suppose you will find your share and some for Miss Hotchkiss with it, as I handed Sheldon the necessary amount. Do not expect me to write any news, for I do not know anyone, and have nothing to write about. I will write to Hattie soon. Give much love to them and every body else.

Write whenever you can. Mary is still here and does not know when she will go home. Must put this up — so Sheldon can take it tonight. We do not go to the office at all. He has been here all the afternoon, as usual, and is coming back tonight to go to church with the girls — I have to depend on Mrs. Smythe's family for escorts.   Love to all   Lina

Sheldon Colton

Adj. Gen. Office.
Columbus O. Aug. 13th 1864.

Dear Father:

In reply to yours of the 4th I would say that Seltzer tells me he has forwarded Nelia's music. If not received let me know.

I would like to have you get Kurtz's figures on a suit of black clothes, coat, pants and vest. I want it for a dress suit, broadcloth coat, doeskin or cassimere pants and silk vest. Let him make his figures on the basis of cash down on receipt of the goods. Some items in my letter to Mother will let you know what they are for. I do not want them for about a month, but might as well begin to see about them.

All well here, Love to all,
Yours truly,   Sheldon Colton.

Lina

Columbus Aug. 28" 1864

Dear Mother,

Third Story — back room — at Mr. H.P. Smythe's will be our "address" again, soon. Isnt it "too funny" how these two neighbors keep changing boarders. Sheldon applied here for board for himself and family and understood for sometime that we were all to stay here, but Mrs. Kelley concluded it would be too crowded for comfort, so gave Hattie and I walking tickets, which I gladly accepted. Mrs. Smythe has agreed to take us about the middle of next month. She spoke of Sheldon coming there just a year ago at this time, to see if she would take Nelia.

We will have to pay 4 1/2. and have coal furnished. It will be impossible to get board cheaper anywhere this Winter. Everybody is groaning over the high prices. Nellie McKinneys husband offered Mrs S. twelve dollars a week if she would take them. But she preferred having two girls. Emma and Myra start for School the 6th of next month. Arthur and Bertie will be in the country some time, so their family will be quite small. I must confess to being very much surprised when Sheldon told me that he and Mary had chosen this for a boarding place. Perhaps I am over particular, (Hattie says I am) but, most assuredly, would I have sought a more refined family to bring a bride into. "Every one to their notion" etc. Am very glad of an opportunity to enter a house where there is more cultivation of mind and manners. Our washer woman says she will continue the washing at $2. a month if we will pay extra for dresses. Hard times makes us sigh too. I console myself with the thought that a little is earned which is better than nothing.

It will be eight weeks next Thursday since I left Milan. Have drawn money twice, and shall draw again next Wednesday, which will amount to about $70. earned during the eight weeks.

Lina

On the 1st of September shall commence work by the month, with a <u>salary</u> of $50. shall have to work but eight hours a day. Having the evenings entirely to myself, which will be much more pleasant and convenient. You will find before finishing, that this letter is all abaout "I" but how can <u>I</u> help it, when you do not know any one else here, as Sheldon is in Granville spending Sunday. Tell the girls that last Wednesday morning at half past seven, Ned Herd, Emma, Myra, Frank, Hattie and myself attended a Catholic wedding. By the way, it was Annie that married her "Soldier boy". Believe Nelia took quite an interest in her affairs last winter at Mrs. Smythe's. The priest went through with the whole morning service before performing the ceremony. Having never been inside of a Catholic Church before, you may well imagine what a scene it was for me. It is wonderful how they can call such performances — Worship — when I got near home, Sheldon was coming out the gate with one-two-three Soldiers. How it frightened me to face such an audience, when I have scarcely met a young man for months. They proved to be three of his boys from the 67th. One was Serg. Owens. They came in the house again and made a call.

Then, Thursday evening, I was standing at the gate alone, and two Soldiers came walking past, but it is such an "every minute occurrence" here that I did not notice them, until they turned around to take the second look at me. Thinking it rather <u>impudent</u> — I <u>looked at them</u> — when lo and behold! there was Capt. Penfield and Horace Stoddard. They, also, came in and <u>I</u> enjoyed the call very much.

Frank McMillen expects to return next Saturday. Mrs. Kelly will take her until she can find another place.

Sheldon expects to return tomorrow.

Much love to all.

Your daughter

Lina

Lina

Columbus Sep. 11" 1864

Dear Delia

You probably will expect a letter from Columbus on Tuesay night, and as Sheldon is in Granville it becomes my painful duty to write to you. This is our last Sunday at the "Kelley House" Mrs. Smythe promises to receive us the middle of the week. Just imagine, about Tuesday night various articles tumbling over the Balcony. Dont you wish you was here to help us move. It would be quite convenient to have a boy about your size to help carry our trunks into the third story. I helped Frank Mc" take one to her room at the Drury's. Then Edgar rushed forward and offered his assistance in carrying the other. Speaking of that family reminds me that "Rumor" says John Drury and Miss Kittridge are <u>engaged</u>. Some folks wonder if she will succeed so well in managing him as she does her father's wild horses.

Hattie and I will miss having a front window to sit by, otherwise the room will be very pleasant. We expect to be in the way, at either house, this week, as numerous friends are coming to attend the State Fair, which will be held the 13" 14" 15" and 16" of this month.

I wish you could have seen the "Splendid Splay" of Fire Works we had here Friday evening. It was a Union meeting, and a grand jollification over recent victories etc etc

Lieut's Denman and Colton called for their Sisters and took them to the west side of the State House where the crowd collected. A <u>hundred Guns</u> were fired. There were two long torch light processions came into the yard and marched around it. Six men carried the <u>dear Old Flag</u>. Others bore mottoes appropriate for the occasion. There was public speaking but we were not near enough to listen to it. There was a Soldier boy stood near me. He could not have been over eighteen, was on crutches and had <u>lost a limb</u>. Some brother Soldier called him to come where he was. "Oh! no," he replied, "I can't mingle with the crowd any more." Poor, dear little fellow, my heart ached for him. The days are gliding swiftly by, and soon I will be with you. The time seems so short till the <u>4"</u> of <u>October</u>. Do you think we can visit fast enough in two weeks? Sheldon cannot be gone from the Office longer than that. There was a letter came to the Office last week from a Mr. Whiting. The General took it to Sheldon, with a sober face, and said "Colton there is a letter from <u>your uncle</u>, he wants a Muster-in Roll."

I shall want Mrs. Story a day or two after we get home, perhaps it would be well to see if I can have her, at any time in the forepart of Oct. Carlos writes that he will come to Granville. I hardly dared hope it for fear of being disappointed, was afraid he could not spend time to come. Now we are certain of seeing Mother too.

Mr. Grammar will preach his farewell sermon next Sunday night. They have no other minister in view. Am afraid they will not succeed in getting one that will preach such interesting sermons as this one. But, he does not equal Mr. Armitage. I have not heard a minister yet that did. I am situated as you was when you last wrote. Have nothing to write about, so will close. Give much love to all. Let me hear from you soon. Sheldon says he will write to Aunt Lucy. He wrote to Aunt Lucinda last Sunday.

Your Sister

Lina

Ned Herd has been up here and taken the measure of <u>that</u> piece of glass. But we hear nothing more about it. Mrs. Kelley says I can do as you did. Leave it for the next boarders that come, to attend to.

Carlos

Toledo Sept 15th 1864

Dear Sister Delia

My last letter to you was duly received some time ago I guess, and I take this opportunity to write another. Lucy & John Blinn were here yesterday and last night (or rather, last night and today) and Lucy went on to Detroit this afternoon to visit Fanny for a short time. Annie had another "Chill" today, and I fear will shake off the "fat" that she accumulated while at the Sea Side. Alpha is getting ready to go to New York.

Tell Father I dont think Mr Kurtz could make a suit that would answer for me to wear at Sheldons <u>funeral</u>! I have ordered a nice coat and vest here. Am surprised Sheldon did not get his <u>Shroud</u> made in Columbus.

My health has improved very much since the cool weather commenced.

If we should have a draft here on Monday I will not "catch cold", as our Ward is out of it.

I send the usual amount $5.00

Love to all from
Carlos

Sept 18th 1864
New Albany Sunday Evening.

My Dear Sister

I have just been reading your long and very welcome letter of the 28th ult, and it is with pleasure I improve the opportunity of writing you this evening. Henry has gone to the Baptist Church, and Nellie is fast asleep. I never fully realized before how hard it is to live without our own Church services. I occassionally attend Presbyterian Church in the morning & Henry takes care of Nellie & of late he has been attending Baptist Church in the evening, there is a young minister there preaching a series of sermons on "the Signs of the times", in which Henry has become interested. I am so glad to have him propose going to any Christian Church, I cheerfully remain with Nellie. I feel very well contented here for a time, but, I would not like to feel it was to be my home I want to settle nearer Home. Henrys business does not yet bring him in much and I suppose it will be some time ere it will, as there are many expenses attending the commencement of such a business but I hope he will realize the profits after awhile, he has faith to believe he will. I am much happier here with him, than I could be anywhere away from him but I should be happier if I was where I could go to any of you in a few hours, as all the rest of the family can except Hiram. I feel bad to be so far from Ma fearing when her time comes to leave us it will be with only a few hours sickness. I received a letter from Lucy the same time I did yours. She was thinking of making Fannie a short visit very soon, as both Mr. Hyde & Fannie were very anxious to see her. I shall hope to hear from her soon, & know if she went & how she found Mr. Hyde. I had no idea when I left there, he would be living now.

I have not had a word from Lucinda since I left there though I wrote to her & Fannie when I first came. Fannie wrote me a mongh ago, but I do not expect letters from her, poor child. She has her hands & heart full. Your letter was very satisfactory for you told me of each member of your family except Carlos & Aunt mentions him in her letters. I suppose he will visit you too next month should Sheldon & Lina come home. How much I would like to compose one of the family circle too at that time. You must please remember me <u>then</u> with love to each and every one of the loved ones. I am comforting my heart with the hope I can make you a little visit next summer. Lucy was also dreading the Draft when she wrote I am hoping neither John, Mr. Carter or any of <u>our</u> family will be affected by it. Henry has not been enrolled here, & I trust he may escape it. How natural it is for us to be selfish when our own dear ones are in danger of leaving us. My greatest dread since I came here, has been the Guerilla warfare, we have not as yet been affected by it. I have seen a great many Kentucky Reffugees on account of them. There will of course be a great deal of excitement all over the country until after our Presidential Election. There was a McClellan Ratification meeting here last Thursday. My sincere prayer is that God may direct the issue of that Election to the honor safety & welfare of our Country. Please let me hear from you whenever you or the girls can communicate. I regret very much that you still suffer from those spasms of your stomach. Is there nothing can cure you. Please give my love to all enquiring <u>friends</u> and accept a good share for both the Heads & Daughters of your Household, including Lottie. Nellie is well & busy as ever each day. Good bye dear Sister

yours

Myra

Lina

Columbus Sep. 25" 1864

Dear Mother.

Sheldon and I felt quite releived yesterday after receiving a few lines from Father, saying that you would report here next Saturday. We were doubly glad to learn that you are coming to Columbus. I was trying to arrange matters in some way so you might come to the city, but did not know how it could be done.

Mrs Smythe says "Write to your Mother to come directly to our house and we will make her as comfortable as possible."

Hattie went home yesterday, I shall be alone all the week, and will be very impatient for the days to pass until Saturday shall come. Wish I could send enough money to pay your fare, but my months wages will not be due until Friday. Then, how rich I shall feel? The happy possessor of fifty dollars. Mrs Smythe requests us not to pay our board, at all, until the Holidays. Sheldon thinks now that he will not have writing for us after that time.

Mr Grammar has left Columbus, a minister from Covington preached here to day. I have taken a seat with a Mr Millers family. Does Nelia know them? He works at the State House. I felt as though it was discommoding Mr Smythes family for me to sit with them, although they have insisted upon it all the time. There is enough of them at any time to fill their seat, and, since Eddie's death they can all attend. Tell the girls to be prepared to hear the worst at any time, from Ned Herd. He is very sick indeed, with Camp fever. The Dr. gives the family little encouragement about him. Mary Herd is in Indiana.

I had a letter from Aunt Clarinda last week, inviting me to accompany Sheldon there on his wedding trips. I respectfully decline, thinking it will be far enough if I go to Milan with them. She writes that Aunt Fanny has been very anxious to have me with her and would have written for me long ago had I not been engaged here. Uncle Hyde is no better. Aunt Lucy is there trying to releive Aunt Fanny some. She intends to return home this week.

There is nothing in particular to write about as we expect to see you all so soon. Sheldon and I will meet you at the cars.

Give much love to all.

> Your Daughter
> Lina

Lina

Wednesday Morning.
Detroit Octo. 1864

Dear Sister.

Do you think it time I was writing to you? I motion that we write to each other all the time with a lead pencil, it is too much trouble to use ink. Well, I left Milan last Saturday morning at five oclock and took passage on the "Parsons" as I well know? It was a stormy day. The boat started late, staid a long time at each Island, and finally reached Detroit at ten oclock at night. Did not stop at Woodward Avenue, & no friends were there (at the boat) to meet me. I have not time to relate all the adventures of the day, but allow me to tell you that I was most wretchedly sea sick and reclined gracefully on the sofa from ten in the morning till ten at night. You of course remember the clerk of the boat. That gentleman who picked up your hat. Well, from some unknown cause we scraped acquaintance. In fact he sat by me an hour in the evening and talked, and talked, and talked. Said he would get me a carriage if Cousin Phin was not on hand. It was so late when we got here there was no carriage to be found, no Phin, nor nobody. So this polite young clerk informed me that he would be most happy to accompany me wherever I wished to go. The darling Soul? I will remember his kindness as long as I live. We reached Uncle Hydes sometime between ten and eleven. Phin was here taking care of Uncle, and Uncle George had been down with his carriage, waiting for the boat until he gave up in despair and concluded not to wait for its arrival. Uncle Hyde is more comfortable. They have some hopes now of his recovery.

How do you prosper with the writing. Do you like it? Are you homesick any.

I have hardly got settled yet, but think I shall like staying here very much. Aunt wanted me for company more than anything else. She keeps two girls all of the time, and there is some gentleman in every night to take care of Uncle. Generally a young man comes to sit up with him. I have made two or three new acquaintances.

There is no news to write, as I have not been about much. Saw "Chandler" in the street yesterday but not to speak.

How do Mr & Mrs Colton flourish? Give them my love, also Mrs Williams & Hattie. Remember me to Mrs Smythes family. What pen are you using? Can have mine if you would like it. Let me know.

Write whenever you can. Excuse short letters until I have been in the city longer.

Your Sister
Lina

300

Milan O. Nov. 19. 1864

My Dear Sister

Your kind letter was received with much pleasure; did not really expect one, yet thought perhaps you would think "that a bad promise is better broken than kept." Should not have blamed you much tho if you had not broken yours; but now I hope we will both let bygones be bygones in the matter of letter writing, and hereafter be on punctual corresponding terms. Am glad you are so well pleased with your situation this time, and hope you will not get home-sick till the time comes for you to come, and I for one will be right glad when you do come.

I miss you very much, in fact we all do; you need not be afraid the children will forget you; when I had read your letter to them, I asked Carrie Belle if I should write to you, she said yes, I asked what I should say for her, she answered immediately without any prompting, "tell Aunt Dele I dont want her to stay to Columbus, I want her to come home," and that is but the echo of the wishes of us all.

Robby Jarvis died last Tuesday evening about ten o'clock, and was buried on Thursday, Mr Marks officiating. Robert had been failing for the last month very rapidly, I was over to see him Tuesday afternoon, and saw that he had but a short time to live; he was sensible of his approaching end, about five in the evening having a fainting spell, he thought he was going, and called all the members of the family and shook hands and kissed each one and bid them good-bye; but he rallied up for a few hours longer.

He seemed perfectly resigned to go; to question from his father, just before he died, if he was willing to die, and if he expected to go and meet his Mother and Hiram in Heaven he answered yes, this is very gratifying to his friends, and serves in a great measure to mitigate the pang of parting.

I suppose you have heard of the return of Adie Poe's husband, he came quite unexpectedly, suppose Adie will be happy now.

Lina writes of terrible times in Detroit concerning the Secesh, wonder if Lina does'nt get frightened, and sometimes wish that she could be at Columbus, or somewhere, away from threatened or immediate danger

We have no Minister in our Church yet, nor no prospect of any as I can see.

This you will say is a short letter, and I agree with you, but I thought you had rather receive a short one, than none at all, and as I had a few moments leisure this morning, thought I would improve it. With much love

I remain
Yours truly
J P. Carter

(Delia)

Columbus Ohio Nov. 20/64

My Dear Father

I received your long looked for letter a few days ago. I was very much surprised and pained to hear of your ill health. If I had known it before, I should not have looked so long for a letter from you. I received a letter from Nelia soon after I came in which she said she was writing for you, as you had the sick-head-ache

I supposed it was one of your usual headaches and that you would be well in a few days and then write for your self. But it seems that it was more than that and from your letter I judge you are not well now. It makes me just want to get home and help you, but never mind. I will be there before long and then I will try and relieve you. Dont think that three months in Columbus will raise me above chopping & sawing wood, bringing water, going for the milk and mail etc. etc. no indeed I believe I can do it all just as well <u>now</u> as I could three years ago, at least I am willing to <u>try</u>.

I may not be home before Christmas and I may be home in about a month or so. I have not decided yet what I shall do.

How I should like to step in and spend next Thursday with you all, but as I cannot go to <u>that</u> home I am going to my <u>other</u> home. They have given us an urgent invitation to spend Thanksgiving in Granville which we have accepted.

And now while I think of it let me say that Mary says she did not say what I said she did, she says she said that she "<u>thought</u> my <u>Mother</u> liked her but that she did not know <u>how</u> it was with <u>Father</u>" If I wrote it differently from what she said I am sorry. I am sure I did not intend to, and <u>I</u> think too, that y<u>ou behaved very well</u> while they were there. I am sure I did not see anything that would lead her to think that you did not like her, and if I wrote any thing that made you think <u>she</u> thought so I am <u>very</u> <u>sorry</u> <u>indeed</u> but hoping that it is all made straight now by what has been said I will say no more about it.

Delia

I suppose you are having quite cool weather up North now. It has not been _very_ cold here yet, not "cold enough to go skating" I do not think I shall have much use for my skates here the short time that I remain.

Does Nelia still intend to go to Detroit? I received a short letter from Carl yesterday. In it he says "I am pleasantly situated in my _new boarding place_" Where has he gone to board? I did not know he had left Aunt's.

Yesterday Mr Williams and some of the folks here tried to plague me about George Whiting, as he had been here that day. I told Sheldon and Mary of it and then Sheldon began, he gave me some more work and told me not to begin it "_Capt George B. Whiting's Company_."A short time after it I found a figure I could not read and took it over to him with out first looking at the name and there right before me in big letters was written "_George Colton_" you may imagine the laugh that was turned on me then.

I have not been for any of Lina's photographs yet as I have had no money to get them with I shall be paid soon how ever for I informed Sheldon that he must get me some or else I cannot go to Granville this week and as he says I _must_ go, why of course I must Does Nelia enjoy teaching now as much as she did before I left? Ask her to write me what new pieces she has got since I came here.

I guess you will be supplied with letters this time as Sheldon and Mary have both written to Milan.

As I wish to put in a note to Mother I will close this, with much love to all and hoping you and Mother, and all, will keep well until we are permitted to meet again I remain as ever your loving

Daughter
Delia

Lina

Dear Delia

I asked for B.F. Hyde's mail and got a letter from you. Am glad you gave me such advice. But, after all, I came very near <u>not</u> getting it, for, just as my hand was upon the letters the Clerk called out "show your check". I, kindly, informed him that "I <u>hadn't</u> <u>any</u> pocketed my mail and disappeared. The Clerks carry the letters around now, and if mine are directed to No. 89 Farmer Street, they will reach me safely. No: I did not tell the Boat Clerk that my Sister was anxious for me to get married, but I <u>did</u> tell him that she lost off her hat one day, and <u>he</u> picked it up for her. He remembered the circumstances. You wanted me to write and tell you all the news, what in the world can I tell you! Hattie has a baby, a bright little boy. Is that news? Mary will please notice that she made a mistake in the person. They have named the baby "Earl". We live in a state of considerable excitement here, expecting any night to be attacked by rebels from Canada. You perhaps have seen it noticed in the papers that they are trying to destroy this City and Buffalo. The people of Detroit think they are well prepared to receive them. They are obliged to be very cautious and watchful all of the time.

How much longer do you intend staying in Columbus? Take my advice and dont leave there <u>to</u> <u>spend</u> <u>the</u> <u>Winter</u> <u>in</u> <u>Detroit</u>. I miss the copying more and more every day. The time ahead seems long to me, but perhaps it will fly faster after awhile.

Hiram Poe and Jordie have both got home, we have not learned the particulars yet. Has Henry "Cant see it" been to see me? Indeed he has. He has been here to dinner. Spent an evening, escorted me to church and to a lecture. But, Delia to tell the truth, I wish he would <u>not</u> come. I verily believe his intentions are <u>serious</u>, and for some reason, unaccountable, I cannot feel more than friendship for him. He is a real good looking, straight forward, honest, hard working, money making, sharp fellow, (so Uncle Hyde says). Am expecting an <u>offer</u>, have viewed the matter in every light, but "<u>cant see it</u>". Keep this letter to yourself or else burn it.

Lina

There is another chap comes here to <u>sit</u> <u>up</u> with Uncle Hyde and takes me to Union meetings. If I chance to rush down stairs before he comes up he embraces the <u>opportunity</u> (<u>and</u> <u>me</u> <u>too</u>) to sigh, press my hand, look his affection in a thousand ways etc. etc. I examine my heart, but it is safe and sound in the right place. In fact, I believe that it is perfectly hardened, and only one person in the world, that I know now, can make an impression on it. So look out for a cross old maid Sister. The lecture I attended, with Henry, was delivered by a female, Miss Hattie Greenwood. The subject, "Whom shall I marry?" It was a grand fizzle. Dont go to hear her, should she chance to visit Columbus. Del Smith sat near me, came forward and shook hands. Says he is coming to see me. Brady Backus, (a cousin of Dr. Cornell's) living here, has been told that <u>I</u> <u>used to know the Dr.</u> He sends word by Louise Truax that he is coming to see me some evening this week. Am anxious to meet the gentleman, on account of relation. How do Mr. & Mrs. Colton prosper?   Have not heard a word from them since they went back to Columbus.   Tell Hattie when that green dress is photographed I expect a copy.

Uncle Hyde is improving all the time. Do not think I am needed here <u>very</u> much. Although Aunt Fanny says it is a great relief to her having me here. The rest of our folks are all well.

Write me whenever you can, and burn this nonsensical epistle.

Your forlorn Sister

Much love to Mary & Robbie   Caroline

[pencilled in <u>tiny</u> script on the back of the envelope]

Walk on my dear, my all, my life,
For I have got another wife.
I cannot come and lie with thee
For I must go to bed to <u>she</u>.

Milan O. Dec 22. 1864

My Dear Sister

Your kind letter was duly received and having a few leisure moments, thought I would improve the time in <u>commencing</u> a letter to you.

I am glad to hear you continue to like your situation, and hope you will stay contentedly as long as Sheldon can find something for "honest hands to do". Now dont say I am glad to have you away, putting the wrong construction on my words, for if I did not think it for your good, I would not have said it, for I tell you we all miss you much, and none more than I.

Your Father & Mother must be very lonely now, for Nelia took her departure Tuesday Morning, however guess they can manage to get along for couple of weeks. Hope Nelia will have a pleasant visit, and think she will, for Detroit is a pleasant City, and then she has many friends there who, I doubt not will do their utmost, to make her visit agreeable. Lina will be pleased, for I think, from her letters home she is somewhat afflicted with that prevaling disease by some called homesickness, at least the symptoms indicate it, now, from having seen good deal of the disease, and witnessed its direful effects in <u>others</u>, I think, I can prescribe a few <u>remedys</u>. In the first place, because it is the most important, if she should form a <u>very</u> <u>intimate</u> acquaintance with some very eligible young man, in the society of whom, she could be led to forget the disease, or the cause of it, or failing in this, let her throw off the feeling that perhaps she is needed there, and go to Hattie's to make as long a visit as she <u>wishes</u>, then she would effectually be cured, or thirdly as the Domine's say, if she should come home feeling that it was really necessary for her to be here, either one of the above <u>remedys</u> would produce a radical cure. This is a gratuitous opinion voluntarily given, for I feel that I shall be well paid, if it should be the cause of doing good in the case in home or in my future case, for they are remedies that by varying little will answer in almost any case.

There is nothing new or particularly interesting transpiring here. They are getting up a Christmas tree in the Episcopal Church which I believe closes up the Sabbath School for a time.

We are particularly lonesome just now, on account of Ma going home, we were much disappointed, for we had made up our minds that she was going to remain with us all Winter, but my Sister with whom Ma makes her home, would not hear to it, and so to "keep peace in the family", we submitted. Here I have to stop for I am interupted so much that it impossible to proceed.

Wednesday afternoon

Not a great deal more to say, went to the concert last evening (had a complimentary ticket) and was well pleased, the Hall was literally crammed. We are having cold weather here, I suppose you are so far down South, cold does not effect you; we have had some skating but not much, the snow has interfered, and we have not had enough of the latter to make good sleighing or rather have not had enough in the right places, for the wind took pleasure in blowing it out of the road; but I must close. I will take this to the house and try and induce Lottie to write something and perhaps if I will keep it over the <u>Sabbath</u> she can find time.

With much love for yourself and <u>others</u>
    I remain
        as ever
           Yours truly
           J P. Carter

Lottie Carter

[written on back sheet of J P. Carter's letter of 12/22/64]

Christmas night. /64

Dear Sister Delia

I hope you have passed a "merry christmas," or at least a happy one. It has been very quiet for us, and all that marred our pleasure was being seperated from our brothers & sisters, at a time when families love to be united, but, as you say you "sent a Substitute" in the shape of presents, which made many hearts glad. We were all so surprised when the box arrived and we discovered its contents, it does not seem right Delia that you should spend your money so dearly earned, for us, however it <u>does</u> make folks happy to receive presents, and I think still happier to <u>give</u> them. I hope "Santa Claus" made you a visit. The children were delighted with their presents, and have kept their "jumping jacks" <u>dancing</u> all day. I put them in their stockings with only the <u>Monkey</u> <u>visible</u> perched on top the stick, and I <u>do</u> <u>wish</u> you could have seen how delighted they were. They understand where all their presents came from and would thank <u>Uncle</u> <u>Sheldon</u> for those pretty cups if they could see him. Carter wishes me to thank you in his name, and thinks <u>with</u> you that he cannot have <u>too</u> <u>many</u>, and now for myself, I fared extra well, the pictures you sent are beautiful, nothing could have pleased me more. I am so fond of pictures, and these will make such pretty ornaments. <u>Accept</u> <u>my</u> <u>thanks</u>. Pa presented me with a covered vegetable dish, and a very pretty Britania soup ladle, and Carter gave me a sett of silver forks. But I must close for want of room to write.

[written upside down at top of page]

I do want to see you <u>so</u> <u>much</u>, hope you may spend a happy New year. The children talk about you a great deal. With much love for Sheldon, sister Mary, and yourself I close.   Lottie

You must excuse this miserable writing for I do not write enough to keep my hand in

Lina

Hattie Mansion
Detroit Dec. 29th 1864

Dear Delia

I have concluded to <u>steal</u> a few moments this morning and write you a line. Nelia arrived last Friday night, and ever since we have been <u>very</u> busy visiting. First, in one place, then, another. Uncle Hyde is so much better that they do not need me, so I follow around after Nelia, and, I <u>tell</u> <u>you</u>, it seems good to have her here. I will describe our Holiday and gifts thus far and shall expect to hear from you soon with a full report of the doings at Columbus. Clarinda had a Christmas dinner on Saturday. Visions of Turkeys and mince pies still haunt my mind! From there we went down to Aunt Fannys and staid over night, at the breakfast table some mysterious packages appeared, one large one in particular, at my plate attracted attention. After undoing two or three papers I found a dish of "pork and beans" with Mrs. Saunders compliments. The next package contained candy. The next a collar, a pair of cuffs, sleeve buttons, and some blue ribbon to "tie up my bonnie brown hair", all from Aunt Fannie. Nelia's was a very pretty neck tie, a sheet of music ("Annie Laurie" with variations), candy, etc. The next day Uncle George took us a long sleigh ride. We went all through the Cemetery, to the Water Works, and every place of note around the City, coming back to Hattie's we found Santa Claus had called there too. Another piece of music "The Patriotic Hymn" for Nelia from Cousin Phin, a handsome bottle of Cologne from him to me, Handkerchiefs for us both from Cousin Hattie, and <u>snuff</u> <u>boxes</u> from Aunt Clarinda. Nelia brought me a beautiful handkerchief case of her own work that I prize highly. She received the music and collar from Sheldon and Mary and sends many thanks for them. We both fared well although it was entirely unexpected. I thought much of you and wished it was in my power to send some token of remembrance. Nelia expects to start homeward next Tuesday. I may go to Trenton, but do not intend to go farther with her at present. They have sent invitations for me to spend the remainder of the Winter in Toledo, however, shall stay here a few weeks longer.
Uncle Hyde is gaining slowly all the time. They consider that he is in no more danger and after the tedious Winter is through he expects to be able to attend to business.
It is dinner time and my note must be closed. All unite in sending love to Sheldon, Mary and yourself. Love to Hattie and Miss Morgan Nelia will write soon.

Your Sister
Lina

1865

Grant orders Sherman to march up through the Carolinas, thus providing the Union a base on the coast.

On February 17, the right wing of Sherman's army occupies Columbia, South Carolina. The city is burned accidentally, leaving a forest of chimneys and ruined State House. Sherman's left wing proceeds, through swollen rivers and swamps, to Hanging Rock — then on to Fayetteville, North Carolina. Goldsboro is occupied on March 23.

Richmond surrenders to Grant and the Army of the Potomac on April 3. A negro regiment is the first to enter the town.

General Lee surrenders at Appomatox on April 9.

On April 14, President Lincoln is assassinated.

General Johnston surrenders at Greensboro on April 26.

In May, Lincoln's coffin (on a catafalque covered with moss and flowers) rests in the State House of Columbus, Ohio.

Carlos continues working in Toledo. His salary is raised to $1,000/year.

Carrie Belle, young daughter of Lottie and J.P. Carter, dies.

Sheldon and Mary have their first son, Walter.

Lina remains in Columbus as a copyist, working with Sheldon.

Nelia resides in Toledo with relatives, finding satisfaction in her piano accomplishments.

Delia attends the Western Reserve Normal School, continuing to assist her parents in the Milan home and garden.

Melinda and Hamilton (as in years past) struggle to maintain the family homestead, receiving their primary financial support from Sheldon and Carlos.

M. S. Cotton

Milan January 1st 1865

Dear darling Dee-dee,

I wish you a very "Happy New Year" — and may every <u>succeeding</u> <u>new</u> <u>year</u> , bring you increasing joy & happiness. Whatever your outward circumstances may be may you <u>ever</u> have that "<u>inward peace</u> & <u>joy</u>" which only those can have, who <u>truly</u> <u>love</u> the Saviour.

As we have no Sunday School to attend to now, and as I have a cold & not feeling very well, also the weather being pretty cold, I concluded I would not try to go to Mr Walters Church today, — although he called a few days ago, & invited us to attend there, while we had no Services in our own Church, also said he would like to have some of our Sunday School Teachers come & assist in the Service, as they have so many scholars now, (over three hundred) that they have a lack of Teachers. But as I am not able to attend regularly in the Winter season, I thought it was hardly worth while for me to go in as Teacher, — And we shall probably have our own started again by Spring, if not sooner. But Mrs Mackey thought that perhaps she would take her own children, & go there for the present.

Several times today I have imagined that I could see you sitting in Trinity Church listening to our good Bishop. And have thought to myself, how glad I am that Delia is now where she can enjoy such privileges. —   And I hope by the time you come home there will be something done towards getting a Minister here. I suppose you know that Bishop McIlvaine has but just returned from a visit to Europe, consequently he has known nothing about our condition here, for some time past. Mr. Minuse wrote to him a few weeks since, telling him how we were situated, & that the Ladies were about giving up the Sunday School. — The Bishop replied that he had always felt a deep interest in this Parish, & that he would very soon try, & see what could be done for us. So we will try to "Hope on & hope ever" for a better time to come —

We have got along very nicely since Nelia went away only that we have <u>sometimes</u> felt a little lonely, but we shall now expect her back again toward the last of this week, & then when your time is out and you get home again, safe and well, we shall try to forget the past in the joy of the present.

M. S. Colton

I presume Nelia will have pretty busy times of it for she will have more new music scholars to commence the new year. Josey Mackey will begin again next week, & she says that Leah Edwards, and Alice Hough, also expect to commence taking lessons at the same time.   At one time we thought that Lina would return with Nelia but we judged from her last letter that she had decided to stay awhile longer, & visit among her "Ellations" —

Mr Carter has decided to go to Chicago, will leave about the middle of next week. But Lottie says she does not wish Lina to hurry home on her account, but would rather she would stay and you will see that I had to turn back to this sheet to finish my letter & have now only room left to say "Happy greeting to all, Mrs Smythe & family included, and love for Nelia & family & yours in particular from your

Affectionate Mother M.S. Colton

I wanted to write to Sheldon & Mary to day also but have now concluded to put it off until a "More Convenient Season" you will please tell them, that I am very much pleased with the <u>book</u> that I received, as a "Christmas gift" from them, and return them many thanks for it Carter & Lottie are now reading it, they are also much pleased with it ———— Carlos sent your Father & I each of us five dollars extra for our Christmas gift, from him. So you see Santa Claus remembered the "Old folks at home" even from different parts of the Country — he also sent Lina five dollars — I suppose the reason of his having so much to give away just now is that on Christmas Morning at the breakfast table he found on his plate a present of fifty dollars, from Messrs Hopkins & Griffith. But the time for which he had engaged to remain with them has now expired. And tomorrow he is to commence again with Mr Strong with two hundred dollars added to his salary, which will now make it one thousand a year, consequently he feels in better spirit, now than he has for some time past —

There has been several cases of Small Pox, over in East Milan but as yet no deaths, some cases in Mr Lockwoods family. And Mr Henry Lockwood (not Uncle Henry) who were to Mr Darlings to help take care of those who were sick with it. It is reported that there is a great deal of it in Sandusky.

Old Mr Mears, who has been sick for a long time with Consumption died Friday Morning. May Abbot was more comfortable when we heard from her a few days since.

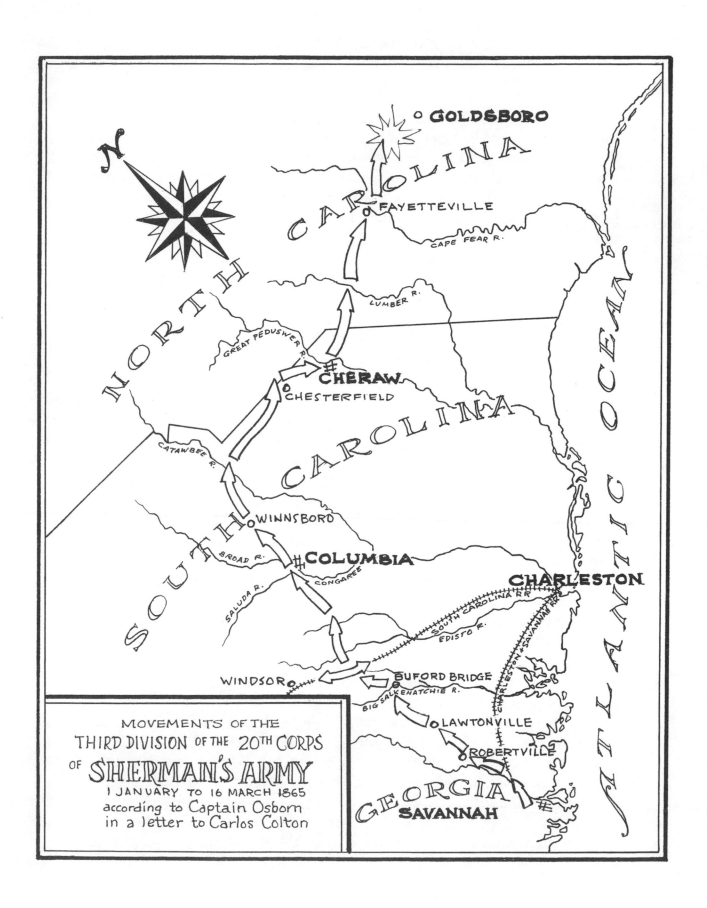

MOVEMENTS OF THE
THIRD DIVISION OF THE 20TH CORPS
OF SHERMAN'S ARMY
1 JANUARY TO 16 MARCH 1865
according to Captain Osborn
in a letter to Carlos Colton

Friend

Dear Carlos

Now that we have got a permanent Camp for a few weeks, I am able to acknowledge the receipt of your letter of the 7th of Feby ~ , and to give you according to my custom some account of Sherman's raid at the glorious termination thereof. Please excuse the dry details I may inflict upon you. You know that some events which would interest me, have little or nothing to please you, and I cannot always judge. Trusting to your charity however I will enter upon the task.

This movement had of course to Gen Sherman quite as clear a beginning as any other campaign, but to those not in the secret, when all the army was in motion is not so clear. Leaving Savannah on the 1st of Jan'y the 3rd Division of the 20th Corps, encamped on South Carolina soil first on the plantation of a Dr Cheves, who from many indications we judged to be an arrant rebel. We soon moved to Cardee's Farm and from thence to Cardeeville a small station on the Charleston & Savannah R.R. The swamps predominate in this section, and the effect of the swamp water on the general health of the men expecially those not yet inured to the service, was very generally deleterious. We enjoyed a good spell of wet weather at this place, but on the 20th of Jan. when we took up our line of march for the interior, the weather was fine. Our next camp was at Robertsville, where forage was plenty. Some of the enemy opposed our foragers here, but they were driven off and the eatables <u>secured</u>. Feb. 2nd found us on the march again and still toward the north. At Lawtonville a town indicated by a cross roads only, some cavalry undertook to check our advance, but were soon sent flying. They fell back unfortunately into a column of the 15th Corps on another road, and were so severely handled, as not to be willing to try that again. As we advanced through Beaufort and Barnwell District, all abandoned houses were burned. The consequence was that between the foragers and the Provost Guards the country was totally ruined. Pursuing a north easterly course through Barnwell Dist. we crossed the Big Salkehatchie at Buford Bridge. This was of course destroyed, and the crossing gave us much trouble as it is through a long and difficult swamp. We had now emerged to a higher country from the swamp, of the low land and although we found swamps occasionally, the travelling was much more pleasant. Feby 7th we struck the S.C. R.R. at Grahams TurnOut and commenced our work of destruction. From this station to near Windsor, a distance of nearly twenty miles I can vouch for the fact that the track was thoroughly destroyed. In addition to bending the rails, they were thoroughly twisted, and rendered totally valueless.

Friend

Feby 11th passing through Williston station we again marched toward the interior. The South Fork of the Edisto was crossed without opposition. Some enterprising soldiers however had cut loose a mill dam and flooded the roads, so that the troops were compelled to wade a considerable distance. The weather was decidedly cool and the sensation of wading in ice cold water over frosty territory, can be better imagined than described. But soldiers must be prepared for experiences, and Sherman's army took the plunge as usual with a yell, and a hearty laugh. The North Fork of the Edisto was crossed after some slight opposition and we entered Lexington District which is certainly the poorest in the State. Through long stretches of sandy soil covered with a dense pine forest we wound our way, only occasionally finding any houses or traces of inhabitants. At last on the 16th inst we camped on the banks of the Congaree with the City of Columbia in full view. A pleasant place it seemed, situated on gently rising ground and beautifully shaded with large trees. The view was just at that time doubtless pleasanter than the reality, for the union guns were sending them compliments into the city, and the little puffs of white smoke in and about the State House, showed that the gunners practice was to say the least not bad. It was not our fortune to see more of the city. The Right Wing passed the Congaree, here, and destroyed the city, leaving a forest of chimneys and a ruined State House to tell where the nest of traitors hatched the serpent of rebellion. The Congaree is formed by the juncture of the Saluda and the Broad Rivers, which combine only a few miles above Columbia. The Left Wing crossed both the last two rivers above their junction. They are rapid streams and of considerable size and are beautifully fringed with willows and other trees which grow out of the steep banks and hang over the water. North of the Broad River the country is characterized by abrupt hills of red clay, but with much more hard timber than we had before seen. On the 21st inst we passed through Winnsboro, a thriving town, and one of the pleasantest I have seen in the South. The district is a rich one, and affords very many fine views. The columns of smoke which rose from every hill denoting the destruction of fair homes and pleasant firesides, added a certain sublimity to scenes such as the South seldom affords. A rapid march of some thirty miles, at last brought us to the Catawbee River which we crossed at midnight on a pontoon bridge by the flaring light of pitch pine fires. It rolls a rapid flood although not very deep and the banks are very precipitous. Happily for us, the clouds withheld their favors until we were safely en route on the hither side. The 14th Corps which followed us had an awful time toiling up the steep hills made slippery by the rain. For about a week however our progress was very slow. The heavy trains cut the roads to pieces and many a mile did we make a corduroy of rails. The only way to get

Friend

them along. At last on a fine day we reached Hanging Rock, the scene of a revolutionary encounter, which is named from a large rock poised upon a narrow base, looking as though about to plunge into the creek far below. On Friday the 3rd of March we entered Chesterfield G.H. the county seat of the Dist of that name. From there our Corps marched north and camped on the North Carolina line, but soon marched to Cheraw where we crossed the Great Peduswer. Cheraw had been the refuge of those who left Charleston upon its occupation by our forces, but they left the frying pan for the fire. The town was badly destroyed an unfortunate explosion of a magazine adding its horror to the scene. From Cheraw to Fayetteville our march was through a barren waste, upon which we could with difficulty live. The whole country is given up to the manufacture of turpentine, which is obtained by scoring the pine trees and collecting the pitch which exudes. Mile on mile of these turpentine groves we passed, the march being only diversified by the occasional swamp or creek. The pitch pine trees burn very readily and I have seen them so burned while standing as to fall. The only comfort we derived from them was the quick fire they made. After having crossed the Lumber River on the 11th of Mrch we reached Fayetteville. The 14th Corps were in the town when we arrived and we found the Michigan Engineers busily engaged in destroying the Arsenal. Scarcely one stone was left upon another although they all agree it was the best constructed set of buildings they ever destroyed. The Cape Fear River was crossed here on a pontoon bridge. The fine wooden bridge having been destroyed by the rebels, and now we were off for Goldsboro. After a march of forty or fifty days, the novelty of the thing wears off, and we were anxiously counting the miles and the days which must necessarily intervene before we could hope for our well earned rest, when on the 15th inst our advances were opposed by the enemy. On the 16th we advanced and had a sharp fight, driving the enemy from two lines of works and capturing three cannon with many prisoners. In this action the line was advanced to within one hundred and fifty paces of the enemys breastworks, with very little cover.

[the remainder of this letter was never found]

[a letter to Delia from Carlos dated April 13th, 1865, identifies the author as — Captain Osborn, serving in General Sherman's army]

Carlos

Toledo Mch 29th 1865

Dear Sister Delia

      I suppose you suppose I got back to Toledo all right and I write to inform you that the supposed supposition is correct, I did. Carter and Lottie and Libbie Moore and the "Dorg" arrived safely Monday night. I had some berths engaged in the sleeping car for all but the dog, and saw them comfortably fixed before the train left. Lottie was well, only a little tired. Libbie Moore was wide awake, and glad to see her "Untle Tarlos" and a couple of oranges that he gave her.

Tell Nelia I delivered her note to Mr Whiting, he said the money enclosed we paid her account <u>two cents!</u> —— The lists of Soldiers names that I got of you was published in the "Blade" tonight. I send back the original list and will send you the "Blade". The name of "Shoemaker" I left out from the list as there is a family here by that name, and by the way Miss Mary Shoemaker enquired very particularly about Nelia a few weeks ago when I attended a little party at their house. She said she and Nelia were good friends once. She is a very pretty girl. ——

Lottie said Grandma and Lucy met them at the cars in Fremont.

The weather has changed again, today being dark and rainy —— The family here are well. Aunt got a letter from George Truax saying Alice is no better, and said he and Lucinda intended soon to visit Toledo Fremont and Milan. I dont know how soon. Annie told me of it on the street, presume you will hear from them before they start —— Please give the enclosed $5— to Father. I have no "Greenback" today but think this goes in trade just as well.

      Much love to all from
           Your brother
           Carlos

Friend

Milan April 7th 1865

Friend Lina.

Of all your acquaintance in Milan you will probably, be most surprised in receiving a letter from me. And that too on a subject, which had passed my mind, untill I was again reminded of it by public gossip.

I refer to the conversation, (or the remarks,) I made to you, in my last call at your mother's. Now Lina, you and I have been acquainted for a long time: and I always esteemed you, Lottie and Sheldon, as among my best, and most choice friend's; And do you wonder Lina, I felt hurt, <u>grieved</u>, to learn that, <u>that</u> conversation had been made public.

My sisters sudden death, and our conversation about her, and in regard to her little motherless children, caused me, unthinkingly to say what I did to you. It appeared my remarks seemed strange: perhaps they were. I should not made them, had I not thought, our long acquaintance, and friendly feelings: warrented me, the respect of privacy: at least, upon so delicate a subject: What I said to you my friend, I would not repeat to the public. Although if the whole of the conversation was taken into consideration it would not seem so very singular after all.

Now Lina, I <u>do not</u> blame you, for rehersing our conversation to your mother, that was but natural for you, but I was not a little surprised, to learn, that your kind and sensible mother, should repeat it to "Miss Harriet Gorden" and "Miss Harriet" repeat it to Mrs "Gaston" (And you know a story carried by fickle Miss "<u>Public Gossip</u>" never looses anything).

Friend

My Mother, heard of it, as well as other of my friends, they told me people were wondering why "Mrs Smith" talked so to "Lina Colton" It was a great wonderment! In fact it was quite a dish of petty scandal: served around to one and another: Do you blame me, dear Lina, or is it strange, that I felt hurt and mortifyed? Let your own kind heart answer.

It was a confidential girlish talk of mine, prompted at the time, by thoughts, and a heart-full of grief, occasioned by the sudden death of my tenderly beloved sister.

Death, is a terrible guest, and my friend after his visitation's, one has many serious thoughts — thoughts, which perhaps, otherwise would never occur. Under such circumstances, it was I made those remarks to you, little thinking of the result.

I regrett that afternoon call. No! pardon me, I will not say I regrett the call. I regrett exceedingly, my own want of discression and thoughtfullness. And lament my natural impulsiveness, but one lives to learn by experience: the lessons in life.

Yours with kind, and friendly regard
Josephine

P.S.

Please remember me to Sheldon, whom my husband and myself, have alway so truly regarded

I believe there is, very few, in society, who posess his love of truth, uprightness, and integrity.

The longer I live, the more I learn, of so called Society those gems of his character shine, with a brighter and more beautiful luster in the memory of his friend.

I have thought of talking with your mother: you can remail this letter to her if you choose, in fact it is my wish that you should, as she knows a part: I wish her to know the whole of our intercourse

Lina

Columbus April 9" 1865

Dear Delia

The housekeepers still prosper, and were greatly rejoiced at seeing their Milan goods yesterday morning. The bureau was considerably scratched, I mention it so that Lottie's can have a thicker covering if it has not already gone. The bedding could not fit better if it had been made expressly for this bedstead. In fact I feel quite proud of my <u>white</u> <u>counterpane</u> and ruffled pillow cases. It was quite laughable to see how we managed before the things did come, minus kitchen table and chairs, crockery, etc. etc. I have been writing and reading since last Tuesday. Have been to the Goodale House, twice, to "read up" Mrs Snively. Also once to the Medical College, up three or four flights of stairs to read with Mrs Stone. We do not know when to expect Hattie as their family have not got settled. I shall be glad to see her, for the eight hours are long sitting up in my room all alone. I have been to the State House a number of times this Spring and am quite well convinced that the clerks in the Office do not work half as steadily as the copyists outside. George Whiting visited us last week. He now intends going to Detroit soon, and rather hinted, to me, that he would like to go by the way of Milan. Shall I invite him to do so? To me, he is Eugene Whitney and Late Lathrop combined. Who does he remind you of? Are you yet in School: and do you enjoy going as much as ever?

The Sandusky paper that Pa sent this week has in it an account of Carrie Belle's death. I had the same statement in a Columbus and Toledo paper, and a shorter notice in the Cleveland Herald that I bought on the cars. Have sent the Columbus paper to Mr. Carter and if you care to keep the acct from the Register will send it to you. Has there been a tomb stone placed at the little grave yet? How is it engraved?

Lina

When news reached here that Richmond was taken, and that a Negro Regiment was the first to enter the town, Sheldon says that Gov. Brough was fairly beside himself with joy and excitement. He would exclaim with an oath "Boys there is poetry in that". I attended the Presbyterian Church this morning. Mr. Morris read the Gov's Proclamation, setting apart next Friday as a day for divine service Thanksgiving and prayer. The evening for the <u>thundering</u> of <u>Artillery</u>, public speaking, bonfires, illuminations and general rejoicing.   In short, it is a Singular proclamation. At the close of it Mr. Morris remarked that there would be services in the church Friday morning but <u>not</u> in the evening. At that point somebody laughed aloud.

I enclose a letter received from Josephine yesterday. It tells its own story. I feel a little mortified about the affair myself, and do not wonder that she feels very much so. I think the report circulated from its being repeated to Mrs Dean, and not to Miss Gordon as she asserts. What does Nelia think about it? Sheldon & Mary think they will never board again. The first named is busy all the time out of office hours, with wood sawing tinkering and <u>fussing</u>. He has bought tools and lumber and worked until ten oclock last night making a wash bench.

Mary has a great deal of ambition. She is busy all the time, and accomplishes a good amount of work in a short space of time. I am writing on the dining table and as it is tea time must lay aside my letter. Has Ma returned from Fremont yet? Give much love to all and write soon

Your Sister

Lina

Had a long call from Mary Herd yesterday. Whenever it is convenient will you send the two receipts for lemon pie, cottage and crowsfoot pudding.

Columbus, O. April 10th 1865

Dear Father:

Enclosed please find a draft on New York for $28.65 payable to order of myself and endorsed to A.P. Mowry, which please hand to him to settle my account with him.

Also find $7.00 of which $3.50 is to be paid to Mr. Ashley and the rest to Halsey Draper.

The town is jubilant to day over the surrender of Lee.

We are all well.

Yours etc.

Sheldon

Carlos

Toledo April 13th 1865

Dear Sister Delia

I am writing with your pen which has been to Detroit and back this week, it seems to be very much improved now. I will enclose it in this letter and hope it will suit you.

I sent a Detroit paper to Mother today, containing a notice of Beely Brigham, it seems he came unexpectedly to George Truaxes, dont know whether he still remains there or not. Aunt Sophia has been expecting a visit from him though she dont seem to desire it particularly. Grandma is still here waiting for Company and pleasant weather to go to Detroit with. Thinking that perhaps you have not seen any Rebel Money I enclose some that was sent to me by Capt Osborn, who is with Genl Shermans army. You may keep it to show to your friends. I also send $4— for Father. At last account Alice Slocum was getting better. Have not heard from Lina nor Lottie yet.

With much love I am   your brother —
Carlos

Lina

Columbus May 7" 1865

Dear Mother

Your letter was received, but I did not find time to reply to it last week. I enclose one to Aunt Fanny that you can do as you wish about sending to her. It is the most I can do for a reply.

Not feeling well enough to attend church this morning have seated myself to writing in "our Sanctum" while Sheldon & Mary are keeping house down stairs. They say they never will board again, never. Our board bill is paid over to Mary and she refuses to accept more than $3 1/2 per week. Of course we do not complain, but are willing to pay more while provisions are so high. There is a prospect now of losing our situations before many months, the war is so nearly closed. Sheldon says we will be crowded with muster out rolls for the present, and he will <u>try</u> to put back the National Guards, so as to make our work last longer, but is not certain yet as he can do it.

Captain Dewitt Whiting was here two or three days last week, having just escaped from prison. He is a second Cousin of Mary's and has been a prisoner over two years. He escaped three times before but was recaptured. His last escape was the most <u>laughable</u> of any I have heard about yet. When they were being convoyed from one prison to another the train stopped at Charlotte N.C. while there, with a knife and file they had cut out a portion of the car floor and got beneath it. When the train started <u>they</u> <u>were</u> <u>left</u> <u>on</u> <u>the</u> <u>ground</u>. They were fired onto from the cars and one poor man was killed. The Capt. went from here to Newark to give the particulars to the wife of the man that was shot. Four of them escaped, travelling by night and hiding through the day. They started in March and have only just reached here. Says they would not have got through this time without help from the darkies. They often hid them in the Haylofts and carrying two meals a day to them. Three officers from their Regiment got away from prison last Winter, they endured such hardships, fatigue, and excitement of mind in escaping that they are now all in the <u>Lunatic</u> <u>Asylum</u>. Capt. Whiting is only 22 but very heavy and measures 6 ft 2 inches. We can hardly

When they were being convoyed from one prison to another the train stopped... with a knife and file they had cut out a portion of the car floor and got beneath it.

imagine him crawling through any <u>very</u> small place. His whole conversation was interesting and we all enjoyed the visit. Sheldon, Hattie, and I spent a part of Tuesday evening at the Blind Asylum with Mr Lindsay, a day or two before he had fallen over a Bass Viol. striking his eye on one of the keys. It has been very painful to him but was better the night we were there. He invited Miss Lipton into the parlor to sing for us. How strange it seemed to be entertained by two blind people. It was sad too, but they so entered into the Spirit of entertaining us and seemed so glad to have us there, that we enjoyed it very much. Mr Lindsay urged us to come out there some afternoon and listen to singing by the choir. We intend to do so and then write in the evening.

The sweet scented Shrub came to hand last week. We have not smelled anything so good before this Spring. The paper that I sent to Nelia describes the Catafalque in the State House as being covered with moss and flowers when the Presidents Coffin rested there. Sheldon brought us some of the moss as a memento. I want to put mine under glass in a very small frame so as to preserve it. Having it pressed first. If Pa has any more of the Stonewall Scrapings, or little shells, I should not object to that style of a frame. I have the Presidents photograph in a "passapateau frame" (Nelia knows what that style is if it isn't spelled right). It is square and about the size of the one that Pa sent Mary's picture in.

Sheldon says he is intending to write and send with mine, so I will let him tell the rest of the news.

Give much love to all.

Your daughter

Lina

Delia need not think that silk cape too short. The shorter the more stylish we find, this season.

It is to be hoped you will not send this letter to Carlos for I have written him about the same thing once.

How strange it seemed to be entertained by two blind people. It was sad too, but they so entered into the Spirit of entertaining us and seemed so glad to have us there, that we enjoyed it very much.

M. S. Cotton

Milan May 7th 1865

Dear Carlos,

      Your little inclosing receipt for Life Insurance, also a "note" for family use, was rec'd last evening. For all of which you will please accept our grateful thanks. All the benefit that I ever hope to receive from these yearly receipts, is the reflection, that I have a dear good Son, who is constantly providing for my present wants, also laying up a sum, for my future necessities, if it should be the will of our Heavenly Father to take him first. And I hope & trust & <u>pray</u> dear Carlos that you will, at the same time, be "laying up for <u>yourself</u> treasures in Heaven". And I know that this, that you are doing for <u>us</u> in our old age, & for your young sisters, you will find hereafter, has been one treasure laid up, on your account which will <u>never</u> be forgotten.

      Yes, your "memory serves you aright" as to "the 7th of May, being the anniversary of that memorable event, your birth day. And do you <u>remember</u>, that, that first, 7th of May, that <u>you</u> <u>ever</u> saw was just such a bright & beautiful <u>Sunday</u>, as this has been? And I hope you will live to see a great many more such quiet & beautiful anniversaries, as this has been to-day.

      Last Friday morning when you imagined that "I was out among the flowers" I was employing my time in a very different manner. The girls & I have been cleaning house for a week or two past, a little at a time, finally found a woman who agreed to come on Friday, to help us about the hardest of it, (the two largest rooms) we got every thing ready for her to go to work, but she did not come, & we were then obliged to go on alone with it.

M. S. Colton

Your Father, for the <u>first</u> <u>time</u>, helping Delia & <u>another</u> boy shake, or beat the carpets. We have always before had help enough, so that it was not necessary for him to do it. I intend with Nelia's help, to try to put new paper on the parlor walls this week.

I have sold that "fifty dollar bond" to Sheldon, & received the cash for it, have already purchased me a new dress, & some other little fixings, also the paper for the parlor. Hope you will approve of the way I have disposed of it. Your Father suggested that I should get myself some good clothes with it, & I have begun to do so ——

I rec'd a letter from Myra last week. She says that Henry's business is so dull this Spring, that she fears, she will not be able to come & visit us as early in the season, as she had hoped to (she had expected to be here in June) but hopes to come some time in the course of the Summer. Am in hopes that Carter & Lottie have got settled in their new home by this time, as when he wrote last the goods had just arrived, & he expected Lottie would be there, by last Friday or Saturday. Am sorry that they could not have settled nearer, it seems now that they are so far away that I can never hope to go there to see them. Accept a great deal of love from your affectionate Mother

M.S. Colton

The enclosed is a sample of the dress — it is the best piece of the kind, there is in this town, paid one dollar a y'd for it, the price was at first one dollar & a quarter —

Lina

Columbus May 21 ~ 1865

Dear Delia

I received a long letter from you awhile ago. It ought to have been long, it was so long in being written. Have not much to write about, so will relate a laugh we had, at Hattie's expense, last night. We have been to "Naughton's" a number of times having our cloth circles cut over. The man that cuts them is exceedingly accomodating and polite. In fact we had said so much about him that Sheldon had begun to joke us considerably about Mr Bell. Hattie has now had her silk mantle made over, and last evening we went to the store after it. Mr B. wanted her to try it on, she did so, but could not fasten the top button neither could I. She seated herself on one of the stools and Mr B. offered his assistance. While he was working at it, I thought she acted rather strangely, and said "Hattie are you sick"? Down, went her head to the counter, off <u>rolled her hat</u>, Mr B. went running down the store for a fan, sent another clerk for water, threw open the back doors, and <u>had</u> a <u>great time</u>. It is ridiculous enough for <u>me</u> to faint, but I <u>do</u> think it more laughable still for <u>her</u> to. Well for us we were at the farther end of the store so not much commotion was raised. She did not faint entirely away, I fanned her awhile, and the water and fresh air revived her shortly. Sheldon said <u>my</u> market was spoiled entirely, when we were relating the incident to them at home. Suddenly Mary burst forth in an <u>uncontrollable fit</u> of <u>laughter</u>, she had been reading the receipt and said it was addressed to <u>Mrs</u> Whiting. Mr Kelly might well say now, p-o-o-r-H-a-t-t-i-e, for she is most too unmercifully teazed. I never had known her to have a faint spell, then to have it happen at such a time, in such a place, when there was no cause

Lina

for it whatever made us consider it "funny." Am afraid you folks worked too hard at house cleaning and papering. Suppose it is too late to talk about that now.

Is Nelia going to answer Will Penfields letter? If he comes here to be mustered out hope he will call at our house, 157 East Spring Street. We are to have a number next Tuesday. So there will not be quite so much trouble in directing our friends.

You ask how I like Columbus this time. It is very little I see of it. We are living a quiet life. A number of young ladies have called on us. But Mary does not feel able to return calls, and Hattie dislikes it about as much as you do. I shall not wait for them any longer but, as <u>soon</u> as <u>my</u> <u>new bonnet</u> is <u>finished,</u> shall start out foot and alone, what is the use of living here and not know anybody. Hattie and I have been around to Mr Coles two or three times. We are all invited there to tea tomorrow afternoon. Am owing Miss St. Clair a call. She starts for Detroit the first of June. She has considerable to say about Brainerd. He boards at her Grandfather's. There has been a Prof. Richards called to fill Mr Grammar's place. He preached here last Sunday but has not yet accepted the call. Everyone likes him <u>very</u> <u>much</u> <u>indeed</u>. Dr. Muenscher preached again to day. I did not go to hear him.

Do you want anything in particular, at present of the money I am owing you? Have loaned some to Sheldon the reason I did not send more last time. Am afraid next pay day the most of my wages will have to go for clothes. I am so nearly out for Summer.

Write when you can. Give much love to all friends.

Your Sister
Lina

Lina

Columbus June 20~ 1865

Dear Delia

I commenced a letter to you Sunday last, but, finding Sheldon was writing home, concluded to wait, until tonight, and now I am owing you one, as yours was received this noon. Talk about "hot weather", Hattie and I do not even wear the "Collar and Spurs" while we are writing. You say that last Saturday was the warmest day you had had this season. Well, Mary and I went up to the State House on the afternoon to see the Regiment, the 176~ perform. The Col. commanding, put the boys through with the Bayonet exercise, in the State yard. It was a sight for us to behold, but, I did pity the poor fellows in that sun. After they "Stacked Arms" Lieut. Joe Owen came to us, with great drops of perspiration rolling off his face. Said he did think they had warm weather in Nashville, but had changed his mind since coming to Columbus. <u>Hereby</u> <u>hangs</u> <u>a</u> <u>tale</u>. Let me relate it to you. Last Summer Hattie told me to count forty white horses, then, the first young man that shook hands with me afterwards, I would surely marry. The first one that did so, was Joe Owen. We were up street some time since and seeing an unusual number of white horses, I told Hattie I would count again and see if I could not shake hands with someone else besides him. Time passed on, and no <u>young</u> man offered his hand until last Saturday, when, who should that be but the "identical Joseph"

While we were on the State House Terrace, I begged Sheldon, if he had any mercy, to call Capt. Crane up first. He was too smart for that, and calls the affair a "rich Joke" I confess that it was a little singular, my meeting him first both times, and about a year had passed between the times. Indeed, I am giving the subject very serious thought.

Sheldon intends inviting the Capt. and Lieut. here to tea tomorrow. I have made some "Love Cake" for the occasion. By the way, is the receipt book, on the sitting room table, under the medicine box, edited by Mrs Haskell or Mrs Scott?

The flowers were fresh and perfectly beautiful when they reached here. Mary thinks it "paid" sending them. Believe Sheldon has written about the berries. I have not seen so many flowers together for two years.

The gloves may be small for Mother, if so, one of her daughters had better take them and let me send another pair. They break easily but I always mend them right away, and in that way can wear them some time.

Mrs. Herd says a good deal to me about having Nelia come here, instead of Mary going to Milan. If she prefers coming now, to later in the season, think it will be very pleasant for her to make it headquarters there.

I regretted very much being away from home when Dr Alling called. Sheldon told me, just before I started out to make some calls, that he was in town, but I did not expect he would come up that evening. Had about five minutes conversation with him in the street. So Will spent an evening at our house! I had been looking for him here until the Dr. told me he was discharged from Hospital.

The next time Hattie writes to George will have her ask him if he intends going to Milan and when!

Will enclose a sample of my new dress.

Mrs. Herd is making it.

Wednesday morning.

This is Lotties birthday, isn't it. I got too sleepy last night to finish my letter, and will now add a line before Sheldon goes to the Office. This is such a beautiful morning that it is hard work to sit down to writing. Tell Ezra, if he will get a straw hat, a little larger than the one he wore to Mrs Butmans that day, trim it with a plaid or scarlet ribbon, with long streamers in the back, that he will be in the height of fashion. Give much love to all, and write when you can. Ella has been promoted in School, I see by the morning paper, so will probably return after a visit East. She starts next Monday.

Your Sister
Lina

Carlos

Toledo July 14th 1865

Dear Mother

      I came back from Detroit last night — day before yesterday (Wednesday) afternoon Aunt and Alpha, Mrs Slocum, Alice and I started together. Alice and her Mother left the train at Trenton. On arriving at Detroit about Six oclock we found that Mr Truax and Fannie had arrived in the City at noon, the body was taken directly to the Chapel in the Cemetery grounds, on account of its condition, unknown to Fannie. The funeral was held yesterday afternoon at 4 oclock from the Chapel. Some 25 or 30 Carriages were in the procession, the Police force were out in uniform, and the Masons, the Masonic Ceremony at the grave was very interesting. Poor Fannie was nearly worn out with travel and watching. She was very glad to see me, they all enquired after you and hoped you would be able to come up yet this fall — Alpha and I staid at Phins. It is 900 miles from Detroit to "Togus Springs" Maine, where they went. He died unexpectedly to Fannie, was sitting on the bed, Fannie saw that he was having a bad turn, and sat by him with her arm around him, he leaned his head on her shoulder and died. She was alone with him and had to cry for help. They had no acquaintances there, but the people proved to be the best of friends, relieving her of every care. Some gentleman accompanied her as far as Montreal, where Geo Truax met them, her little boy Harry is an uncommon child, one of the most winning little fellows I ever saw. I dont know that there have been any plans formed for her future. Grandma seemed well as usual. Fannie wanted Lucy to stay over Sunday with her she has written to Nelia to telegraph her if she wants her to come before Monday.

      Kent Hamilton is here today and says he saw Myra on the Cars at Shelbyville yesterday, enroute for Cleveland. Aunt Sophia thinks of returning with Lucy. Aunt S & Lucy, Mr Slocum and I occupied one of the Carriages at the funeral. Fannie was with Mr Truax and O.M. Hyde, Lucinda was with Ben

    I send a "Harper" in this mail for Delia.
                 Your affectionate Son
                   Carlos

Lina

Tuesday Afternoon
Columbus July 18" 1865

Dear Mother.

Unto <u>us</u> a Son is born. Mary is quite comfortable this afternoon. She had a bad night. The Dr. was here from ten last evening until ten this morning. The boy made his appearance about half past nine this morning. Mrs Kelly has been very kind. She came early last night and staid until noon today. Working all the time, I took a dispatch this morning to the Office about eight oclock, for Mrs Whiting to come. She arrived at two this afternoon. Either she or Mrs Denman will stay until Mary is better. Sheldon has not been to the Office since yesterday noon. Will probably commence work again tomorrow. I have not been writing any to day, but am very tired, so will not try to make out a letter.
George Whiting reached home last night. Mrs W. says he was much pleased with his visit in Milan and Fremont. Will write again soon, to let you know about the sick folks.

Your daughter
Lina

Lottie Carter

Dear Sister Delia

This has been <u>baking</u> day for me, and as I am tired, do not feel much like writing, but I have let a longer time pass, than usual, without writing home, and judging your feelings on the subject, by my own, think you are growing anxious to hear from me. This cannot be mailed until tomorrow but I write now so as to have it ready to send by Carter in the morning. We received good letters from Sheldon & Lina last week, how strange it seems, to think of him as "Papa", he seems quite proud of his <u>heir</u>, it is natural, are not you proud that you are "<u>Auntie</u>" again We have <u>four</u> days now, of <u>dry</u>, <u>warm</u> weather, which is <u>thankfully</u> <u>received</u>. I suppose Aunt Myra is with you now, and you are taking a great deal of pleasure, how much I should like to see her, and little Nellie too. I wish she would make <u>us</u> a visit before she goes home, <u>urge</u> her to do so, it would seem so good to have someone come here <u>right</u> <u>from</u> <u>home</u>, she could let us know what day she would start and Carter would meet her at the Depot, so she would not be bothered finding us.

The mail carrier just hand me a letter from Nelia, when I saw the hand writing I <u>thought</u> it was Nelia's, but from the postmark concluded it was from you, and <u>was</u> surprised, and pleased to know that she is home again was intending this morning to write her today, and shall do so very soon. Am sorry to hear that Ma's health is so poor, hope you do not let her <u>work</u> <u>too</u> <u>hard</u>.

Tell Nelia I have got the Picture framed she made for me and am very proud of it. When Carter was bringing it home, it attracted great attention by passengers on the street car, one man in particular took it, and after examining it closely, asked how it was made. Carter told him, and then he asked what was the price of such a picture. he answered <u>very</u> <u>proudly</u>, that he <u>did</u> <u>not</u> <u>know</u>, <u>as</u> <u>his</u> <u>sister</u> made it. The frame to the Picture is Rosewood lined with Gilt, very much like our looking glass, he told them, he wanted a Gilt frame, but they missunderstood him, and when it was finished, it looked so pretty, that we concluded to let it remain so. What house does Delight live in now, do they and his father still live together. I have thought many times of writing to her, and think I shall do so soon.

Libbie Moore sends a kiss to Nellie and <u>wants</u> <u>you</u> <u>to</u> <u>tell</u> <u>her</u> <u>to</u> <u>come</u> <u>here</u>
With much love for Aunt Myra little Nellie, Alice, and <u>all</u> the loved ones at home.

> I remain
> your loving sister
> "Lottie"

Lina

Columbus Aug. 6" 1865

Dear Delia,

Mr Richards has gone away. It is raining. Mary is alone. Taking all things into consideration I concluded to sit down and write to you instead of going to church. Yes, I did some expect a letter last Tuesday morning, and on my way to read with Mrs Stone, called at the Office to get it. The postmaster refused to hand one over. I do not want any of you to think that you <u>must</u> write at just such a time, whether you feel like it or not, so the letter will reach here Tuesday morning. I am glad to hear from home at any time, but, can endure it <u>if</u> a letter does fail to reach here regularly every week. I know you think about every time you take up pen and paper, that it is so dull in Milan there is nothing to write about. Sometimes I am troubled in that way here. It would not take long to tell how the copyists spend their time. For, in the morning, it is, get breakfast, wash dishes, make beds, do the sweeping, go to writing at noon, get dinner wash dishes commence writing again, at night, get supper and wash dishes. If you feel like it sew a little while, if not, go to bed. There is seldom any variation, so how much more have I to write about than you have?

Mary has not had a single drawback as yet. She is quite herself again, and takes care of the baby as though it was the fourth instead of the first one. Thus far, the child has been very good indeed. We only hope he will continue so.

As soon as Mary is well enough to do the work alone, Hattie and I are going to Granville to spend a few days. I <u>must</u> get some sewing done, and would as soon lose a little time as to board and pay a sewing girl. Father sends an invitation for Sheldon, Mary, and the young man, to visit Milan this month. Sheldon says he cannot leave the Office. Perhaps he knows best, but I know that Genl. Cowen would not raise one single objection to his taking a play spell. The Genl. has been absent for two weeks on a pleasure excursion. Carleton White has just returned from a trip up the Lake. Col. Mercer has been visiting in New York. Mr. Miller and Scarrit have gone East. When they return, we say it will be Sheldon's time to go. There is no use of his staying there week in and week out, while all the others take a vacation. Hattie and I would just as soon keep house alone, and let them go, as not. Perhaps we can get them started in the grape season if not before.

Is Late Lathrope in Milan now? ask him if he is personally acquainted with E.H. Powers, late Lieut Col. of the 55th. What sort of a man is he? How does he like him etc. etc. It is you that wants to know, not me, but you may write me what he says, then I will tell you why I want to know. Tell Nelia that Mrs Cochrane (once Miss Sabine) called here last evening. She inquired, particularly, about my sister that was here taking music lessons.

Sheldon wanted to invite them here to tea. But, Mary was occupying the parlor and not well enough to see them, and I knew they would not enjoy coming, while we were so situated. We have moved Mary up stairs again and it seems a little more like living to have the parlor clear again. If I conclude there is anything more to write, will add it tomorrow morning. So farewell. Your letter, with Father's was received last week. Sheldon also had a letter from Father.

I have found a Drug Store here where they keep "Adams & Fays" hair oil. Hurrah! Do not think I have made way with that full bottle so quick. The whole community here have been using it freely.

Give much love to all,

Your Sister

Lina

Lottie Carter

Dear Father & Mother

We received the good things, and the good letter accompanying them, last night, that you sent by Mrs Otis. Mr Otis met Mr Carter in the street and told him the things were at his house and so he went right away and got them. Mrs Otis told him that she should come very soon to see me. Perhaps she will.

The Grapes came all right, and are just as fresh as though they had just been picked from the vines, when we opened them Libbie exclaimed, wasn't that a good Grandpa to send us such nice grapes. I had made some Catsup of a part of the Grapes, we are all so fond of it, and you can judge of my delight when I found that you had sent me a can of the Gooseberry, for I always thought it equal to if not a little nicer than Grape Catsup. I opened the can the first thing this morning and put it into an earthen jar and sealed it up again, for I shall use it sparingly, and the corn, to think that you should have sent me so much of it, when it was such hard work to dry it, it made our mouths fairly water to look at it. I think we are nicely fixed for winter, through your loving kindness, and words cannot express the pleasure it gives us, or the thanks we feel. We take so much comfort eating the Grapes, and they taste all the sweeter coming from home. Libbie has not seen the chestnuts yet, as she has a severe cold and I know they are not good for her, but she will be delighted when she sees them, and I thank Delia in her name.

Mrs Abbot & Everton called here today, she has been in Chicago a week or more, but I did not know it until night before last. I had such a good visit with her that it really did me good, she spoke of having seen you all recently, said Nelia came to see her often and had been a great comfort to her this summer. I have been very busy today in my general housework & ironing I could not get my washing done until yesterday. I have commenced cleaning house, and tomorrow am going to have whitewashing done. I commenced this late this afternoon, and if I had had the time could have written a good deal more, as it is, being evening and Carter sitting here hurrying me, guess I will draw this to a close. We did not have any Peaches at Joliet but had all the apples we could eat, they said they would send us a barrel full bye and bye if we would pay the Express, and that we are willing to do.

The neighbors that were living nearest to us when we came here have moved lately, and the family that has taken the house I like very much I think she (Mrs Farson) is her name, will be a companion and a friend for me they have two boys ten & sixteen years of age and a little girl about five months younger than Libbie, they are almost inseparable. I am acquainted with most of the neighbors round now so that I feel more at home.

With much love, many kisses, and kind wishes, I remain your loving daughter
"Lottie Carter.

Carlos

Toledo Aug 18th 65

Dear Delia

I got a letter from Nelia this week. Since then have sent her "Harpers Weekly". Will now drop you a line or two.

Tell her, Aunt said "they would be satisfied with $5 for the Piano Stool, inasmuch as the Piano itself brought a good price" ——

Alice Boehm of Cumberland, now "Mrs Dr Barnes", has been here two or three days, for a visit — her husband is a Homeopathic physician of Delaware (this State) but has recently removed to Maumee. She has improved very much since her marriage. I didnt dream when I used to frolic with her as a Soldier in Maryland that three years would bring such a change but you know the world is full of change. Wish I could say as much for my pockets — excuse brevity I have got some work to do.

I enclose $5.00 and Love

Your Brother
Carlos

Mr Waggoner has sold out his interest in the "Blade"——

Lottie Carter

Chicago Aug 18 th/65

Dear sister Delia

     <u>Not</u> a le<u>tter</u> <u>from</u> <u>home</u> <u>for</u> <u>me</u> <u>this</u> <u>week</u>.
Well I suppose you all have some good reason for <u>not</u>
writing, perhaps you have company that keeps you busy, it
seems a long time since I recieved a letter from you.
What do you busy yourself about. I suppose it is about
time for school to commence again , shall you attend?
I wish you could take a trip into our quiet little town to
ru<u>sticate</u> for a season. I think it would do you more good
than a <u>term</u> <u>of</u> sc<u>hooling</u>, but it costs money to travel, and
I know you have'nt it to spare, when I get rich I will send
for you, is not that <u>consoling</u>.
I do not feel in a writing mood, and consequently ca<u>nnot</u>
w<u>rite</u> — more this time. We are all very well and the
weather is deli<u>ghtful</u>. Please excuse this disconnected <u>little</u>
<u>note</u>, if I had more time perhaps I could do better, but it
is about time for the mail to close, & hope you are all well
and that I shall hear from you soon.
     With much love from all to all — I remain
                    your affectionate sister
                    Lottie Carter

Chicago Aug. 19. 1865

My Dear Sister Delia

Your letter written yesterday was received this morning, and it gave me such pleasure that I hasten to answer it, tho I shall not probably mail this till Monday. We have been looking all the week for something from home, each night. I would answer Lottie's question, "any letters from home", with "no but I think you may expect one to-morrow without fail", and each day have been mistaken till last night, for so I have the long looked for epistle: And here let me say a word or two about your letter, and I hope you will not take what I say in any way disparaging to your other letters, for they are always very acceptable and interesting, but this one is so easy, so much like yourself that it almost seems as if you were present talking with or to me, and as I read it, which by the way I have done several times, the illusion is only dispelled by looking at the top and see that it is headed "Milan", so you can judge for yourself how much pleasure it gives me, and the pleasure is greatly enhanced by feeling how delighted Lottie will be when she reads it, and I would say what perhaps you have already guessed, that my pleasure is not half enjoyed by me unless Lottie can unite with me in its enjoyment.

No, I think, you are mistaken, for if my memory is not at fault you wrote last, but I shall rebel at once, and will not send yours back, for 'tis too good to lose, so to compromise the matter I send this one.

Judging from your letter there are certainly a great many improvements going on in your place. I wonder if all the rest of the Town are making as many alterations, if so we should hardly know it a year or two hence, unless you or some other kind friend should keep us posted. Am glad you are learning telegraphing, for it will be nothing lost, even should you never wish to make it pecuniarily profitable.

I thank Nelia and you for information concerning Cousin Delight.

You will probably receive a letter from Lottie this evening, and I heartily endorse her wish that you might be induced to come and make us a long visit the longer the better, but am sorry my endorsement cannot come in a more substantial manner.

We are all well, we think Libbie Moore's health was never as good as now, and the same of Lottie, and as for me, why I am plodding along in the even tenor of my way, occasionaly grunting with the headache, but with one or two exceptions nothing very serious.

So with much love for yourself Father, Mother and Sister Nelia

I suscribe

Affectionately

Your Brother

J P. Carter

Monday 21st

I left half of this sheet thinking perhaps Lottie would like to add a few lines, but Saturday evening she was busy, and she does not like to write Sundays for she prefers to visit with me she says. It was as I anticipated, she was delighted that I had letters from home, she says she had made up her mind to write home twice a week if possible, but as this one goes the fore-part of the week, she will defer writing till the latter part writing but once. and in the meantime she expects to receive one from home, which she can answer.

Lottie has been making the acquaintance of some of our neighbors, and I am glad, for 'twill not seem so lonely when I am away especially when it storms, for you know she has a great dread of storms particularly of thunder showers. I think I never saw one who is so much afraid of them, and Saturday afternoon we had a heavy shower and I felt worried about her, but she told me that she had been baking and was just doing up the work, when she noticed the storm coming, and knew she would not have time to come to the office, so she left her work just as it was, and took Libbie Moore and ran into a neighbors till the storm was over, she was feeling very elated over it, and thinks now she will not feel so bad hereafter, and 'twill relieve my mind materially to feel that she is not alone.

But no more at this time

As ever

J.P.C.

Lina

Columbus Aug 25. 1865.

Dear Delia,

      I will commence my letter by relating a little affair, which is now quite laughable, but might have proved very serious to the copyists on Spring Street.

A short time ago I purchased a bottle of "Adams & Fays" Hair oil but used none of it until after we got to Granville. While there, I took some out once. The day we came away I tied it up tight again, put it inside of my work box, together with the <u>rats</u>, belonging to my hair, and put it inside of my trunk. Hattie watched the operation, remarking that it was a good way to carry the bottle so it would not get broken. The trunk arrived Thursday after noon right side up etc. I opened it and was a little surprised to see the work box upset, on taking it up was completely dumb founded at its lightness, on opening it, was "dumb <u>foundeder</u>" at its emptiness. The contents consisted of one <u>rat</u> only. My first thought was of George, as we "played tricks" upon each other <u>occasionally</u> out there, so we searched the trunk through but no Oil could be found. The mystery was great, for I knew he would not be so ungentlemanly as to take it from the trunk entirely. About five oclock Hattie says "Lina where did you put all those clean handkerchiefs of mine"? My reply was "I put them next to my work box but they were not there when I unpacked." Then, our eyes began to open and we were suspicious there had been "<u>foul</u> <u>play</u>". I did not think far enough to examine the lock to the trunk until about ten oclock in the evening when lo & behold! the catch was broken or filed entirely apart. Sheldon says it was pried open and thinks the thief must have become frightened and only made away with those articles, as we have not yet missed anything else. Was not that a narrow escape? Our most valuable summer clothing was at the mercy of the thief. Silk basques, parasols, muslin dresses, summer bonnets, gaiters under clothing etc. etc. I honor their judgement in taking the hair oil, and nice handkerchiefs, and thank them for leaving articles of greater value. It must have been done at Union as the trunk was there over night. George is using "Adams & Fays" so I wrote asking him to go over to Union and "smell of the heads" about the Station. Without joking, I do think it would be an easy way to detect the guilty one. The oil is an uncommon one, and any one accustomed to it, could tell very quick who had been using it.

Going over to Granville Hattie had her pocket book, containing between eight & nine dollars, and a fine handkerchief taken from her. She was fully convinced, before this last performance, that it was done in the Hack from Union to Granville. Rather an unprofitable trip for her! Well, I have made out a long story, and think it time to change the subject.

Monday morning

I changed the subject immediately by going to bed, and have not found a moment since to write until now. Mr St Clair agreed to put a faucet in the boiler to that stove, and I regret very much that it was neglected, as it is said to be a very great improvement. Suppose it can be done in Milan but the expense will be greater. If it is not too much trouble will you send me a list of the articles received with the stove. I want to know if all was sent that is paid for.

How do you like telegraphing? Shall you attend to that and school too? Is Alice going to marry Ed Parker? Sheldon is ready to start up street, so this must be closed. George came out Saturday afternoon. Do not know how long he will stay.

Love to all
Lina

Nelia's music goes in this mail.

H. Colton

Milan August 28~ 1865

Dear Carlos

Your letter of 26~ was recd Saturday evening
containing as customary my weekly wages — I had like to
have written <u>earnings</u> — but thought the other might be
the more appropriate word

My health has been better the past summer than for
several years and I have labored pretty diligently but so far
as earning anything in the way of support is concerned my
work amounts to but little — I do not of course hope for
the same degree of health when the stormy Fall weather
comes on, but am thankful for what I have enjoyed through
the Summer — I am trying to fix up things generally
about the House and find as I expected many small as
much as some large jobs, <u>it</u> is not strange considering that
it has borne the storms of more than twenty years without
repairs ——

Your Mother recieved last week from Lina and
Sheldon a new cooking stove of the most modern style
which cost fifty dollars in Columbus — It has not been in
operation yet but if it will cook without provision or fuel I
shall be exceeding glad ——

Charley Hitchcock, who married Sarah Minuse died
in Minnesota a few days since leaving her a two thousand
dollars Insurance policy and a baby, the former at least will
be comfortable ——

We are glad to hear of your health, and industry —
Affectionately
H. Colton

Chicago August 31st 18—

My Dear Mother

Such a dear good Mother as we have, is not to be met with every day, when we are in Milan you are always doing something for us, and now, although there a hundred miles away as you are always doing something—

The fruit you sent by Little Lizzie Carter brought home last night. I was surprised & delighted beyond expression, but I feel all the time as though it was not right, feeble as you are, to be working so for us. After you sent something to just Eddies, Carter's performance sending some money, as that if you should feel like putting so much into...

We are not only willing but anxious to pay a part of the expenses there, but cannot find out how much it is so she will not not tell

Your affectionate daughter

Little Carter

I have at last decided to go to Detroit and make a visit. Carter thinks it would be better for Lizzie and I to go there and spend a couple of weeks during the warm season. He will take his meals over in town and sleep at the house. I think now if it is a pleasantly we will start next next Thursday—

With much love and many kindnesses

I remain

Your affectionate daughter

Little Carter

Please remember me to Kate and when you are her, and tell her I wish she would come here to live

I received your good long letter last night, what a comfort it is to have ones to write and receive letters.

Lottie Carter

My Dear Mother

Such a dear, good, Mother as we have, is not to be met with every day, when we were in Milan you was always doing something for us, and now, although three hundred miles seperate us, you are always sending something. The fruit you sent by Libbie Lewis Carter brought home last night — I was surprised & delighted beyond expression, but I feel all the time, as though it was not right, feeble as you are, to be working so for us, after you sent fruit the first time. Carter proposed sending some money, so that if you should feel like putting up more, any time it need not cost you anything, but I told him, I had rather not, for fear you might put yourselves out, too much, to do it. I had no idea you would think of sending more. I have not been to see Libbie yet, because it has been so very warm I could not venture out, but it is cloudy today and if it does not rain, I am going this afternoon. Carter went to the house to get the fruit, and she told him that just as they were going to put the box on to the car's, she noticed that it was broken so that she left it, and told them to send it by express, it came night before last, all the cans are jammed a little and beat some, but I shall take care of them right away. O! but how proud I feel, so nicely fed for winter, but what troubles me most is, that I have nothing to send home, but Mother dear, we hope "there's a good time coming", and until it comes, all we can do, is to send thanks, and good wishes. Mr Penfield came here on business, was taken sick, and we insisted to our home, he has been with us for ten days past, starts for home tonight, he said he would call right away and see you, and tell you all about us, he can tell you better the how and where we are living better than any one else, because he has been with us more, so ask him all the questions you can think of. How sad that Sarah Hitchcock should be left a widdow so young. I feel deeply for her in her sorrow, her baby will be a great comfort to her, in her sorrow it is well that he has left her so independant — please remember me to Kate Norton when you see her, and tell her I wish she would come here to live too.

I received your good long letter last night, what a comfort it is for absent ones to write and receive letters.

I have at last decided to go to Jolliet and make a visit. Carter thinks it would be better for Libbie and I to go then and spend a couple of weeks, during the sickly season, he will take his meals over in town and sleep at the house. I think now if it is a pleasant day we will start next week Thursday.

With much love and many kind wishes
       I remain   Your affectionate daughter
              "Lottie Carter.

We are not only willing but anxious to pay a part of the express charges, but cannot find out how much it is — she will not tell.

Sheldon Upton (signature)

Columbus, O.
Sept. 3rd 1865.

Dear Brother:

I am under the impression that I am owing you a letter and will avail myself of the present opportunity to write a few lines, not so much on account of having anything particular to tell you as for the purpose of letting you know that we still live and enjoy ourselves.

The young man is flourishing finely; increasing in weight and wisdom and proving himself to be one of the best natured little fellows that ever made home noisy. He does not disturb us any of any consequence at night, by fretfulness and crying, as gentlemen of his age are apt to do. I have not lost an hour's sleep on his account since the young man came to stay with us.

Mary's health is good, much better than could be expected. She travels around now about as well as usual and takes the young man out calling with her.

Lina and Hattie are almost always well, and it would do you good to be in the same house with them. I think I never saw two girls so generally happy and capable of enjoying themselves, before.

I don't believe that anything like an unkind word or thought ever passes between them. They are a pretty good match for each other in size and strength and are a "full team" for fun, besides being my best assistants in the work on which they are engaged.

I wrote to Abram some time ago in regard to the Piano, I bought of him in "years gone by," offering to pay him the amount then agreed on $75. or send him the money as I received it from the sale of the piano, which was sold on time for $80. He said I might send him $50. and call it even. I had to go to buying furniture about that time and could not well send it. I was about to write to him again today and make my offer over again, as I could not close with his in what I deemed proper time, and was willing to send him the full amount first specified, which I could do in a few days but I have just received a letter from Father in which he mentions having sent $50. to you for me, on account of the piano. If Abram still thinks that amount sufficient, of course I have nothing more to say but if he has any hesitancy at all in closing the account in this manner or Aunt is likely to think it too small an amount, I would rather send the rest. You can say so to him and let me know what he says about it or, if you prefer I will write to him myself.

Remember me to the family and friends, generally,
Yours truly
Sheldon.

Lina

Columbus Sept. 10" 1865.

Dear "Folks at Home"

Before me is lying a letter from each member of the Colton family, now in Milan. I address all together as each must have had a share in preparing the very excellent fruit and pickles received by us last Friday afternoon. They were all in good condition except one can of peaches, that we used right away, those were not soured at all, but were leaking, and we were just wanting some sauce for tea, so used them. We tried the pickles to day too. They suit my taste exactly. I think Mother has done too much, during poor health and warm weather. Mary ought to be sufficiently thankful for the labor that she has been saved, yes, and expense too. She has tried putting up tomato's. The first night four of the corks flew out from the jugs. She heated the fruit and <u>jugged</u> them over again, then two more popped out and the tomatos soured. So her first experience in canning fruit was not very agreeable. I am disappointed that Mother does not accept the invitation to Columbus. Think the journey and rest might both do her good. Sheldon thinks he cannot afford to take his family to Milan this Fall, and it is very doubtful about my going, although, at present, I feel inclined to do so. Mrs Snively, our best and most rapid copyist, has resigned on account of poor health. That will cause our writing to last much longer, unless the Genl. orders new copyist's to be obtained, which is not very likely. If I find by the last of October that we will be employed two or three months longer, then I shall be tempted to spend about two weeks at home. That will be an absence of seven months from Milan for me. When Father's letter was received, last Thursday afternoon, I was entertaining a young man from the Adjutant's Office. Sheldon thought I needed "Spurring" and invited him up here to tea. Perhaps Delia will remember him. It was Cyrus Strahl. His desk is at the first window. But, I was going to say <u>that</u> Mr. S. told me <u>that</u>, the Asst Adj't. told him, that Mr Colton was working entirely too hard and ought to take rest. Says there are two or three men in the Office that Shirk, and Sheldon will take hold and do their work. We have said all we intend to about his taking a vacation. There would be not a single objection raised from either the Col. or Adj't.

The State Fair commences this week on Tuesday. Mr Whiting is coming out to attend it, and Mary expects to return home with him. Do not know how long she will be gone. Probably two weeks or more. Sheldon expects to spend a few days there with her.

Hattie wanted to know how Nelia liked the music I sent her. I was a little mortified to reply that she not even mentioned having received it. What have you all been doing to have so much toothache? You must make Dr Perrys business quite profitable.

Nelia, if going riding does cure the toothache, it sometimes causes heartache, so beware!!

Hattie will wait until hearing further particulars from Youngstown before she sends any reply. What is Julia doing now?

Do not know why Sheldon & Mary decided to change their boy's name. I once wrote that George sent some message to his namesake. He denies sending any such word, it came from his Aunt. He was more surprised than the rest of us at their calling the baby — George. Perhaps Delia will smile at my experience in writing to the other Lina Colton. The letter was given to me four times at least, and finally returned to me yesterday from the Dead letter Office. Now the question arises, who & what is she that has been opening my letters? It is an "unfathomed mystery."

Mary just finds I am writing and wishes me to return many thanks for the canned fruit. I agreed to pay express charges, but am obliged to wait until pay day comes around again.

Accept much love,
Lina.

Chicago Oct 19. 1865

My Dear Sister
   I thought I would write you a few lines to-day fearing Lottie would not have time to-morrow, but I cannot give you any very good news especially about Libbie Moore; she was taken over a week ago with a severe cold which continued to increase notwithstanding all we could do, and last Friday morning she got up with a high fever and for two or three days we thought it was one of her usual worm attacks, but we finally called a Physician, and he pronounced it Diptheria in a very severe form, but gave good deal of encouragement in the fact that it had not gone too long, she appeared to grow better under his treatment, but the disease is a very treacherous one, sometimes she would appear quite smart in the morning when I left, and then at noon I would find her very bad, but to-day she is manifestly better and the Dr says if we can keep her from taking cold she will get along without further trouble. The poor little thing is as patient as she can be, she hardly utters a word of complaint, yet the inside of her mouth is almost raw all over, she does not keep her bed, you know it is difficult to keep children, on the bed, but she has had to be held the most of the time, and strange to say, she has not kept us awake scarcely any nights. But I must close, will let you know if she grows worse, would not have written now, but for fear the worst might happen and this would in a measure prepare your minds for it, but I am sincere in thinking the danger is past; if I can get time will write to-morrow and let you know how she is, and will <u>take</u> time if she is worse. Lottie and I are both well and send much love to all
     Your Brother with affection
      J <u>P. Carter</u>

Please direct all letters to 577 Carroll St — till further notice

Lottie Carter (signature)

Chicago Oct 29th/65

Dear Delia

     This is a delightful day, though cool. We have had a stormy week, and it seems good to see the sun shine again, we had a light fall of snow night before last, and last night was <u>bitter</u> <u>cold</u>. We received Nelia's letter last Wednesday, telling how many folks you had there. What nice times you must have had. I am glad Carlos went home for a visit, he wrote us that he was intending to do so. Libbie is now quite well again you would be <u>surprised</u> to see how <u>tall</u> she has grown, since we came here. <u>I</u> think she resembles <u>you</u>, more than Lina now, and I call her "<u>little</u> <u>Delia</u>" to tease her.

In one of Pa's letters once, he said something about your wearing your hair done up now, how do you fix it. I cannot imagine you any way but with it shingled. Do you think Sheldon & Mary will be home for a visit this winter. I hope so. I know you must be anxious to see the "little Colton". I <u>am</u>.

Monday   I commenced this letter yesterday but Carter and Libbie, together, kept up such a "<u>hubbub</u>" that I could not write, and so laid it aside, and now as I am boiling meat for "<u>Mince</u> <u>Pies</u>" and going to make soup for dinner too, (don't you wish you was here) I must be at work, so <u>good</u> <u>bye</u>, with much love for <u>all</u> and hoping to hear from you soon, I remain your loving sister

               Lottie Carter

Dear Sister Delia

     Did not think I would have time to write you this time, but as there is a few minutes to spare before the Mail closes will say a word or two.

     So Lottie has excusing herself from writing a long letter by laying the blame on Libbie Moore and me, well we who know her so well could not expect anything else from her but to attempt to screen herself from censure by blaming others, when the truth of the matter is, that I urged her to write yesterday, and I would amuse Libbie to be sure we did not sit still without saying a word, but being naturally very fond of music we thought we would have a good time singing whistling & playing the flute and very often we would pause in our music to tell Lottie to hurry & finish her letter for soon 'twould be time to get supper and she is pleased to call it all a "hubbub." Well how ungrateful people can be! But I must not complain I suppose for we must all expect persecution.

     But I must close, thought this had not ought to go without vindicating Libbie & myself.

           With much love
               Your Brother
                 J P. Carter

Nelia,

Dear Mother,

I suppose you wont object to my writing home as often as I feel like it, provided I dont require you folks to answer all my letters. But you know I have no one to talk to here, and I get lonesome and want to talk to you, so I write. I do not wish to tell Aunt anything more than I can help for it is so hard to make her take things as I mean them.

I want to tell you of what a pleasant time I had last evening. George Haskell had a little musical soiree at his mother's house, and asked Carl to bring me. I had told <u>Aunt</u> <u>what</u> <u>everybody</u> <u>wore</u>, <u>what</u> <u>the</u> <u>refreshments</u> were and <u>how</u> <u>the</u> <u>parlors</u> <u>were</u> <u>furnished</u>, how many persons inquired after Annie etc. Now I will tell <u>you</u> what interested me, far more. There is a Mr and Mrs Shephard boarding at Mrs Wood's, who have a cousin here from New York, Charley Force, a superior pianist, and it was in his honor that the gathering of musicians took place. Carl and I went and soon after arriving George and his Mother urged me to play. I declined at first, but finally consented and played the "Stairish Waltzes" without mistakes or embarassment. There were very few in the room then and I felt sure that George Haskell would not criticize me. But what was my astonishment to find after wards that the quiet young man behind me who listened so attentively was none other than the great musician himself, Mr Force. Well the evening passed off delightfully. I never, in my life heard such music from a piano as that young New Yorker played. His cousin Mr Shepherd told me, that it was no wonder he excelled for he had taken lessons all his life and paid 70 to 80 dollars a time for instruction. George Haskell is also a very fine performer, then Mary Osborne and Will Smith played the piano together accompanied by Hartwell Osborne with the flute, and Mr Thurston with the violin. It was grand. Kent Hamilton was there. He said he had become a great musician, could now tell one tune from another if they <u>showed</u> <u>him</u> <u>the</u> <u>music</u> <u>with</u> <u>the</u> <u>name</u> <u>written</u> <u>over</u> <u>the</u> <u>top</u>. Mr and Mrs M.R. Waite were there and treated me with the greatest cordiality, as "Carl's sister." Carl told me coming home that Mrs W. said to him — "Your sister has got a <u>real</u> <u>good</u> <u>face</u>." I told Carlos it was no doubt sincere for Mr W. told me I did not look <u>at</u> <u>all</u> <u>like</u> <u>my</u> <u>brother</u>.

When we started to come away, as I told Mrs Daniels and George good night, the latter said low, to me "Miss Colton I think you ought to know what Mr Force said of your playing, he said you had an excellent touch and would make a superior musician." That made me feel quite encouraged. I did not suppose he would notice my playing among so many. I have told you all this because I want some body to talk to, and Aunt is so <u>touchy</u> about the Waite's and Carlos, that I have said nothing to her except that they were there. We are to have another gathering at Mrs Wood's the first of the week, before Mr Force returns to New York, you can imagine what an advantage these gatherings will be to me, if they continue them. And somehow I felt perfectly at my ease last night and they all showed me a great deal of attention. Carlos is a great favorite every where, I should judge and in very best society too. Mary Osborne said she could show me in a very few lessons, how to use the organ and we are going to the church once or twice for that purpose.

I find I left several things at home that I intended to bring. My napkin ring, for one thing and my Bible and Prayerbook. I have found a Bible among the books in the back room which will answer every purpose, though I always preferred my own.

Aunt took such a fancy to that large white apron that I gave it to her, and she takes so much comfort in wearing it, I cannot regret the sacrifice on my part, and she is always saying that <u>nobody</u> <u>ever</u> <u>gives</u> <u>her</u> <u>anything</u>. She is the queerest specimen to talk I ever heard, and when she cant find anything else to talk about she turns and scolds at me for <u>practising</u> when she wants to talk to me. It is too funny. I have to keep my temper, and then do as I please after she gets through. Yet I know she thinks a great deal of me and would do anything for me. Well, now I have had a chat with you I will close. We started for church this morning but found when we got there that Mr Walbridge had a <u>slight</u> <u>cold</u> and could not preach, so Aunt and I went to the Congregational church where I intend to go with Carl this evening. They had a letter from Annie and Alphens yesterday. It seems Annie went there to see Mr Daughady, as he could not leave to come here this Fall, which seems to me a funny proceeding as she cannot yet fully make up her mind whether she loves him or not. Alphens pays eight dollars a week for board and $100. for instruction for three months, or rather his Father pays it.

With much love
I remain
your aff. Dau.
Nelia.

Lina

Dear Delia

The last I saw of you at Norwalk you was trying a race with the Cars. Think you could not have run <u>very</u> far as I saw nothing of you at Grafton. The sight of your comical appearance, left me shaking in my seat, for quite awhile after leaving the Station. Here I am settled down to work again, with nothing in particular, to relate. It hardly seems as though I had been away at all. Were it not for the remembrance of the pleasant two weeks spent at home, almost, could I convince myself that I have been sitting at this stand, writing day in and day out, since the first of last April.

Mary wrote while I was gone, and writes part of the time now. She has been trying to get a kitchen girl, but has not succeeded yet! Hattie was much pleased with the mat. All of the mats came into instant use, as Mary had been purchasing a quantity of shells during my absence. They look very fine with shells on them.

I neglected taking the street and number that Mr Carter gave as a direction for our letters Wish you would send it to me so I can write to them.

Sheldon and Hattie are about starting for choir meeting so I must descend and keep Mary company until they return.

Sunday afternoon

You may observe that this letter was not finished last night. After going down stairs I concluded to tend baby and let Mary fix her bonnet for Sunday. He would keep his eyes open until ten oclock, and as I have not learned yet to hold the baby and write at the same time, my letter was left unfinished. This morning I went to church, and oh! my how cold the weather was. It did seem like a real winter day. You are probably feeling it in Milan, a little. I dread the cold, dark days that are coming, more than ever before. Growing old, — growing old. No, I do not think that is what's the matter, but think I am more anxious for life, some fun, and a little more society, than there is any prospect of having here. You will see plainly, that my visit home has spoiled me. Unexpectedly, I received a long letter from Frank McMillen last week. She is teaching a small district school near Waverly Ind. 15 miles from Indianapolis. Says "she is perfectly happy as she is one that does not care at all for society." If my memory serves me right, she is not the person to be contented in a small country school, and without any society. She wrote a very cheerful letter, however, and I hope she is enjoying herself.

Suppose the Normal will close this week. How about the Exhibition? Shall expect full particulars in the course of time. Are you going next term? Did not think to ask when at home. Sheldon promises me work until the middle of January, so my "Holidays" will be spent here. How will it be with yours? I looked earnestly for Henry at Camden, but he was not "visible to the naked eye."

Have been writing to Carlos, and have still another letter to write, so you will please excuse me from saying anything more, particularly as I have nothing more to say, except, that, the five enclosed is to pay any debts with. (Suppose there will be no difficulty in dividing it as half belongs to Ma.)

And that I have fully recovered my health.

Love to all.

Your Sister

Lina

(Delia.)

Milan Nov. 19th 1865

Dear Nelia

Your letter was received last evening, and I take a few moments this morning to reply to it.

So you are lonely too, occasionally are you? Dont believe you are as lonely as I am. Last evening is the first one I have spent away from home since you left. A little different from the week before, wasn't it?

Casper came home last Friday and Mary King is going back with him tomorrow morning. Yesterday afternoon Lucy Dean came up here to invite me down there in the evening. As Mary wanted to have a little company before she went home. I could not decide whether to go or not, as I did not want to go alone. Pa said he was going down for the mail (as Josey was away) and would go down to the house with me, if I wanted to go.

I finally made up my mind that I would rather stay at home. Just before night George Eddy and Belle rode up here, when they went to go, Geo. wanted me to go down town with him, and he thought perhaps I would get a chance to ride back again. After we rode round town a while we took Belle home then came up here. He wanted me to go to the party with him. As he could not find anyone else to go, and there was no one else to go with me. I consented, and we went, had a very pleasant time. Now I suppose you would like to know who were there, well there were, Belle, Julia, Jenine and Ella Burman, Georgia Ayers, Miss Wright, Mattie Ashley and myself. Geo. Eddy Dut Page, Ezra Oliver, Charlie Moury and Sam Ayers. Between Dut, Ezra, and Casper, we had enough to laugh at. That is spree No 1 When No 2 comes I will let you know.

Guess George will think I have not got over my spree last night, as I did not go to church this morning. I have not had a glimpse of Will since you left, and he was coming to see me all so fast, as soon as you got away. Oh well never mind, you will be home before long and then the folks will begin to come here again.

Mattie said last night, that she was looking for a letter from you, but had not seen it yet. Mary King says "Tell Nelia, she may write to _me_."

(Delia)

Jenine said "Give Nelia my love when you write," etc. etc. So you see others do not forget you, even if your own family do. Yes and another thing, Charley Moury wanted to know if Nelia had gone to Toledo yet? And when she went, and when she is coming home, etc. Dont you feel better now?　　　As Mother wishes to write a few lines on this I will close. Mr Newman told Mother the other day that he is not going to marry Mary Simmons. So I think the town folks will some of them slip up on some of their conjectures. Mr Newman said he heard the other day, that he intended using the proceeds of the Exhibition to pay his wedding expenses. He took in about $98.

One more piece of news and then I will close. Mary Rostwell has a little daughter.

With much love, and hoping to hear from you soon I will stop.

Delia

Dear Nelia

　　　We think, that while you are staying with your Uncle, you ought to do as he thinks best, & act according to his <u>sense</u> of <u>propriety</u>. We did not at first know <u>why</u> he wished you to take music lessons at the Nunery, but since knowing his reasons, & considering the matter over our judgement coincides with his. You know that before you left home we all thought, that if you could get what instruction you wished, without patronizing a Roman Catholic institution we should prefer your doing so — But now we think, that, as you have to go there to take your French lessons, it would be better to take your music lessons there also — It seems to me, all that is necessary for you to say to Mr Mathias, is that your Parents do not approve of your taking lessons at a "private room". Then <u>if</u> he "is a perfect gentleman" he will think none the less of you, nor will he have any hard feelings toward you for it — You and other <u>young</u> folks of Toledo may think that <u>ours</u>, is only an "old fashioned" <u>idea</u> of <u>propriety</u>. But you may sometime, be led to see that is not a very <u>wrong</u> one ———

　　　That you may enjoy yourself all that you possibly can while there, and learn all the good you can, is the earnest wish of your

affectionate

Mother

M.S. Colton

Lina

Columbus Nov. 19" 1865.

Dear Delia,

I find I am owing you a letter and a five dollar bill so will endeavor to cancel the indebtedness this time.

You are probably lonesome today without your Sister. How long does Nelia expect to remain in Toledo? Will try and write to her today. Will you please send me Mr Carters address so I can write there. Think from what he wrote that he does not wish letters directed to the box and I cannot remember the number of the house. Did you ever see more delightful weather for this time of the year? As a man said to me, the other day, "It is the remarkablest Fall I ever knew."

Last Monday noon Hattie and I were up street and came to the conclusion that the day was too temptingly beautiful for us to remain in the house. So we hurried home and informed our employer that it would be more conducive to our health and happiness to go out and see Delia Mix, than to spend the afternoon in copying. He made no objections, consequently in about an hour we were seated in an Omnibus enroute for Camp Chase. The drivers are not willing to go farther than the Camp for fear of losing passengers back to the City. So we walked the other two miles.

The folks seemed delighted to see us. We had a very pleasant time, staid over night, and one of the neighbors brought us home the next morning. Emmit intended to bring us, but went off to work supposing we would not want to return, until afternoon, anyway. Delia and her Mother both inquired about you. Emmits wife is good, but not very handsome.

We were all invited to Mr Smythe's to tea last night. Mary went about three oclock and took the baby. By the time we got through writing it was raining so hard that we decided to stay at home. Frank Williams is there with her baby. They have named it "Anna Wilson." Mr Williams brother is here too, the one that was wounded in the Army. The "Wilson" is for him. We have received two more letters from Granville insisting upon our spending Thanksgiving there. I have no desire, whatever, to go. Mary says she will not go without me, so one of us will have to give up before the 7" of December. I was there a week this Summer and at home two weeks this Fall, feel now as though I had rather use my three dollars in some other way and not lose any more time in copying.

George expects to go to Atlanta with Frank Wright, about the middle of December, to open a Wholesale Grocery Store. Mr Whiting is anxious to have the family all together again before he goes. Not being a member of the family is another reason why I do not wish to go.

Think it is pleasanter on such occasions to have only the relatives present.

Am sorry the Exhibition did not pass off well. The Temple must be a poor place for any such performance. Why did Mr Newman choose it in preference to the Hall? How can you get along without any Holidays this Winter? It will be dull business, won't it?

The "Widower" has not appeared yet, but I can still live on hope, as he said he might not get here until the 1st. Sheldon says I will have to be "dressed up" and have a fire in the parlor every day for two weeks. I do not expect ever to see him again, but still "stranger things than that have happened" Our copyist, Mrs Stone, was lately married to Judge Metcalf, a youthful couple!! He knew where to look for beauty.

Having other letters to write I will bid you adieu, with much love to all,
            Your Sister

                    Lina

Toledo Nov 22nd 1865

Dear Sister Delia

      I got your letter saying that you got mine, etc. Now as that was so well received I will write another, also send another vignette same as the other, only finished in a different style — Also enclose a "note" for Father — The weather which has for sometime past been all smiles and sunshine commenced to be cool yesterday, and continues to be cooler today. I suppose you hear often from Nelia and doubtly have had an account of the musical meeting at George Haskells house — The young man from New York whose playing was so much liked told a friend of mine that Nelia was the best player there — She has had a good many very fine compliments — I have no doubt she will deserve and receive a good many more after finishing her course of instructions with Mr Matthias — He is considered the best instructor here, and withat is an unassuming quiet gentlemanly German — I think he will take special pains with Nelia as I have known him for several years and have often met him at Mortimers — I mailed a "Harper" to you last night which I suppose you will receive this evening ———

      I intend going with Nelia this evening to a lecture by Revd Dr Willets on "Sunshine and happiness" it being the first lecture for the Winter Season ———

          With much love for all
              I am
              Your Brother
              Carl

Please tell "Belle" when you see her that I <u>thank</u> her for the photograph I took from Lina's album ———
I have only one "profile" picture and think as it is a one sided affair altogether I will keep it to myself ———

Delia

My Dear Sister Nelia

        I have come up to my room this morning to have a little talk with you. How I wish you were here, so I could <u>talk</u> with you, for I have so much I want to tell you, which I cannot say with pen and ink. Last Wednesday night when the mail came there were only two papers, for me. One was the "Harper" from Carl, and upon opening the other I found it to be "Godey's Ladys Mag." I looked at the writing again and again, and also at the postmark, but could not tell where it was from. The engraving in the magazine was of a schoolhouse and the children going to it, and under it, it said, "The Country School," and after that, was <u>written</u>, "<u>Milan</u>" That writing I recognized in an instant, and looked through the book to find more, on the first page, at the commencement of the first piece was written "<u>E</u>. <u>R</u>. <u>H</u>." I then made out the post mark on the wrapper as Norwalk, but it was not Ed's direction. Father made some laughing remark about it, and that's all that has been said. He has been unusually pleasant ever since school was out. Why Nelia, Charley Hoyt came down alone last night, and staid till <u>after</u> <u>half</u> <u>past</u> <u>nine</u>, and Pa went to bed without coming into the room. I never was so astonished. But I have not time or room to talk about these <u>little</u> things now, as there is something more I want to say.

Emma Clark starts for Oberlin this morning. I went in to see her last night, in the course of conversation, I asked her if she knew why Mary G. was not at her house that night? She said she did. I asked her why? she replied, "<u>She</u> says she was sick." She told Em. she had intended to come with <u>Mr Drinkwater</u> but was sick and could not. I then told her the truth of it, she had not heard that before. I told Em that Mary had written some things to Ed about me that vexed him a little, so he did as he did. She said, "Now Delia there are some things I want to tell you. You know it is not my way, to repeat things that are told me, but for all that I am going to tell <u>you</u> all I know about this affair, for I consider you a better friend to me than Mary." She said one day she was up to school and Mary was there too. M. came to her and said "Oh Em. I want to tell you something" she then said, she was in the P.O. the night before for the mail, and did not get any letter as she had expected, and expressed her disappointment at not getting it. Ed was in the Office, and heard her speak about it, so that night he wrote to her. She showed the letter to Em. and the reply she had written, (which is one of the two I have) Ed replied immediately to that. Em said of course all he wrote was all in fun, and Mary ought to have taken it as such, but instead of that she took offence, and said she would pay him back as good as he gave. So the next day she came to Em's and wrote a reply, the one I have in which she speaks of "the luck that bound us together" etc.

(Delia)

Em advised her not to send it, told her it was too hard and unlady like, the tone of the whole letter, but she would send it. I then asked Em. if she understood about the "link" etc. She laughed and said she did, that Mary had told her all about it. I asked her what she said, and she told me, M. said that, "there was plenty of room on the seat, but for all that I would sit in his lap, and he had his arms around me, and we talked there together all the way home, and he would hardly say a word to her, ("Em. says to me, "jealousy, nothing but jealousy, why Dele that girl was so jealous of you. I thought sometimes, she never could stand it." I told her all about how I happened to sit on his lap, and she said, "there was nothing out the way in it at all." I then told her what Ed told me about taking Mary out to Nelia's that night why he did it, etc. She said "Good I'm glad he did it." She then said, I am not very well acquainted with M. but what little I do know of her, I dont like, and never can. She said Mary told her, that she invited the boys to go out to Stuart's that night. "And" Em added, "all she did it for, was to get Ed away from you, she thought if she could only get him out in company where you were not there, she could have him all to herself." She said "I have been an outsider myself and have watched the game all the way through, then Mary would come to me and tell me everything." Says she, "I saw how the game was all working and I was glad of it." She said, Mary said to her once, "I tell you Em Dele just looks daggers at me when she thinks I have been with Ed, or have had anything to say to him" that pleases me. Em says Ed asked Mary to write to him and she told him she would. "But" says "Em I knew at the time he would not write, for it was after she had written him that about you and he was too mad, but just asked her to fool her." "At any rate," says she he has not written to her yet, and if he intended to he would have written before now," and I think so too. But Nele things are getting messed up more and more every day and I do not know what to make of them. If Ed does write to me I shall just write in a friendly way, and not say anything to lead him to think I think more of him than he knows I do now. But I cannot think he has been fooling with me. If he has he has carried his part better than W.W.W. did his, time only can tell and I must wait, wait.

No I cannot believe he was fooling me, but I have no reason to trust him any more than any one else. Oh if you were only here so I could talk to you as I want to, but I shall have to wait for that time, too. I begin to believe more than ever that we have very, very, few, true friends on earth. I feel quite blue this morning as you will doubtless judge from the tone of this. But it is too cold for me to stay up here any longer. So good bye till next time. Will try and write more some other time. I am as ever your Sister   Dele

Lina

Columbus Nov. 26" 1865

Dear Mother

Your long letter was received last Tuesday, and as I am nurse girl this morning will commence writing while my baby sleeps. Did not feel hardly well enough to go to church to day, having taken a severe cold, and it is too annoying for other people, to have some one by them, coughing, all through services.

You need not conclude, at once, that I have been imprudent, for I have not been outside of the gate, but once, for a week, and then it was a pleasant afternoon.

Think I mentioned, when at home, that I had been trying to get a seat in church but could not find one. I noticed lately, a young man, sitting alone ———————   Sunday afternoon

Mary came down stairs ready for church but said she had such a toothache she could not go — So I, suddenly, changed my mind, flew around and was dressed for church by the time the bell rung. Sheldon went with me, and that reminds me of the sentence I left unfinished at the commencement. That young man is Mr Butler, I have met him at Squire Millers. Told Sheldon I was going to him to see if he had any objections to my occupying a part of his seat. Sheldon said "you need not go, I will see him myself" I wondered a little at his objecting as he is an acquaintance of mine. At noon Sheldon said "Lina I have seen Charley Butler and spoken for seats for <u>both</u> of us with him." Am afraid Mary will blame me greatly, and consider that I enticed him from her church. I have been very careful not to ask him out right to go with me but, whenever Mary could not go, have asked "which church he intended going to," knowing that he preferred the Episcopal. If I had not been here he would have continued at the Presbyterian, so she has a right to think I led him astray. Our minister, Mr Richards, made me a long call last week. He is the most agreeable minister both in and out of the pulpit, that I ever met.

Mr and Mrs Smythe, Mrs Williams and baby were here to tea last Wednesday. We had a very pleasant visit with them. Frank wants to know if Delia ever says anything about her baby. Delia must remember that, to keep in the good graces of these young mothers she must send frequent kisses to the babies. Have had two letters from Nelia since she went to Toledo! Think at the time of writing both, she felt somewhat homesick. It is nothing strange however! The severest punishment any one could inflict on me, would be to compel me to stay in that house two weeks. Am very glad the girls got cloth for Basquines. Did Nelia will her water proof to you? If Delia has not finished that under garment yet, and would like some crochet edging for it, I will agree to send her some of my own make, that I like very much for trimming. Hattie taught me the stitch.

Mary has about given up going home to spend Thanksgiving. Sheldon thinks he had not better leave the Office, and she does not want to go without him.

The baby is very well, very good, and grows fast. Mary did not succeed in getting a girl for the kitchen. Do not know as she will try any more. Girls are scarce, and can get just as high wages in a family smaller than this.

I receive papers from Father every week. The evening Mrs Smythes folks were here, Mary opened a can of your Strawberries for tea. They all pronounced them "perfectly deliscious."

Give much love to all.

Your daughter

Lina

(Delia.)

Milan November 26th 1865

Dear Sister Nelia

As Father told you I would write in a few days to tell you all the news I suppose I must, not that there is any news to tell, for I do not know of anything important that has taken place since I wrote you last, unless it is the opening of the Winter term of the Western Reserve Normal School.

I went up to school Tuesday morning, as I supposed, early. I expected to see a good many there, but was some what astonished when I walked up stairs to see every seat full on the other side of the house, and all as quiet as if school had begun. They are nearly all strangers, and the greenest looking set I have seen in some time.

There are not so many of them strangers on our side of the house, there being many of the town girls there. Wednesday Mr Newman had enrolled 112. More than we had last time at the first. Herbert Hickey and Arthur Osborne are about the only familiar faces except those who were here last term, as Benschooter, Greene, Frank Moore, Ellsworth etc. I only go in the afternoon, have commenced 2nd part Algebra, and will study Chemistry when the class is started. Going up in the afternoon so, and not being there when the roll is called I shall not get much acquainted. I sit with Ella Butman and Mary Bangs, when I am there. You see the seats are all full, and ours is not the only one with <u>three</u> in.

Yesterday afternoon when I went down town, I stopped at Mrs Hamilton's with some things, she was not at home. Miss Palmer came to the door. I left the things with her and had got outside the gate, when the door opened and some one said, "Are you going off without speaking to me"? I looked up and there stood <u>Lile</u> <u>Taintor</u>! I never was more astonished at seeing any one in my life, than I was at seeing her, she had come down for her Melodion and was going back that afternoon. It does not seem possible that it is only <u>two</u> weeks ago that I went up to their room to tell them good bye. Lila says she has not heard from Ach since she commenced her school.

(Delia.

But Miss Simons, who is here again this term, told me Friday that Ach is teaching in their district, and that she is real home sick, her school is much smaller than she expected, as she will only have about 16 scholars.

Yesterday I helped Pa build <u>part</u> <u>of</u> a fence, from the big gates down by the barn, making a lane down to the lot. It is the first work of that kind that I have done in some time and I got rather tired.

I have not seen Will since you left here. Charley spent Friday evening with me. George Eddy called a few moments last evening.

I had begun to think that now was the time to tell which one, folks came to see, <u>and</u> I <u>guess</u> <u>it</u> <u>tells</u>. As Will has not been here and Charley and Geo. have.

I have got my Sack done. Mrs Perry stiched it for me. Think I shall like it. George said last night that he had got <u>him</u> a new over coat too, and he would wear his to church today if I would mine, but not having any one here to go to church with me, and not caring to go alone, I remained at home.

As I wish to write to Mr Carter this morning and having nothing more to say to you I will close

Write soon, Give much love to Carl from your Sister
                    Delia

Rob Daly has gone to Ann Arbour to school.

It was not enough for Mr Hough to buy our lot and cut down all the trees, but this morning (Monday) Mr Croft is at work with pick and spade leveling that little hill, at the foot of the big one. "Twas ever thus etc."

We are all well here this morning, except a cold, belonging to me, hope to get rid of it before long Dr Alling gave me some liquorice yesterday in Sunday School, and said he gave it to me as much for his comfort as mine, so I would not disturb him in church coughing. I was very glad I had it last night, for after lying awake about two hours coughing, a small piece of it stopped my coughing and put me to sleep.

Write soon and often to your Sister
                    Delia.

Lina

Columbus Dec. 12" 1865

Dear Delia.

My letter "came up missing" that was written last Sunday, didn't it? At least, you could not have received it for I saw it going into the fire instead of the Office. I commenced a letter to you, but not feeling at all well, left it unfinished, supposing Sheldon would write Monday Morning. Finding he did not, I concluded to wait until this noon so as to see what news there would be from home this morning. I got your letter, and find you are in the same predicament I am, that is, suffering with a cold.

I went to Dr Loving for some cough medicine, he gave me "sixteen powders" and said if they did not relieve me to call again in a few days. Last Saturday I went again, he gave me twelve more, and said if I was not better by Tuesday, and should be passing by, to give him a call. Last night I coughed harder than ever, so went again this morning to talk with the Dr. He said, "Miss Colton if you want to save yourself a months sickness, go home and stay there, give up work and go to bed, if possible."

I do not write this to excite any alarm, but to assure you that I do not feel much more like writing than you did last Sunday.

You know I seldom have a cold, and when I do it takes hold of me rather hard. "Powdering" and staying in the house for a few days, will, probably, bring me about all right.

You must have had rather a quiet time Thanksgiving day. Mary invited Mr Kellys family here to dinner. We had a very pleasant visit with them. Mr Kelly always inquires particularly, about Delia.

I have that Edge, for Pa's [this part of page torn off] if wished, and expect to send it, in a paper, the latter part of the week.

Hattie has just returned from home, she says her father intends making another desperate effort to get his family together on Christmas. If the rest go, suppose I shall, but had much rather stay here.

George has given up going to Atlanta, for the present, and will remain in College the remainder of the Winter.

It seems as though I had much to say but cannot think of anything now, to "consider my feelings" and excuse a miserable letter. I have no intention of being down sick, so none of you need worry about me at all. Should I be, however, will have some of the folks write immediately. Had a long letter from Nelia this morning.

Your Sister
Lina.

Am feeling much better this Wednesday morning.

Lina

Thursday Evening
Columbus Dec. 21" 1865.

Dear Mother.

It is after ten oclock and I am in no writing mood, but thought there had better be a line written to tell you that a small box will be sent from here tomorrow morning, by Express, which we design having reach you on Christmas. It may get there before, perhaps not until after. We thought best to send word that you might know it was some where on the road, or, so that it would not stay in Norwalk a week or two.

One of the girls spoke of wanting that black plume, so I put it in the box. It needs recurling. Suppose Nelia knows how to fix it. Was sorry to hear you had been sick again. Hope you will entirely recover before Christmas arrives.

Am getting quite disgusted with my cold, or <u>myself</u>. Do not know which. I stopped Doctoring this week, thinking I was about well, but seem to take cold every time I look out the door. The folks here have all concluded to spend the Holidays in Columbus. Mary rather expects her brother and Cousin next Saturday to spend Christmas.

Sheldon had more photographs taken quite awhile ago, and intended sending one to Mrs Hough. Will put one in this letter if I can think of it. Am very glad you got a merino dress this Winter. Will send a piece of mine, that you may see it is a shade lighter.

Will answer Delia's letter some time next week.

Suppose Nelia and Carlos will both be at home by the time this reaches you. Well, I would like to be there too, but <u>cant</u>.

Wishing all a "Merry Christmas." I will close this hastily written note.
Your daughter
Lina.

[included in this letter is a small piece of brown merino cloth]

Lina

Columbus Dec. 30" 1865

Dear Delia

I will commence a letter tonight as I may not have time to write much tomorrow. How are you enjoying the Holidays? We had a play spell from Friday night until Tuesday noon, after Christmas. George and his Cousin Nina were here during the time. An opportunity offered at last, for me to visit some of the public places, as Nina never had been here before and George was ready to accompany us. Saturday we went through the Penitentiary, you and Nelia have both been there and know to just what an extent I was interested and instructed. I do not think a person can form any idea of the amount of work done there until visiting the place.

Tuesday morning we went to the deaf and dumb and Blind Asylum. I saw Mr Lindsey, Davie Abbott and Miss Tipton only had a short conversation with each, as they were busy with their recitations. David did not seem in very good spirits. He said, "Do y<u>ou</u> hear from Milan often! I have not heard from there but once since I came here, last October."

Christmas morning, George, Nina, Hattie and I, got up at half past four and went with our irish girl to the Catholic church. It was brilliantly lighted and "beautifully" crowded, that is the most I can say about it as the exercises were all in Latin. But we came away with a better idea of how they performed.

Sheldon had a letter from Nelia, this week, in which she expressed a wish to know who sent what in the box received by you.

Mary sent Mother the "Hanging basket." The handkerchief to Father, and the two bows to you and Nelia. The rest will have to be (charged) to me, as Sheldon made no presents this year, except a book to his wife.

I was very glad to hear that you liked the picture. I felt that it would please you all better than to send individual presents that might, together, amount to the same in price. It was my intention to have it standing, the same as the photograph, but the Original was so poorly taken that the Artist positively refused to try more than the face. All here liked the expression very much. Sheldon said first thing "Mother will want to send that to Lottie." If they ever do want

Lina

one I think a much better picture can be obtained by copying from that, than by using the Original.

For Mother's benefit I will say that, when I was under Dr Loving's care I talked with him about my "catarrh." She wanted me to go to a Dr some time ago. He said I had not "catarrh" nor anything like it. Gave me a perscription and said it would entirely cure me in six weeks. I feel a change for the better already and will return sincere and heartfelt thanks to him if I am cured. You think I have had enough of <u>Loving Dr's</u>. They are the best, Delia, by far, the best. Speaking of "physicians" reminds me that I had an introduction to one, last night, and he astounded me by saying that, he had never been in Milan, but he wrote a letter to <u>my Mother</u> not long ago. After getting my curiosity sufficiently aroused he informed me that it was in regard to some Sanitary Stores, that were supposed to be lost. His name is Dr Wheaton, perhaps Ma will remember the circumstance.

Ella Morgan and Emma Smythe were here to tea last Thursday. Ella thinks you have forgotten her entirely. Myra starts for School again next Wednesday.

I received Nelia's photograph and like it, only that it looks older than she does. I would like to see another picture she proposed sending me.

Mrs Col. Arthur Wilcox sent me word to day that she was in the City. Shall call on her the forepart of the week. Am glad she is to be here this Winter. Sheldon and I called on our minister this week. His wife is almost as lovable as himself. We had a very pleasant call.

I should not object to seeing "Uncle H'r" Especially as he has been promised to me for so long a time, just my luck, isnt it? to be away when he at last comes home.

Perhaps Belle thinks I am owing her a letter.

Sunday afternoon

I seem to have made out a letter last evening. So will only add "Happy New Year" and close with love to all.
Your Sister
Lina.

The Route Through Which These Letters Travelled

Melinda Sophia (Mrs. Hamilton Colton)

conveyed the letters in the 1880's
to her daughter **Cornelia** (Mrs. Asa Raymond Cole)

who transmitted the letters in the 1920's
to her daughter **Lina Louise** (Mrs. Elmore L. McLane)

who transferred the letters in the 1940's
to her daughter **Gertrude Caroline** (Mrs. Charles Gates)

who presented the letters in the 1960's and 1980's
to her daughter-in-law **Betsey** (Mrs. Sheldon Gates)

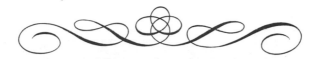

APPENDIX

OFFICIAL ROSTER

OF THE

SOLDIERS OF THE STATE OF OHIO

IN THE

WAR OF THE REBELLION,

1861—1866.

VOL. V.

54TH–69TH REGIMENTS—INFANTRY.

COMPILED UNDER DIRECTION OF THE ROSTER COMMISSION:

JOSEPH B. FORAKER, GOVERNOR,   **JAMES. S. ROBINSON,** SEC'Y OF STATE
H. A. AXLINE, ADJUTANT-GENERAL.

PUBLISHED BY AUTHORITY OF THE GENERAL ASSEMBLY.

AKRON, O.:
THE WERNER PTG. AND MFG. CO.
1887.

Sixty-seventh Regiment Ohio Volunteer Infantry.

THREE YEARS' SERVICE.

This Regiment was organized in the State of Ohio, at large, from October, 1861, to January, 1862, to serve three years. On the expiration of its term of service the original members (except veterans) were mustered out, and the organization, composed of veterans and recruits, retained in the service. The 62nd Regiment Ohio Infantry was consolidated with it September 1, 1865. It was mustered out December 7, 1865, in accordance with orders from the War Department.

The official list of battles, in which this Regiment bore an honorable part, is not yet published by the War Department, but the following list has been compiled, after careful research, during the preparation of this work :

WINCHESTER, VA. (Kearnstown),	March 23, 1862.
STRASBURG, VA.,	March 27, 1862.
FRONT ROYAL, VA.,	May 30, 1862.
HARRISON'S LANDING, VA.,	July 4, 1862.
MALVERN HILL, VA.,	August 5, 1862.
FRANKLIN, VA.,	October 5, 1862.
BLACKWATER, VA.,	December 11–12, 1862.
FORT WAGNER, S. C. (Siege of),	July 10 to September 6, 1863.
FORT WAGNER, S. C. (Second Assault),	July 18, 1863.
CHESTER STATION, VA.,	May 9–10, 1864.
BERMUDA HUNDRED, VA.,	May 16–30, 1864.
WIER BOTTOM CHURCH, VA.,	May 20, 1864.
PETERSBURG, VA. (Siege of),	June 15, 1864, to April 2, 1865.
WIER BOTTOM CHURCH, VA.,	June 17–18, 1864.
DEEP BOTTOM RUN, VA.,	August 14–18, 1864.
DARBYTOWN ROAD, VA.,	October 17–28, 1864.
PETERSBURG, VA. (Fall of),	April 2, 1865.
APPOMATTOX, VA.,	April 8–9, 1865.

(563)

Names.	Rank.	Age.	Date of Entering the Service.	Period of Service.	Remarks.
Starr, John W.	Private	19	Oct. 19, 1861	3 yrs.	Transferred from Co. E, 62d O. V. I., Sept. 1, 1865; mustered out with company Dec. 7, 1865; veteran.
Taylor, Asbury G.	do	19	Jan. 6, 1862	3 yrs.	Killed Aug. 16, 1864, in battle of Deep Bottom Run, Va.; see Co. E, 62d O. V. I.; veteran.
Terry, Silas, Sr.	do	40	Oct. 28, 1861	3 yrs.	Discharged July 2, 1863, at Folly Island, S. C., on Surgeon's certificate of disability.
Thomas, Zepheniah	do	24	Feb. 8, 1864	3 yrs.	Transferred from Co. E, 62d O. V. I., Sept. 1, 1865; mustered out with company Dec. 7, 1865.
Vongonton, David	do	18	Dec. 26, 1861	3 yrs.	Wounded Feb. 22, 1864, in action at Wilmington Island, Ga.; also Sept. 29, 1864, in action at Deep Bottom Run, Va., and Oct. 13, 1864, in action near Richmond, Va.; mustered out Dec. 31, 1864, at Columbus, O., on expiration of term of service.
Vine, John	do	42	Dec. 21, 1861	3 yrs.	Discharged Aug. 4, 1862, at Alexandria, Va., on Surgeon's certificate of disability.
Wiley, Samuel	do	44	Oct. 20, 1864	1 yr.	Drafted; mustered out May 31, 1865, at Camp Lee, Va., by order of War Department.
Wiley, Leander	do	19	Oct. 17, 1861	3 yrs.	Transferred from Co. E, 62d O. V. I., Sept. 1, 1865; mustered out with company Dec. 7, 1865; veteran.
Weyand, Henry J.	do	24	Feb. 24, 1864	3 yrs.	Transferred from Co. E, 62d O. V. I., Sept. 1, 1865; mustered out with company Dec. 7, 1865.
Williams, John	do	38	Nov. 4, 1864	1 yr.	Substitute; transferred from Co. E, 62d O. V. I., Sept. 1, 1865; mustered out Nov. 9, 1865, at Richmond, Va., on expiration of term of service.
Whiteman, William	do	38	Oct. 18, 1864	1 yr.	Drafted; transferred from Co. E, 62d O. V. I., Sept. 1, 1865; mustered out Sept. 14, 1865, at Camp Dennison, O., as of Co. G, 62d O. V. I.
Wilson, Henry	do	21	Oct. 18, 1864	1 yr.	Drafted; transferred from Co. E, 62d O. V. I., Sept. 1, 1865; mustered out Sept. 14, 1865, at Camp Dennison, O., as of Co. G, 62d O. V. I.
Welsh, Harrison	do	20	Dec. 12, 1861	3 yrs.	Discharged June 6, 1865, at Cleveland, O., on Surgeon's certificate of disability; veteran.
Weber, John	do	19	Dec. 5, 1861	3 yrs.	Wounded Aug. 16, 1864, in action at Deep Bottom, Va.; mustered out Dec. 5, 1864, at Columbus, O., on expiration of term of service.
Wrinzler, John	do	23	Dec. 7, 1861	3 yrs.	Wounded Oct. 13, 1864, in action; mustered out Jan. 17, 1865, at Columbus, O., on expiration of term of service.
Wolf, Jacob	do	21	Dec. 9, 1861	3 yrs.	Died March 28, 1862, in hospital at Winchester, Virginia.
Waldron, P. W.	do	20	Oct. 18, 1861	3 yrs.	Wounded May 10, 1864, in action at Chester Station, Va.; no further record found.
Winans, Theodore	do				
Yocum, Joseph	do	18	Sept. 17, 1861	3 yrs.	Transferred from Co. E, 62d O. V. I., Sept. 1, 1865; mustered out with company Dec. 7, 1865; veteran.

COMPANY K.

Mustered in Jan. 2, 1862, at Camp Chase, O., by C. C. Lewis, 2d Lieutenant; Sheldon Colton, 2d Lieutenant, and John Faskin, 2d Lieutenant, and U. S. A. Mustering Officers. Mustered out Dec. 7, 1865, at City Point, Va., by J. Remington, Captain, and A. C. M. Department of Virginia.

Names.	Rank.	Age.	Date of Entering the Service.	Period of Service.	Remarks.
Charles C. Lewis	Captain	27	Oct. 4, 1861	3 yrs.	Appointed Dec. 18, 1861.
Sidney G. Brock	do	25	Nov. 18, 1861	3 yrs.	Transferred from Co. D May 25, 1864; mustered out Jan. 7, 1865, on expiration of term of service.
William H. Kief	do	19	Dec. 1, 1861	3 yrs.	Promoted from 1st Lieutenant Co. F Dec. 9, 1864; discharged Sept. 1, 1865, by reason of consolidation.
John D. Kennedy	do	32	Oct. 19, 1861	3 yrs.	Transferred from Co. K, 62d O. V. I., Sept. 1, 1865; mustered out with company Dec. 7, 1865.
Sheldon Colton	1st Lieut.	26	Oct. 4, 1861	3 yrs.	Appointed Dec. 8, 1861; discharged Oct. 9, 1862.
John C. Cochrane	do	31	Oct. 14, 1861	3 yrs.	Promoted to 2d Lieutenant from Com. Sergeant April 15, 1862; 1st Lieutenant to date Oct. 5, 1862; died May 29, 1864, at Fortress Monroe, Va., of wounds received in action.

Western Reserve Normal School!

"The greatest calamity which can befall the education of a people, is, to have teachers without competent knowledge ; with no aptness to teach or govern ; and who feel no strong desire to improve themselves."—*Bishop Potter*.

How can teachers be properly qualified for their work, unless they have access to schools, whose design it is, to give the instruction requisite for this object?

The subscribers intend to open, at MILAN, on the 1st Monday of January next, a school for the purpose of training teachers. This being their *express* and *only* object, their whole attention and effort will be directed to its accomplishment. Mr. B., having had charge of a Normal School some twenty years, brings, to aid in its accomplishment, the results of long experience.

In addition to a most *thorough* drill in the studies to be taught, instruction will be given on the organization, management, discipline, and instruction of common schools. To accomplish this, a much larger amount of labor, than usual, must be devoted to the scholars.

The school will be open to all who wish to acquire a *thorough* English education ; an education best adapted to all the practical purposes of life.

Milan is a pleasant, healthy, and moral village ; situate four miles from the Depot at Norwalk —to which a hack runs several times a day, to convey passengers.

The building formerly occupied by the Huron Institute, is now being re-modeled and repaired for this purpose. It is situated in a pleasant grove, with spacious grounds.

TUITION, *(to be paid in advance,)* per term of twelve weeks—$8,00.

BOARD in good families, $2,00 per week.

ROOMS can be had by those who wish to board themselves.

FOR INFORMATION respecting board or rooms, apply to Dr. Stuart.

The school will be furnished with a new Chemical and Philosophical apparatus, Globes, Maps, and Physiological Charts.

ASA BRAINERD,
SAMUEL F. NEWMAN.

MILAN, October 12th, 1858.

Agency

Agricultural Insurance Company
of Watertown, N.Y.

Norwalk, O. July 8- 1895

Miss H.S. Eddy
Milan, O.

January 1858, Rev. Asa Brainard and myself started a Normal School in the old Institute building in Milan. Mr Brainard remained with me that year, and also 1859.

I continued to have charge of the School from 1859 until 1870. During that time my Assistants were Dr Geo. Cornell, Miss Hattie Ashley, Mr and Mrs Seymour, Miss Delia Palmer, Miss Lydia Dimon, Miss Agnes Ingersoll, and Mr Spencer, the Author of the Spencerian system of penmanship. Mr. Spencer and Miss Ingersoll taught penmanship only.

I think Miss Palmer was my Assistant for five years, and Dr Cornell about the same length of time; the other teachers mentioned about one year each.

I do not remember the name of the young man who succeeded me —— perhaps Mr Perrin or Mr Fish can tell you. He was killed by a horse; and lived I think, near Sandusky.

I had no acquaintance whatever with the teachers who preceded me.

Yours truly,
S.F. Newman

Miss Cornelia Colton also assisted me a short time.

Newspaper clipping found in Cornelia Colton Cole's scrapbook:

September 2, 1899

Carlos Colton, THE VICTIM OF INTERNAL HEMORRHAGE

Served in the Civil War and has resided in Toledo for many years.

"Carlos Colton was found dead in his room at the Imperial Stag Hotel this morning. How long he had been dead, no one knows, except that the messenger came sometime during the lonely hours of the night. The discovery of Mr. Colton's death was made at 8 o'clock this morning by one of the servants of the hotel who went to his room to place it in order. Acting Coroner, Abele, was summoned, and, after viewing the remains, had them removed to his undertaking establishment on Cherry Street. Internal hemorrhage is given as the cause of Mr. Colton's death. So far as can be learned the deceased was in his usual health last evening, although Gus Haas, proprietor of the Imperial Hotel, says that he had not seen him for a day or two.

Mr. Colton was born at Milan, and was about 60 years of age. He was one of the pioneers of Toledo, and few men were better known here. He saw service in the civil war, and after peace between the States had been restored, he came to Toledo, which was his home up to the time of his death. For sometime he was a member of the insurance firm known as Brown and Colton, and was still later employed in General Hamilton's law office. Mr. Colton also had some newspaper experience, being at one time employed on the staff of the Blade.

Mr. Colton was a bachelor, but is survived by two sisters, residing in Norwalk, and one brother, a resident of Columbus. He was a cousin of A.W. Colton, Manager of the Lake Erie Transportation Company.

The remains will be taken this afternoon to Norwalk, Ohio, where the funeral will be held to-morrow."

The newspaper obituary for Sheldon was reported as follows:

TRIBUTE TO WAR HERO

Lieutenant Sheldon Colton died at his home in Columbus, O., Sunday morning, June 5, 1904, at 8:20 o'clock, after a ten days' illness with pneumonia.

He was born at "The Landing", near Milan, O., January 9, 1835 and the most of his years were spent in Milan and Toledo, O., until the outbreak of the civil war, when in 1861 he enlisted and was commissioned Second Lieutenant of Co. K, 67th O.V.I., and December 8, 1861, was appointed 1st Lieutenant, which position he held until at the battle of Winchester, or "Kernstown" March 23, 1862, he received a wound which disabled him for further army service. When sufficiently recovered he went to Columbus, O., where he had since made his home. He served as private secretary to Governor Tod and afterwards had charge of the Confederate prisoners at Camp Chase. For several years he was chief clerk in the Adjutant General's office, but the wound in his hip became so painful he was obliged to resign the position and seek rest for a time. For the past twenty-five years he was employed in the auditor's office of the Hocking Valley R.R. Co. and the same uprightness of character and steadfastness to duty which marked his army career followed him through all his life and made him respected and beloved by all with whom he came in contact.

He was identified with the ex-soldiers and sailors association of Franklin county from the time of its organization in 1878, and was very active in securing a lot in Green Lawn Cemetery in Columbus, for the association and in having a $7,500 monument erected thereon. He was a member of J.C. McCoy post, of the G.A.R. and of the Union Veteran Legion encampment, No. 78 of which he was chaplain at the time of his death.

His love for his comrades and their memory was so strong that on Memorial Day he asked his physician to allow him to attend the services, saying it might be his last opportunity. It was the first time he had missed marching with the living to pay tribute to the dead.

A widow and five children survive him, Arthur, of El Paso, Texas, Walter, Fred, Mrs. Paul Luce and Louise, all of Columbus, O. One son, Allen, died recently in Texas.

The funeral services were held from his late home Tuesday afternoon, June 7, in charge of the Union Veteran Legion, Rev. Dr. S.S. Palmer, of the Broad Street Presbyterian church officiating and under the cover of the flag he so dearly loved and cherished, he was borne, with military honors to his last resting place in Green Lawn Cemetery at Columbus.

Mr. Colton was a brother of the Misses Lina and Delia Colton, of Norwalk, of Mrs. J.P. Carter, of Milan, O., and of Mrs. A.R. Cole, of Port Huron, Michigan.

[Compiled from information provided by David Morgan/Milan Public Library]

THE MILAN LEDGER

Milan, Erie County, Ohio

Thursday, January 10, 1924

The Death of An
Estimable Lady

Mrs. Charlotte Colton Carter, widow of James P. Carter, aged 84 years, 6 months and 16 days passed away at her home Monday morning at 5:40 o'clock.

Charlotte Colton Carter was born in Monroe, Mich., June 21, 1839. She was married on June 21, 1859 to James Powers Carter who preceeded her twelve years ago. She died Jan. 7, 1924, leaving to mourn their loss one daughter, Miss Elizabeth and three sisters, Mrs. Cole of Detroit the Misses Lina and Delia Colton of Milan.

Funeral services were held from her late home Wednesday afternoon at 1:45 o'clock, conducted by Rev. J.W. Myers of Tontogany. The remains were placed in the receiving vault.

Friday, January 14, 1927

Remains of Lina Colton
Brought to Milan

The remains of Miss Lina Colton, who died at the home of Mr. and Mrs. W. A. Woodward, in Norwalk, last Saturday, were brought to Milan on Monday and placed in the receiving vault until spring, when burial will be made in the family lot.

Miss Colton died of old age, being about eighty-five years of age. She lived in Milan for many years, but for the past four years resided with Mr. and Mrs. W.A. Woodward at 70 West Main street, Norwalk. She is well-known here and highly respected by all. Mrs. Donivan of Milan lived with her as a girl and says, "I was never approached by Miss Colton with a cross word or a frown on her face," and that her friendship will never be forgotten, as she was a perfect lady. Miss Colton was a life-long member of the Episcopalian church.

Friday, February 10, 1928

BROUGHT TO MILAN FOR
BURIAL

Mrs. Cornelia Colton Cole died at her home in Detroit, Mich., Tuesday evening, February 7th at 9 o'clock, after an illness of four weeks. She was eighty-three years of age. Burial will be held in the Milan cemetery beside her late husband, Mr. Asa R. Cole.

Mrs. Cole was born in Milan and lived here until her marriage to Mr. Cole, since which time she has lived in Port Huron and Detroit, Mich.

She is survived by one son, Giles, of Detroit, two daughters Mrs. D.L. Ballentine of Detroit and Mrs. E.L. McLane of Royal Oak, Mich. Six grandchildren and three great grandchildren, of Milan also one sister, Miss Delia Colton and a number of nieces and nephews.

Friday, January 29, 1937

Funeral Wed'sday
for Cordelia Colton

Miss Cordelia L. Colton, 89, last surviving member of a prominent pioneer Milan family, died in her home on Elm St. at 2:15 P.M. Sunday.

She had been ill five weeks. Death occurred in the home where she was born, the daughter of the late Hamilton and Melinda Colton. For more than 25 years Miss Colton was employed at the Huron County court house in Norwalk.

Surviving are four nephews, Walter Colton of Ashland, Fred Colton of Columbus, Arthur Colton of California and H.C. Carter of Akron, and four nieces, Mrs. D.L. Ballentine and Mrs. Elmore McLane of Detroit, Mrs. Louise Colton Appell of California and Miss Elizabeth Carter of Milan.

Funeral services were conducted in the home Wednesday afternoon at two o'clock. Rev. C.H. Gross Pastor of St. Paul's Episcopal church Norwalk, officiated. Burial was in Milan cemetery.

Those from out of town attending the funeral were: Fred Colton and son, Robert of Columbus, Mr. Walter Colton, Mr. and Mrs. Alpha and Langley Colton of Ashland. Mrs. Lynn Kellogg and house guest from Norwalk.

SELECTED

GLOSSARY

&

INDEX

SELECTED GLOSSARY

Alapaca (alpaca): a thin cloth woven from the fleecy brown or black wool of a South American mammal related to the llama; a glossy, dark cloth of wool and cotton, used for linings, suits, etc.

Ancient Abraham: Abraham Lincoln

Adams & Fays: a scented hair oil

Basquine: a woman's tight-fitting bodice, or petticoat

Calico: a coarse, printed cotton cloth

Cassimiere: cashmere

Catafalque: a platform of wood, usually draped, upon which a coffin is placed while the body lies in state

Chemise: a loose dress or undergarment with no waistline

Collar & Spurs: protective cuffs used by copyists or bookkeepers

Continental: paper money issued during the Revolutionary war

Continentals, the: a singing group

Contraband: a slave who escaped into, or was smuggled into Union territory

Copperhead: an expression used in the North, to designate a Northerner in sympathy with the South

Copyists: individuals hired to transcribe records and documents by hand

Counterpane: coverlet, or embroidered quilt

Crockery: dishes, jars, bowls etc.

Dropsy: a swelling of the body due to abnormal accumulation of fluid in cells or tissues

Dyspepsia: indigestion

Ferrotype: tintype, or early photograph taken directly on a sensitized plate of enamelled tin or iron

Gaiters: leather or cloth coverings for the instep, ankle, and sometimes the calf of the leg

"Gottschalk": possible reference to the medieval German theologian who espoused the doctrine of absolute predestination, and was convicted of heresy

Greenback: a treasury note, issued originally as fiat money in 1862; made redeemable in gold or silver by the Specie Resumption Act of 1875

Hack: a coach or carriage for hire

Havelock: a military cap cover made of light cloth, designed to protect the back of the neck

Haversack: a soldier's bag, usually worn over one shoulder, used to carry rations

Home Affection: depression at being separated from one's family; homesickness

Homeopathy: a medical, therapeutic treatment introduced by S.C.F. Hahnemann of Germany

India Rubber Cap: protective supporter for an injured joint, such as a kneecap

Knights Templar: a member of a religious and military order, or a certain order of Masons

Lovetaps: a gentle spanking given on a birthday, one tap for each year

Melodion: a small keyboard organ using reeds and bellows

Merino: cloth made from the fine, silky wool of a special breed of sheep

Old Secesh: Jefferson Davis

Omnibus: a public carriage

Parish Visitors: church publications

Passapateau: a decorative or engraved picture frame

Pest House: an isolation hospital for people with contagious or epidemic diseases

Picket: a soldier posted to protect a body of troops from surprise attack

Portmonnaie: a pocketbook or purse

Rats: small pads used to enhance women's coiffures and make the hair look thicker

R.S.S.: a youth organization

Sacque: a garment

Secesh: Confederates

Secession: withdrawal of the Southern states from the Federal Union

Shilling: coins or money

Shirt Chandler: retailer of shirts

Snuff Box: a decorative, miniature box crafted of materials such as gold, silver, brass, tortoise shell or wood; in the 17th and 18th centuries, used to contain a powdered preparation of tobacco used for inhalation

Spencer: a short jacket

Spencer, Platt Rogers: author of the Spencerian style of penmanship, using well formed, rounded letters

Stoop: a small porch or platform with steps

Take the Cars: travel on the railroad

Tatting: a fine lace created by knotting and looping thread, using a hand shuttle

Traps: goods, or articles of clothing or adornment

Weaver's Salt Rheum syrup: a remedy, possibly for cold or rhinitis symptoms

"What is it": a carnival curiosity

SELECTED INDEX

Betsey Gates grew up in a small town on the shores of Lake Michigan. She received her B.A. degree from the University of Michigan, continuing graduate studies at the University of Chicago and Arizona State University. Betsey has been an active volunteer at the Scottsdale Center for the Arts, the Heard Museum of Anthropology and the Frank Lloyd Wright Foundation, (where she assists in the Archives and Docent program). Her other interests include reading, travel, and writing poetry.

Illustrations and map of Sherman's raid by **Quick Carlson**.

Cover painting and military portrait of Sheldon Colton by **Tom O'Mary**.

NOTE: A larger-than-normal type has been selected for the body of this volume, for the convenience of readers of all ages.